Advance Praise

This book offers a refreshingly new analysis of Sri Lanka's ethnic civil war and the problem of post-civil-war political transition. Bart Klem builds a rich analysis on the premise that multiple contestations over sovereignty and identity cannot be adequately explained purely from constitutional or institutional perspectives. He adopts a performative perspective to analyse how political claims and counterclaims are enacted at many levels.

Based on extensive ethnographic fieldwork in Sri Lanka, the author views the continuing conflict as an ensemble of contentious enactments of political order performed through the practices of a range of actors – politicians, bureaucrats, insurgents, community leaders, voters and other participants of political life. This book fills a significant interpretive gap in the scholarship on Sri Lanka's ethnic conflict.

Jayadeva Uyangoda, University of Colombo

Bart Klem covers the grand themes of Sri Lanka's contemporary history – nationalist politics, provincial devolution and the friction between the constitutional, administrative and political realities of the state – with his feet firmly planted on the ground and his eye on the smallest ethnographic detail. The result is a gripping, theoretically sophisticated and genuinely insightful account of the country.

Mukulika Banerjee, London School of Economics and Political Science

Bart Klem aptly illustrates how the state is simultaneously being destroyed and created during Sri Lanka's armed conflict. The Tamil militants delegitimise, dismantle and indeed destroy the state, while constructing an alternate version of their own. The author elegantly describes the performance of the state in the making. Sadly, the real people in whose name the war was fought became the material surface on which such abstractions are played out. Having closely interacted with the Tamil leaders before and after the conflict, Bart Klem offers a unique vantage point to explore the concepts at play. For that reason alone, this book will alter the analytical landscape of the Sri Lankan ethnic conflict.

Yuvi Thangarajah, Eastern University, Sri Lanka

This original book combines sensitive ethnography collected over a period of twenty years and imaginative analysis to tell the story of Tamil nationalist politics. It is a brilliant analysis of the particularities of separatist insurgents' sovereignties by casting the eyes on performative politics. A must-read for all who seek a better and more holistic understanding of rebel governance, civil wars and strongmen repertoires of authority in Sri Lanka and beyond.

Lucia Michelutti, University College London

Performing Sovereign Aspirations

In a society that experiences secessionist conflict, many things are not what they seem. *Performing Sovereign Aspirations* adopts a performative perspective to understand the peculiar institutional landscape that ensued around the Tamil separatist conflict in Sri Lanka, both during and after the civil war. It draws on two decades of fieldwork across towns and villages in northern and eastern Sri Lanka, ethnography within Sri Lanka's civil service, and privileged access to the Norwegian-facilitated peace process. This yields a compelling analytical narrative that shows how political institutions are enacted and witnessed, rather than cataloguing them in the strictures of the law. This provides a fertile vantage point to address the to-be-or-not-to-be dilemmas that we face when seeking to interpret the legitimacy, legality and validity of the institutions that separatist movements create in aspiration of sovereign status. And as such, this book provides food for thought for broader conceptual debates concerning armed conflict and insurgency.

Bart Klem is an Associate Professor in Peace and Development Studies at Gothenburg University, Sweden. He writes about everyday life and politics amidst armed conflict. He has conducted fieldwork across Sri Lanka's northeast since 2000. He co-authored *Checkpoint, Temple, Church and Mosque* (2015) and co-edited journal issues on insurgent politics (*Modern Asian Studies*, 2018) and on legal identity under insurgencies (*Citizenship Studies*, 2024).

SOUTH ASIA IN THE SOCIAL SCIENCES

South Asia has become a laboratory for devising new institutions and practices of modern social life. Forms of capitalist enterprise, providing welfare and social services, the public role of religion, the management of ethnic conflict, popular culture and mass democracy in the countries of the region have shown a marked divergence from known patterns in other parts of the world. South Asia is now being studied for its relevance to the general theoretical understanding of modernity itself.

South Asia in the Social Sciences features books that offer innovative research on contemporary South Asia. It focuses on the place of the region in the various global disciplines of the social sciences and highlights research that uses unconventional sources of information and novel research methods. While recognising that most current research is focused on the larger countries, the series attempts to showcase research on the smaller countries of the region.

General Editor
Partha Chatterjee
Columbia University

Editorial Board
Pranabh Bardhan
University of California, Berkeley

Stuart Corbridge
Durham University

Satish Deshpande
University of Delhi

Christophe Jaffrelot
Centre d'etudes et de recherches internationales, Paris

Nivedita Menon
Jawaharlal Nehru University

Books in the series:

Government as Practice: Democratic Left in a Transforming India
Dwaipayan Bhattacharyya

Courting the People: Public Interest Litigation in Post-Emergency India
Anuj Bhuwania

Development after Statism: Industrial Firms and the Political Economy of South Asia
Adnan Naseemullah

Politics of the Poor: Negotiating Democracy in Contemporary India
Indrajit Roy

Performing Sovereign Aspirations

Tamil Insurgency and Postwar Transition in Sri Lanka

Bart Klem

CAMBRIDGE
UNIVERSITY PRESS

Shaftesbury Road, Cambridge CB2 8EA, United Kingdom

One Liberty Plaza, 20th Floor, New York, NY 10006, USA

477 Williamstown Road, Port Melbourne, VIC 3207, Australia

314–321, 3rd Floor, Plot No. 3, Splendor Forum, Jasola District Centre, New Delhi – 110025, India

103 Penang Road, #05–06/07, Visioncrest Commercial, Singapore 238467

Cambridge University Press is part of Cambridge University Press & Assessment, a department of the University of Cambridge.

We share the University's mission to contribute to society through the pursuit of education, learning and research at the highest international levels of excellence.

www.cambridge.org
Information on this title: www.cambridge.org/9781009442466
DOI: 10.1017/9781009442459

First published 2024

Printed in India by Avantika Printers Pvt. Ltd.

A catalogue record for this publication is available from the British Library

ISBN 978-1-009-44246-6 Hardback

To Shahul Hasbullah (1950–2018),
my mentor in navigating northeastern Sri Lanka

Contents

Illustrations

Map

Photographs

Table

Acknowledgements

The writing and re-writing of this book spanned several years. The research presented in it took many more. Though most of my material was gathered in the 2010s, the oldest fieldwork notes in fact date back to 2000 – Sri Lanka was a different place then, and I was less than half the age I am now. My own maturation as an academic has occurred alongside the gestation of this book, and therefore the list of people who have helped me in this process is long.

Above all, Sri Lankans from all kinds of backgrounds have met me with a generous kindness. In Adivasipuram, Sampur, Trincomalee, Jaffna, Colombo and many other places. Many of them shared details that were intimate, painful or distressing. Some of these encounters involved risks or hardship. Thankfully, many also involved jokes, enthusiasm and heartfelt connections.

Several persons were instrumental in helping me navigate Sri Lanka's convoluted landscape of insurgency and postwar transition. First and foremost, I want to acknowledge Shahul Hasbullah, to whom I have dedicated this book. His friendly generosity and depth of knowledge have guided me, right from when we first met in 2008 until after his sudden death in 2018. I would also like to mention Jeremy, Jasmy, Deen and Munazir, each of whom made a vital contribution to my fieldwork – helping me get access, arrange interviews, find documents, clarify what's going on, translate, making me feel welcome, keeping me safe.

There is a handful of people who have left a strong mark on the way I think, how I work and how I write. Apart from Hasbullah, these are Georg Frerks (who was omnipresent in the early stages of my career and remained a dear colleague ever since), Jonathan Goodhand (who guided me into a much larger, international research community), Benedikt Korf (who facilitated my conversion from a hit-and-run consultant into an academic), and Jonathan Spencer (who remains my main source of inspiration and aspiration, in terms of dedication to Sri Lanka, crafting research that is driven by ideas and curiosity rather than academic scheming and an aesthetic of writing that contrasts with the awkward sequence I just squeezed into these parentheses).

In addition to these mentors, I want to mention three friends with whom I have a long history of sharing ideas, non-ideas, puzzles, worries and accomplishments. Sidharthan Maunaguru has shaped the central concepts and ideas presented in this book, perhaps more than anyone else, through our joint writing and many other exchanges and asides. Dinesha Samararatne has been a huge help in terms of trying out perspectives and finding creative ways to understand laws, judicial bodies and constitutions. Bert Suykens, finally, managed to make me happy even when we talked about the most troublesome things. Our collaborative work on contested public authority in South Asia has helped me widen my gaze beyond Sri Lanka.

Maris Gillette and Rebecca Bryant, in their own personal ways, offered me inspiration and encouragement when I really needed it. I suspect they both remember their encounters with me as a workaday collegial exchange, but I want them to know that they gave me renewed enthusiasm and confidence when my book project had comprehensively derailed.

I received constructive feedback from countless colleagues on drafts, pre-drafts and off-shoots of this book. Two anonymous reviewers for Cambridge University Press helped me give the manuscript a final lift, by pointing me to errors, omissions and missed opportunities. Before that, two anonymous reviewers for Stanford University Press, particularly the one who offered two rounds of meticulous and thoughtful feedback, gave me enormous food for thought and helped me convert a scattershot manuscript into a book with more focus, consistency and depth – even if that review process eventually resulted in what I considered an abrupt and unfortunate rejection.

I want to acknowledge discussions with and feedback from many cherished colleagues, including Ahilan Kadirgamar, Amanda Gilbertson, Ambika Satkunanathan, Asanga Welikala, Camilla Orjuela, Chulani Kodikara, Farzana Haniffa, Jayadeva Uyangoda, Maria Stern, Mukulika Banerjee, Neloufer de Mel, Sunil Bastian, Swati Parashar, and Thomas Hansen. Though her textual editing, Jennifer Bartmess not only improved the quality of my manuscript but she also helped me clarify my thoughts and improve my command of the English language. I am grateful to Hisham Rifai, who did the artwork on the front cover.

I have been fortunate to work in very supportive and collegial academic communities in Zurich, Melbourne and Gothenburg. I received helpful questions and comments when I presented parts and versions of this book at a whole range of places and venues, including the Geography Department at Peradeniya University, the Sociology Department at Colombo University, several iterations of the Sri Lanka Roundtable, the research seminars at Peace and Development and Human Geography (both at Gothenburg University), the Varieties of Peace community (Umeå University), the Centre for Conflict Studies (Utrecht University), the Melbourne South Asian Studies Reading Group, the Australia India Institute and the Societies and Culture Seminar (all at Melbourne University), and at the School of Political and Social Sciences (Catholic University Lille).

A DECRA grant from Australian Research Council (DE180101161) enabled me to do the core of the field research and write up the book. My work on postwar Sampur was facilitated by a grant from the Swiss National Science Foundation (grant number 149183). A later grant from the Swedish Research Council (UFORSK 2020-03318) allowed me to widen my perspective and deepen my analysis. In addition, I benefited from a smaller grant from Gothenburg University, which enabled me to contract editorial support. Two universities generously hosted me as a visiting scholar. My fellowship Sociology department at the University of Colombo facilitated fruitful exchange and it was vital for my fieldwork. The fellowship at the Anthropology department at the University of Amsterdam acquainted me with some wonderful academics and it offered me a fantastic place to write.

I thank the editorial team at Cambridge University Press in Delhi. Anwesha Rana guided me through the process of review and publication with kindness, skill and diligence. Priya Das did a fantastic job editing my manuscript.

Finally, I want to acknowledge the people most dear to me, starting with my parents. My mom, who has wondered all along what has taken me so much time, will be particularly happy that this work is finally complete. The same may be true for my wife Rachel – I'm not entirely sure. I want to thank her for her patience, support and companionship throughout the ups and downs of this project and my regular spells of absentmindedness. At the age of 4 and 6, our sons Ole and Ismaël will not (yet) be able to appreciate the nuances of this book, but their open-minded gaze and their thoughtful questions have at times been as thought-provoking as the research seminars mentioned above – and certainly more refreshing. Their wondrous jokes and inquiries help me take the world, and the academy, with a pinch of salt.

A Typographical Note on Separatism

Questions of sovereign recognition – the central concern of this book – have far-reaching ramifications. One of these is the question of capitalisation in the English language. The problem of recognised officialdom is folded into the difference between common and proper nouns: official institutions, when referred to as a single entity, are usually considered to be proper nouns and are therefore capitalised (the *P*resident; the *C*onstitution); non-official institutions or nonspecific terms are considered common nouns and are therefore not capitalised (*t*eam *m*eeting; my *k*itchen *r*ules). Given that this book challenges the categorical differentiation between recognised states and sovereign aspirants, this interpretation of proper and common nouns raises a problem of interpretation. It would yield a text where the authorities of the Sri Lankan state are capitalised but the institutional forms of Tamil separatism would remain in lowercase. To grapple with dilemmas of categorisation and institutional interpretation, which abound when discussing Sri Lanka's civil war, we often resort to prefixes or scare quotes to describe insurgent political forms – *pseudo*-states; rebel 'courts' – but these analytical qualms cannot be evaded with a typographical proviso (see Bryant and Hatay [2020: 6–8] for a conceptual discussion on this issue in relation to the liminalities of northern Cyprus). I therefore seek to confront these problems of classification explicitly in my text, and I minimise the use of capitalisation for all institutions in this book (I do capitalise proper nouns like Sri Lanka, Liberation Tigers of Tamil Eelam, Northern Provincial Council and Peace Secretariat). Similarly, I do not use scare quotes for capturing the purported difference between recognised (the Sri Lankan state and nation) and unrecognised (a Tamil 'state' and 'nation') political realities. However, I do use scare quotes for vernacular phrases that I principally disagree with (such as 'high' or 'low' caste).

Abbreviations

ACMC	All Ceylon Muslim Congress
ACTC	All Ceylon Tamil Congress, the mainstream Tamil party
AIADMK	All India Anna Dravida Munnetra Kazhagam, a 1972 breakaway of India's main Dravidian party DMK
DMK	Dravida Munnetra Kazhagam, a major party in India's federal state of Tamil Nadu
ENDLF	Eelam National Democratic Liberation Front, an offshoot of EPRLF for the 1988 elections for the NEPC
EPRLF	Eelam People's Revolutionary Liberation Front, split from EROS in the early 1980s
EROS	Eelam Revolutionary Organisation of Students, a key militant Tamil group in the 1970s and 1980s
IPKF	Indian Peacekeeping Force, deployed in Sri Lanka by the Indian federal government to uphold the 1987 Indo-Lankan Accord
ISGA	Interim Self-Governing Authority, proposed but unimplemented framework for a political structure with far-reaching autonomous self-government for north-eastern Sri Lanka
ITAK	Ilankai Tamil Arasu Kadchi, the main Tamil nationalist party in Sri Lanka, especially from the 1950s to the 1970s (known in English as the Federal Party)
JVP	Janatha Vimukthi Peramuna, or People's Liberation Front, a Sinhala-nationalist leftist revolutionary movement that staged violent uprisings in the early 1970s and late 1980s

LTTE	Liberation Tigers of Tamil Eelam, the main armed insurgency fighting for a separate Tamil state (defeated in 2009)
NC	National Congress
NEPC	North-Eastern Provincial Council, a merger of the eastern and northern council, created through the 1987 Indo-Lankan accord with the aim to remedy Tamil nationalist grievances
PLOTE	People's Liberation Organisation of Tamil Eelam, an armed movement split from the LTTE in the early 1980s
RDS	Rural Development Society, a village-level community platform
SADR	Sahrawi Arab Democratic Republic
SLFP	Sri Lanka Freedom Party
SLMC	Sri Lanka Muslim Congress, the main Muslim party in Sri Lanka (created 1981)
SLPP	Sri Lanka Podujana Peramuna, or Sri Lanka People's Front, the electoral vehicle of the Rajapaksa family
TELO	Tamil Eelam Liberation Organisation, a key group in the 1970s
TgiE	Tibetan Government in Exile
TMVP	Tamil Makkal Viduthalai Pulikal, or Tamil People Liberation Tigers, the party of renegade LTTE commander Karuna, mainly catering to eastern Tamils
TNA	Tamil National Alliance, an alliance of the main Tamil nationalist parties, created in 2001 (not to be confused with the Tamil National Army, a short-lived attempt by the Indian government to arm the Tamil groups rivalling the LTTE in 1989–1990)
TRNC	Turkish Republic of Northern Cyprus
TUF	Tamil United Front (which later became the TULF), within which ITAK played a leading role
TULF	Tamil United Liberation Front, formerly the TUF, created by all major Tamil parties to adopt a separatist position (the 1976 Vaddukoddai resolution)
UNP	United National Party

1   Introduction

One could start the story of an insurgent movement with a vignette of the frontline or a first encounter with some enigmatic rebel office. In fact, the deleted text that was once on this page did precisely that. While such an initial vantage point helpfully offers the reader a glimpse of the convoluted ground reality of an emerging state, it also risks depicting these territories as exotic and the author as an adventurous protagonist with privileged up-close knowledge of dangerous outposts. Indiana Jones turning to the camera to look his audience in the eyes one more time, before he enters a land of mystery and peril. To start on this footing would disguise that the depiction of these supposedly quaint and anomalous places derives in part from the peculiarities of international perceptions and from the compromised knowledge curve of people like me who seek to understand insurgencies. Let me therefore not start in Sampur or Omanthai or Jaffna but at the picturesque gardens on the northern outskirts of The Hague.

These parklands are home to the Clingendael Institute. As a junior researcher of the institute – perhaps best described as an academic outboard motor to the Dutch Ministry of Foreign Affairs – I had been put on a team of consultants that had been commissioned by a group of aid donors to write a 'Strategic Conflict Analysis' about Sri Lanka. It was 2005, and these donors had enthusiastically jumped aboard the bandwagon of the Norwegian-facilitated peace process between the Sri Lankan government and the Liberation Tigers of Tamil Eelam (LTTE), which had started three years prior. However, the process appeared to be going off the rails, and donors were desperate to consider their options. Hence our assignment. Having completed several visits, interviews and consultations in previous months, I was sitting at my desk overlooking the ponds and greenery of the Clingendael estate to write up our report when the phone rang. In hindsight, my struggle with the interpretative problems around the Tamil insurgency in Sri Lanka that has become this book started with that phone call.

My team leader Jonathan Goodhand – soon to become a friend and colleague – telephoned from London to coordinate our writing and discuss the remaining gaps in our draft text. One of these concerned the significance of the de facto LTTE state that had emerged in different parts of northeastern Sri Lanka, and which had started to consolidate under the auspices of the peace process. Having spent some time in LTTE-controlled territory doing field research for my master's thesis and for various applied assignments, I had gained some credibility on this topic in the Colombo expat circuit, or so I thought anyway. Due to security regulations and diplomatic protocol, employees of embassies and international agencies were confined to official vehicles and orchestrated visits to offices or field sites – wandering around LTTE-controlled areas or sleeping over in villages was a no-go for them. I told Jonathan I would get on with writing a few paragraphs on the implications of the LTTE's institutional landscape, with the breezing can-do confidence of a young, ambitious professional. But when I hung up and opened a new word document, I found myself ferreting for the right idiom.

It was widely known among activists, journalists, aid workers, academics and diplomats working in Sri Lanka that the LTTE had moved from a rudimentary taxation and policing regime to a more elaborate governing framework with an array of departments. Most of us had driven out to the Vanni, the primary site of the LTTE's sovereign experiment, to visit offices and shake hands with LTTE officials. The movement presented itself like a state, and the Norwegian peace facilitators appeared to treat them accordingly, but we all seemed to agree that this was not, you know, a real state. After all, it had no legal status or diplomatic recognition, and while the Tamil cause clearly had some legitimacy, the LTTE had a track record of violence and intolerance. Moreover, this supposed Tamil state was rife with overlaps and ambiguities. The tentacles of the Sri Lankan state continued to function in its territories. The provincial council, a state body that purported to give the Tamil-dominated regions a degree of autonomy, had effectively been pulled into the LTTE's orbit. Government teachers, nurses and bureaucrats went about their work in LTTE areas. The supposed subjects of the Tamil homeland exercised their franchise in Sri Lankan elections. If Tamil Eelam was a de facto state, it was a murky one; one with blurry boundaries and Janus-faced entities. LTTE offices in the Vanni were the talk of the town in Colombo, precisely because they were *not* normal but nonetheless presented and treated as if they were. And because of that unsettled character, nobody knew what would come next. The transformation towards a recognised state? A federal framework? A complete collapse? A new twist with another unanticipated fissure? This was real-time historiography, and it read like a page-turner.

Institutions abounded in the convoluted political landscape of northeastern Sri Lanka, but what they actually did, on whose instructions and on what legal basis was often ambiguous. This book sets out to navigate this apparent institutional jungle and the associated discursive double binds. It is concerned with understanding the LTTE, a movement that has attracted lots of attention but little thorough scholarly study. However, my analysis places the movement within the larger historical trajectory of Tamil nationalist politics: the contestation before the armed insurgency (the political contentions from which the movement emerged), the contestation in parallel to it (alternative and rival enactments of Tamil nationalism) and the contestation that continued afterwards (the struggles of Tamil nationalism in the LTTE's void after its military defeat in 2009). In particular, I am interested in the interaction between the parallel trajectory of armed separatism and the North-Eastern Provincial Council (NEPC), an entity created under Indian duress to accommodate Tamil nationalist aspirations within Sri Lanka's democratic framework.

The political order around Tamil separatist aspirations poses an interpretative dilemma: representing the affected institutions as what they are *supposed* to be (based on their legal underpinnings) yields a skewed, if not plain misleading, picture because these underpinnings are themselves embattled. Conversely, describing institutions as what they *claim* to be (the aspirations projected in propaganda) yields an overly naïve, and equally misleading, rendition. Both approaches raise moral dilemmas around the validating effects of categorisation. After all, the difference between recognised sovereign states and other political actors is fundamental to the way we understand the world. States pass laws, other actors make up rules; states levy tax, other actors extort money; states exercise a legitimate monopoly of violence, other actors engage in unlawful intimidation, thuggery or terrorism; states impart sovereignty by recognising other states, non-state armed actors implicate the parties they engage with. Framing the institutions studied in this book as a State, as a state, as a 'state', as a state with prefixes (pseudo-, quasi-, de facto), a state-in-the-making or not a state at all is not a minor question of categorisation. For the people I describe in this book, rather more was at stake than for me, struggling to find the right words for a donor report. What we render these institutions to be is central to the ethno-political conflict in Sri Lanka. Blindly adopting LTTE propaganda raises both analytical and moral problems, but using the framework of the Sri Lankan state, the constitution and its democratic system to understand this embattled political landscape would miss the point. These supposed foundations are the concepts that are violently placed in question.

Rebel governance, violent democracy and everyday life amidst war

This challenge is not new. Many scholars have attended to forms of order and authority that exist beyond and in overlap with the state. The three bodies of work that stand out respectively focus on wartime order and rebel governance, violent politics within democratic arenas and the everyday lived realities of civil war.

The first body of work emerged as a response to debates of the 1990s which left the inadequate impression that societies experiencing war are zones of anarchy, barbarism and state failure. There is logic and order in civil war, these authors countered, even if it diverges from the good governance handbook. A first wave of interventions coined terms like 'mediated state' (Menkhaus 2006), 'hybrid order' (Boege et al. 2009) and 'political marketplace' (De Waal 2009), 'warscape' (Korf, Engeler and Hagman 2010) and a welter of interventions around the term 'hybridity' (Egnell and Haldén 2013; Justin and Verkoren 2022; Mac Ginty and Richmond 2016; Meagher 2012). These terms are good to think with, but they often remain fluid. The word *hybridity* highlights that things are mixed up, but without further operationalisation it tells us little about why and how that is the case.

The growing literature on rebel governance addresses this concern by delineating the mechanisms and institutions that insurgent movements and de facto states use to govern the territories and populations under their control (Arjona 2016; Arjona, Kasfir and Mampilly 2015; Caspersen 2012; Hoffman and Verweijen 2019; Huang 2016; Mampilly and Stewart 2021; Staniland 2014). Some of this research touches on the LTTE (Mampilly 2011; Provost 2021; Stokke 2006; Terpstra and Frerks 2018). This scholarship describes how insurgent movements impose rules on the civilian population, establish a police and judiciary to uphold them, enforce loyalty, levy taxes, recruit cadres and foster legitimacy through minimal forms of service provision. Some insurgencies go to great lengths to establish an institutional mode of governing that resembles bureaucratic order. Part of this literature is so preoccupied with specifying and categorising the logics of insurgent rule that it appears to underemphasise the political energy vested in these practices. After all, the relentless efforts by insurgents to project a sense of normalcy coexists with their unruliness. Insurgent rule is often experienced as transgressive, spectacular, captivating and capricious. There is almost invariably a lingering anticipation of violence – how sure can one be that an armed movement sticks to its own rules?

The second body of work – on political strongmen, thuggery, mafia practices and violent democratic politics – is centrally preoccupied with this abstruse coalescence of governable order and unruly capacities for violence. Many political figures straddle the divide between electoral politics and transgressive violence, between state governance and the networks of informality, patronage and corruption. And this transversal character is no political liability to them; it is what they derive their political relevance from. Effective politicians bend or break the rules, and though this is widely perceived as a dirty business, it is what many people understand 'normal politics' to be (Arias and Goldstein 2010; Bratton and Van de Walle 1994; Hagmann and Péclard 2010; Lund 2006), not least in South Asia (Breman 1974; Byrne and Klem 2015; Chandra 2004; Chowdhury 2003; Das and Poole 2004; Fuller and Bénéï 2009; Gupta 1995; Klem and Suykens 2018; Spencer 2007; Vaishnav 2017; Witsoe 2013). Political strongmen are capable of unleashing violence, and this ferocity fosters an aura of potency (Berenschot 2011; Hansen 1999, 2001; Michelutti 2010; Michelutti et al. 2018; Peabody 2009; Singh 2012; Suykens 2018; Tambiah 1996). Mafia-like leaders, parties, vigilantes, criminal networks – or some combination thereof – may impose rules, extract resources and enforce loyalty (Malik 2018; Michelutti et al. 2018; Piliavsky 2014a; Price and Ruud 2014; A. Sen 2007). They become 'de facto sovereign' (Hansen and Stepputat 2005, 2006).

This literature offers conceptual inspiration for studying the contested political landscapes of civil war, but there is an important distinction: while some of the de facto sovereigns of 'Mafia Raj' (Michelutti et al. 2018) develop a degree of autonomy, there is no aspiration to be sovereign in the sense of establishing a recognised independent state. The parasitism on state institutions is not a make-do practice in the transition towards a formal sovereign status; it is – and it remains – central to the whole strongman pursuit. This is different for insurgencies that pursue revolutionary, religious or separatist objectives of fundamentally reconstituting the state. South Asia is rife with such movements, as is evident from dedicated studies of the Maoists movement in Nepal (Gellner 2007; Lecomte-Tilouine 2013), the Naxalites (Kunnath 2012; Shah 2019), uprisings in northeast India (Baruah 2007) and cross-cutting and comparative work (Gayer and Jaffrelot 2009; Sen and Pratten 2008; Staniland 2014). Many of these movements adopt some of the above strongman practices, but they combine them with the establishment of proto-state institutions to advance an ideological aspiration that fundamentally challenges the state. Although the distinction between political strongmen and separatist militants matters, it would be a mistake to erect an epistemic wall between societies at war and purportedly peaceful societies and study political contestation in both universes as fundamentally distinct phenomena.

The third strand of literature ponders the lived experiences of the supposed subjects of competing claimants to sovereign power. This scholarship may be rubricked as the anthropology of war (Duschinski et al. 2018; Kelly 2008; Lubkemann 2008; Pettygrew 2013; Richards 2004; Spencer 2007; S. Thiranagama 2011), but similar insights may be gleaned from cognate fields like critical international relations and geography (Brubaker 2004; Cockburn and Zarkov 2002; Hasbullah and Korf 2013; Kirsch and Flint 2011; Stern 2005; Sylvester 2011, 2013). The defining feature of this literature is that it takes society's everyday reality as the primary analytical vantage point. It brackets the master narratives of war and asks how people understand and navigate the reality of war as it manifests in their lives. This perspective interrogates the divide between war and peace and highlights the manifold forms of normalcy that persist amidst a violent insurgency.[1] People go to school, work their lands, get a job, get married, celebrate religious events and so on (Kelly 2008; Pettygrew 2013; Sur 2021; Sylvester 2011; Walker 2013). More pertinent for the focus of this book, this also means that an insurgency does not simply shrug aside the institutions, hierarchies, subjectivities and authorities that exist in a society. These social, cultural, religious or economic forms of order may coexist, overlap, complicate or challenge governing attempts by an insurgent movement.

The rich anthropological scholarship of Sri Lanka's civil war offers many examples of this. There are ethnographies of wartime Hindu temples (Maunaguru and Spencer 2013; Whitaker 1997), social kinship and caste structures (McGilvray 2008), women's social activism (Walker 2013), inter-ethnic irrigation management (Gaasbeek 2010; Hasbullah and Geiser 2019), the transnational engagement by diaspora (Amarasingam 2015; Fuglerud 1991) and the lived experience of violence that persists in society (Daniel 1996). Sharika Thiranagama's work (2010, 2011) is perhaps most illuminating with regard to how social subjectivities, and associated institutions and hierarchies, transformed amidst the political landscape of the Tamil insurgency. She shows that the Tamil militancy constructed different kinds of life and death for different kinds of people: heroic lives and martyred deaths for cadres, precarious docility for Tamil civilians, ruthless eradication for traitors and coercive eviction for non-Tamils (S. Thiranagama 2010). Ultimately, war transforms all subjectivities, not just those associated with ethnicity. Larger political transformations are thus inevitably tied up with more personal contentions of gender, generation, caste, class, locality and ideology. And by consequence, the postwar predicament is one where personal and collective identities have to be negotiated anew because pre-war subjectivities have been irreversibly affected and wartime identities lose their grip.

This book contributes to each of these three scholarly fields by studying the evolution of Tamil nationalist politics – the aspiration of Tamil self-government – from the conceptual vantage point of performative politics. As discussed ahead, this enables me to place political institutions (and the tussles over their legitimacy and legality) in the context of everyday practices and experiences. Rather than delineating rebel governance as a discrete phenomenon, my analysis highlights the interactions and overlaps with parallel repertoires of order and authority, including those of caste and clan strictures, bureaucratic hierarchies and party politics. And as such, the book highlights the longevity of institutional practices. The repertoires of order and authority that we observe during civil war have antecedents that preceded the war and ramifications that outlast it.

A performative perspective on separatist insurgency

The literatures cited earlier offer helpful analytical perspectives and analogies to explore the institutional manifestations of Tamil separatism. However, they do not resolve the analytical dilemma around a movement that pursues a sovereign status but lacks a legal foundation, a democratic mandate and international recognition. It acts like a state but is not one. As discussed at the outset, this leaves us with an interpretative problem because much of our analytical idiom is conjugated with the language of the state. I will adopt a performative perspective to grapple with this problem. More concretely, this book will approach the pursuit of Tamil nationalist aspirations as contentious enactments of political order through the practices of politicians, bureaucrats, insurgents, community leaders, voters and other participants of political life that enter the scene. This does not resolve the 'to be or not to be' dilemma around the state or non-state status of Tamil separatist activities; instead, it usefully places that unsettledness at the heart of the analysis.

A performative perspective helps us see that the manifestation of the state in people's everyday experience can diverge rather dramatically from the formal design of the state's institutional apparatus. This is especially true in a South Asian context, where everybody knows that politics does not stick to the supposed bounds (Chatterjee 2004; Klem and Suykens 2018; Michelutti et al. 2018; Piliavsky 2014a; Ruud 2009). Legally mandated institutions can be rendered politically impotent, while informal institutions without a legal basis can become powerful political platforms. A government department may be responsible for administering the allocation of roads, schools or hospitals, but political patrons may wrest that role from them when they impose themselves as public benefactor. Government prerogatives may be decentralised to peripheral regions, but the ability to action these prerogatives may continue to reside in the capital. Such cunning and trickery is widely perceived as 'normal' South Asian politics, but it becomes particularly significant in a context where duplicity and transgression are not just about the distribution of government resources but about the shape of the sovereign arrangement at large. When an insurgent movement initiates its own set of state institutions or co-opts existing ones, it makes little sense to premise our analysis on an institutional diagram with formal governance structures.

Instead, we need to focus on how political institutions, irrespective of their legal mandate, are enacted. Political anthropologists (Geertz 1980; Gilmartin 2012; Hansen 2009; Hocart 1941 [1927]; D. Rutherford 2012) have underlined that the organised spectacle, symbolic repertoires and the mystification of courts and kings should not be understood as accessories that obfuscate an otherwise rational core of the state; rather, they *are what the state is.*[2] This is perhaps most evident in the way bureaucratic institutions persistently churn out displays of orderly categorisation and procedure to grapple with the rather more unruly power dynamics that continuously percolate their work (Amarasuriya 2010; Bear and Mathur 2015; Das and Poole 2004; Gupta 2012; Hansen 2009; Hull 2012a, 2012b; Jeffrey 2013; Klem 2012; Mathur 2015). Importantly, institutional performance can have both validating or invalidating effects: it may bestow institutions with power, significance and legitimacy, or display impotence, precarity, demise and humiliation.

A performative perspective on political institutions dislodges the official frameworks that purport to direct state operations. Instead, it uses a theatrical idiom to describe how the meaning and significance of state institutions are continuously reproduced through citational practice (Weber 1995), mimicry (Bhabha 1994) and institutional bricolage (Douglas 1970). While some of these dynamics operate at the mundane level of everyday routines and are perhaps best described as institutional *practice*, others have much more theatrical qualities and involve institutional *performance* with an identifiable stage, script and audience. The perspective of performative politics has many intellectual parents, including not only the political anthropologists cited above but also Goffman's (1959) dramaturgical conception of everyday life and Butler's (1990) notion of performativity. Several recent interventions have applied these ideas to political movements that contest the state, in contexts as diverse as Tibet (McConnell 2016), Western Sahara (Alice Wilson 2016), Cyprus (Bryant and Hatay 2020) and Turkey (Watts 2010). Related work focuses on the performative efforts manifest in peace accords and post-accord state-building.[3] Given the close resonance with my own analysis, I will discuss these contributions in some detail.

Fiona McConnell's (2016) account of the Tibetan Government in Exile (TGiE) conceptualises the administration around the Dalai Lama in northern India as a 'dress rehearsal' for a state to come. She uses concepts like scene-setting, stage, playwright, cast, script and audience to describe how this exiled administration replicates state-like conduct while grappling with the challenges of a mobile diasporic population, the lack of international recognition and the inability to operate in the Chinese-occupied Tibetan homeland. Because of its protracted liminality, questions of veracity and fakery hang over the TGiE's performative practices like the sword of Damocles, but it is partly from this precarity and uncertainty that they derive their meaning. Even when the prospects of performing an actual recognised state become ever dimmer, the practice of rehearsing a state-to-come produces tangible effects, McConnell argues. It instils legitimacy, erects a screen for national aspirations and gives material shape to the political theology around the Dalai Lama, the administration's holy playwright. A very similar line of reasoning – though without a saintly monarchic figure in plum-coloured robes – may be found in Alice Wilson's (2016) book on the Sahrawi Arab Democratic Republic (SADR), a government in exile linked to Polisario that aspires a separate state in Western Sahara.

Rebecca Bryant and Mete Hatay (2020) theorise the anomaly of the Turkish Republic of Northern Cyprus (TRNC) as an 'aporetic state', an aspirational entity that is riven by irresolvable contradictions. Referring to the TRNC's institutions as de facto presents them as both real and not real; it simultaneously acknowledges and denies them as fact. They factually exist, but they are perceived as made-up and thus factitious. They comprise a performance of state conduct that emphasises its own provisional status, and by exhibiting this quality of still being in-the-making – a condition of being incomplete or stuck – such performances question their own veracity. While this is especially salient in the TRNC, Bryant and Hatay underline that this contingency of status is inherent to sovereignty. The performance of sovereignty requires an audience to validate its credibility, to confer recognition, but no matter how convincing the performance, sovereignty always remains contingent and incomplete. Its purported end state is endlessly deferred.

For the Kurdish political parties in Turkey that Nicole Watts (2010) describes, this deferral takes place in a more repressive setting. The Turkish republic affords minimal legal and political margins, but Kurdish parties participate in elections and assume governing responsibilities in Kurdish-majority provinces. Watts argues that these parties entered office to use Turkish state bodies as loudspeakers for Kurdish nationalism and to project an alternative governmentality. They engaged in 'as-if politics' (a term she draws from Wedeen [1999] but then applies in a more subaltern manner) to nurture

Kurdish subjectivity and undermine Turkish authority. The stakes of these subaltern strategies were high. As-if politics gave oxygen to the Kurdish struggle, but many of the protagonists faced state retribution and imprisonment.

The approach taken in this book builds on these accounts, though the contexts of a government in exile (TGiE, SADR), a consolidated de facto state (TRNC) and cross-border separatism (Turkish Kurdistan) are quite different. The performative perspective that these authors take helpfully addresses the problematic binaries of state versus non-state, real recognised sovereignty versus aspirational sovereignty. As becomes clear from these books, a performative lens defies the implied opposition between performance and reality. It does *not* view performance as *real* persons who enact *fictional* characters to stage an *imaginary* script which is then interpreted back to reality by *real* people in the audience. Rather, the point of a performative perspective is to deliberately side-step the question of veracity and explore the effects of staged practices. It assumes an inter-subjective reality: meaning and knowledge of ourselves and the world around us are continuously reproduced through the citational practice of discourse. Performance is simultaneously an interpretation of social reality and a part of it.

Interpretating the institutional efforts of an insurgency in performative terms, therefore, does not imply affirmation of whatever act is being staged. This is important for normative reasons, lest my account of Tamil nationalist politics be misunderstood for a Tamil nationalist account.[4] But it also has analytical dimensions: an approach that is overly preoccupied with insurgent performativity could fall prey to a form of fetishism that elides the contingent and precarious nature of these efforts. Insurgent performance is not a stand-alone phenomenon that is isolated from the world by the parameters of the stage. It interacts with diverse audiences and rivals, and it is situated in a political landscape of armed conflict that shapes the bandwidth of what can be credibly performed. To understand the performative efforts of an insurgency, we need to look beyond the phenomenon itself because it involves off-stage coercion and violence to keep performances and audiences in check and ward off competition. Moreover, it derives meaning from other junctures in space and time. It involves citational practice and mimicry of previous or contending repertoires. It competes and overlaps with the efforts of state institutions. The trappings of the state can be turned into platforms of agitation, and the language and institutions of the state can be redeployed for a contrarian political project. The state's technology of power, to use a Foucauldian phrase, comprises dual use technology; insurgent movements may co-opt or replicate the state apparatus for contrarian sovereign ends.

Argument and contribution

This study explores how the Tamil nationalist movement in Sri Lanka has enacted, imposed, contested, reworked, flipped and erased the institutions of legitimate government. It juxtaposes divergent enactments of sovereignty, which unfold both in competition and partial overlap with each other. The LTTE's attempt to establish an incipient Tamil state was the most pronounced example, but in parallel to this, the NEPC enacted a hampered form of shared sovereignty, and Tamil political parties projected nationalist aspirations from within the democratic arena. The frictions, stand-offs and amalgamations between these assertions of sovereignty decisively shaped the history of conflict in Sri Lanka and the dynamics of Tamil nationalism. The 2009 end of the war marked the defeat of the LTTE state and the triumph of a singular Sri Lankan sovereignty while the notion of shared sovereignty – along with what remained of the provincial councils – was left to crumble. This watershed moment profoundly reconfigured Tamil nationalist politics, but the contradictions and overlaps continued, albeit in different ways.

Focusing on the way sovereign aspirations are staged, dramatised and publicly consumed helps us see how political dynamics can transgress, undermine or reverse the institutional logics of the democratic landscape. Political performativity has the capacity to unmoor the foundational premises of the state. It can bolster (or undercut) the potency and legitimacy of a state institution; it can serve to re-enact that institution for contrarian ends; and it can instil insurgent institutions with the potency and legitimacy to supplant those of the state. Transgression and violence are a central element of these contentious political repertoires. By implication, the political performativity that I describe is often precarious. Political authority can unravel, sometimes with breathtaking speed: scripts may take an unexpected turn, the curtain may fall more quickly than anticipated, protagonists may be killed, valorising drama can degenerate into a farce or a mockery, it can fall prey to satire.

My basic contention in this book is that we need to understand separatist militancy as an arena of contingent political performance. Rather than assuming that institutions are constructed on legal foundations, we must consider them as aspirational enactments capable of establishing legitimacy, which may grow legal roots afterwards. Questions around the veracity and authenticity of insurgent institutions remain unadjudicated because of the violent contingencies around these performative efforts. This ambivalence accounts for the political energy around the insurgent experimentation with sovereign rule: the awe, excitement, perturbation and anxiety. More specifically, I argue that the trajectory of

Tamil separatist politics in Sri Lanka comprises several competing repertoires, including the sovereign experiment of the LTTE, but also the institutional forms of a compromised Tamil bureaucracy and the performativity of Tamil political parties. Each of these efforts entailed contingent and precarious performance, and as such they experienced moments of buoyancy, spectacle and triumph as well as rupture and defeat. And as their fortunes changed over the course of the conflict, the repertoires of Tamil separatism shifted vessel, some performative spaces expanded, while others were overrun, and this required new forms of improvisation, self-moderation or regained prowess.

This argument broadly corroborates the existing performative accounts of sovereign aspirants, including governments in exile (McConnell 2016; Alice Wilson 2016), de facto states (Bryant and Hatay 2020) and ethno-nationalist militancy (Watts 2010). My analysis expands the focus from the insurgent state performance itself to other Tamil nationalist endeavours, which existed before, alongside and after the LTTE militancy. The trajectory of the conflict is not confined to the rise and fall of the LTTE militancy; it encompasses tensions, overlaps and bricolage between performances of Tamil aspirations, which are subject to mutual encroachment and dissociation, erasure and reassemblage, legacies and rival heirs. The temporal span of this book also adds an important dimension to the extant scholarship. The potential of rupture or defeat is firmly present in the existing accounts but primarily as a continuously deferred threat: the North Cypriot state is incomplete (Bryant and Hatay 2020), the Tibetan government is constantly aware of its possible downfall (McConnell 2016), Kurdish politics entails a continuous cat-and-mouse dynamic with state repression (Watts 2010). In this book, the ruptures of sovereign erasure, through the 2009 defeat of the LTTE, stand at the heart of the analysis. It is in the wake of this watershed moment that the Tamil nationalist repertoires beyond the LTTE gained new traction and significance. Tamil performative experimentation did not end with the war; it changed vessel and form.

The empirical narrative presented in this book is based on multi-sited and multi-scaler qualitative fieldwork conducted over a period of twenty years. Perspectives are drawn from the everyday encounters in public space, workaday engagement with state officials, discussions with political figures at all scales, from village-level organisers to party leaders, peace envoys and presidents. The four main pillars undergirding this book are long-term fieldwork around the village Sampur in the east coast district of Trincomalee; ethnographic research on the provincial council apparatus in the east and north; fieldwork on several election campaigns; and a cluster of interviews and archival analysis on the Norwegian-facilitated peace process.[5] These methods are subject to limitations, and they harbour dilemmas around the interpretation, representation and attribution of sources.[6] However, they derive strength from the interconnections between diverse empirical strands and a sustained engagement over a long period of time.

Organisation

This book is organised into a conceptual discussion (Chapter 2), followed by four empirical chapters and a conclusion. The empirical part starts out with the rise and fall of the LTTE's sovereign experiment (Chapter 3). The three subsequent chapters study Tamil nationalist struggles in the wake of the 2009 LTTE defeat, through village-level scuffles over socio-cultural delineations of Tamil purity (Chapter 4), manoeuvring and realignment within the provincial bureaucracy (Chapter 5) and attempts by Tamil political parties to project a nationalism for which there was no space in the postwar democratic order (Chapter 6).

More specifically, Chapter 2 addresses the foundational challenges of interpretating separatist politics. It builds on the recent literature on sovereignty, and it offers a more thorough discussion of the qualities and merits of a performative perspective on separatist experimentation. It also offers rudimentary contextual and historical background: Sri Lanka's troubled engagement with the notion of shared sovereignty as a proposed antidote to ethno-nationalist conflict and the escalation from conflict into war.

Chapter 3 comprises the empirical mounting block for the rest of the book. It builds on observations in LTTE-controlled territory to describe how the movement became a de facto sovereign formation that mimicked the state. It highlights the tensions and paradoxes inherent to this endeavour. LTTE rule was simultaneously orderly and capricious: alongside its state-like institutions and procedures, it nurtured a cult of violence, with the *talaivar* (leader) as its supreme referent. In parallel to the creation of its own institutions, the LTTE engaged in sovereign encroachment through fuzzy boundaries, institutional overlap and tactical restraint. The chapter goes on to show how the Norwegian-facilitated peace process of the 2000s offered the LTTE a conduit to elevate its sovereign mimicry to the international stage, thus eliciting an implied international recognition and parity of status with the Sri Lankan government. The spectacle of this Tamil state-to-be captivated many foreign observers. The LTTE's ability to act on the international stage was facilitated by the Norwegian mediators preserving the appearance of symmetry in the peace talks. However, when the peace process started to disintegrate, this apparent symmetry was overrun by the staunch asymmetries in the prevalent policy outlooks in Delhi,

Washington and elsewhere. The LTTE continued to project a Tamil state-to-be, but due to the change in context, its performative efforts lost their authoritative charm and in fact came dangerously close to being perceived as a farce.

Chapter 4 conceptualises the 2009 defeat of the LTTE as a moment of sovereign erasure. It studies postwar Sampur, which was reduced to rubble when the military wrested it from the LTTE and subsequently became an inaccessible military zone. The chapter explores the common local reference to Sampur as a 'pure Tamil' place, and it describes how the residents struggled to reconstitute this purity after their return in 2015 – a prism for postwar Tamil society at large. This struggle harbours cultural disorientation and moral panic amidst *intra*-Tamil divisions of caste and *kudi* (clan): struggles over unwanted mixture and purification that Tamil militants had denounced but which came up again after the war.

Chapter 5 highlights the remarkable pliability of state institutions by showing how the NEPC was first staged as a moderated form of Tamil government instigated by India, then became a politically beheaded bureaucratic entity that was gradually drawn into the LTTE's orbit and finally emerged as a site for competing efforts of staging political normalcy after the war. The heart of the chapter comprises an ethnographic study of postwar administrative life in the Eastern Provincial Council (now de-merged from the north). I illustrate how the tenacity of this entity centres on the bureaucratic inclination to try and keep politics out. Ironically, this contradicts the purported role of the councils as a lesser form of Tamil self-determination. What was conceived as a platform of shared sovereignty with significant powers and law-making competencies has evolved into a truncated channel for the distribution of state resources in pursuit of balanced regional development. As a result, the provincial councils are institutionally resilient but politically impotent.

Chapter 6 looks at postwar positioning of Ilankai Tamil Arasu Kadchi (ITAK), the foremost Tamil political party. ITAK suffered from political schizophrenia: it pitted itself against Sri Lanka's democratic framework but simultaneously participated in it. To grapple with this contradiction, I posit, ITAK resorted to three anti-political repertoires: oath-of-allegiance politics, political abstinence and the politics of performing institutional deficiency. Bereft of recourse to the LTTE's sovereign experiment and faced with growing competition within the Tamil political arena, these anti-political repertoires came under severe strain. ITAK's schizophrenic challenges culminated in the spectacular breakdown of the Northern Provincial Council, which ceased to function in the final year of its term due to ruptures within the Tamil nationalist coalition.

The final chapter recapitulates my findings and draws overall conclusions.

Notes

1   The question of normalcy has spawned some debate on the interpretative place of violence – to emphasise or de-emphasise it, to normalise or abnormalise it. In response to Nordstrom (1997, 2004), who apportions a crucial role to violence in her ethnography, Lubkemann takes issue with the presumed 'hegemony of violence' and proposes to consider 'war as a social condition' (2008: 12–15), thus highlighting the centrality of local struggles, which may interact with the wide dynamics of war but are no derivative of it. In a similar vein, Richards (1996, 2004: 11) argues that war 'needs to be understood in terms of the patterns of violence already embedded in society'. Partly as a result of that, the spatial and temporal demarcations of war and peace are often fuzzy and contested: many people find themselves in the social condition of 'no war, no peace' (Richards 2004).

2   In parallel, and closer to home for the Westphalian state order, post-structural interpretations of the state have gained currency (Abrams 1988 [1977]; Foucault 1997; Mitchell 1991).

3   Jeffrey's (2013) account of the civil servants in post-accord Bosnia Hercegovina studies how bureaucrats (and other state officers) 'improvise' state sovereignty, as they navigate the compromised nature of the new-born state, the competing nationalist forces and the continued presence of international overlordship. See also Dixon's (2019) work for a performative angle on front- and backstage politics around the Northern Irish peace process.

4   I endeavour to take Tamil nationalist positions seriously and to question state-centric perspectives of sovereignty. In Sri Lanka's embattled discursive landscape, this could easily be interpreted as a political stance. My interest, however, is not to advocate Tamil nationalism or separatism (as should be clear from the many instances where I critically interrogate the Tamil nationalist project) but rather to analyse it as a phenomenon in its own right.

5   This book draws on a sequence of research engagement over the last two decades, and as such the data gathering evolved in parallel to my own academic maturation. More specifically, the data gathering process started – in hindsight – with six months fieldwork for my master's thesis in Trincomalee and Jaffna in 2000–2001. The next major effort comprised my doctoral research in different parts of eastern Sri Lanka, including Trincomalee (about six months over the period 2007–2011). A third significant portion of fieldwork was undertaken as part of a Swiss-funded project on settlement politics in eastern Sri Lanka, where I mainly focused on Sampur (during visits of several weeks in 2013, 2015 and 2016). The final effort, which has retrospectively shaped this book as a whole (and Chapter 5 in particular), was an Australian-funded project focused on Sri Lanka's provincial councils. This involved an effort of institutional ethnography among provincial bureaucrats and took place in 2018 and 2019. In addition, one applied research project significantly contributed to this book:

the evaluation of Norwegian peace efforts commissioned by the Norwegian government (2010–2011), which offered my colleagues and me unrivalled access to the highest levels of government in Sri Lanka, Norway, India and elsewhere, as well as access to classified Norwegian archives. Finally, I gathered material during event-driven visits – notably after the tsunami in 2005 and for the first-ever Northern Provincial Council elections in 2013 – as well as during applied research assignments when I worked for the Clingendael Institute, a think-tank in The Hague (from 2004 to 2006).

6   There are significant methodological challenges and limitations. I was unable to speak with many key figures (including some of the senior LTTE leaders), and I did not have access to some of the most significant occurrences of the war (most obviously the massacres at the end of the war). Much of my analysis relies on interview material. As always, such accounts may be prone to biases from the normative colouring of conflict and an inclination of informants to enlarge or reduce their own contribution. Many of these interviews moreover focused on the past and thus relied on people's memory. I have tried to confront these challenges and limitations through triangulation and careful reflection on the basis of my collection of diverse perspectives, at several locations and levels, over a relatively long period of time. A final challenge concerns the treatment of sources: balancing the imperative of being empirically specific and protecting people's privacy, welfare and safety. My approach has been to name informants who occupy such important positions that anonymisation would become absurd ('a Sri Lankan president said') and who are moreover well positioned to go on record. This is a small group. For a slightly larger group of people, who are featured at several instances throughout a chapter or several chapters, I use pseudonyms. I have left all other informants anonymous by referring to them by the categories that matter to the section at hand ('a senior bureaucrat said', 'an older Tamil man from Jaffna said').

2 Sovereignty, Performativity and Tamil Nationalism in Sri Lanka

This chapter establishes the theoretical underpinnings of this book and clarifies key concepts and ideas. More specifically, it reviews debates on the question of sovereignty and its murky status as the central referent of global political order, and it advances the perspective of performative politics to grapple with the contradictions and ambiguities that prevail in the context of sovereign contestation. The chapter then proceeds to apply this perspective to the Tamil nationalist movement in Sri Lanka. In doing so, it also provides the reader with essential contextual and historical background to the chapters that follow.

The notion of the sovereign state as the legitimate authority over people and territory is deeply inscribed in prevalent understandings of the world today – as the referent of law, authorised force, national citizenship, democratic rule and international order. It is embedded in a whole architecture of norms and claimed entitlements. However, this framework of legitimation is ultimately circular: sovereign states are sovereign because they are. This circularity becomes exposed when the fundamentals of a state are challenged (Pegg 1998, 2017). Such confrontations come in myriad forms – indigenous communities resisting settler states, such as in Australia (Schaap 2004), Canada and the United States (A. Simpson 2014); occupied territories with a government in exile, like Tibet (McConnell 2016) or Western Sahara (Alice Wilson 2016), or a constellation like the Syrian Interim Government (Gangwala 2015; Sosnowski, under review); governments with incomplete or faltering sovereign recognition, such as the Palestinian Authority (Feldman 2008; Kelly 2006), the Turkish Republic of North Cyprus (Bryant and Hatay 2020; Navaro-Yashin 2003), Transnistria (Bobick 2017), Abkhazia (Preltz-Oltramonti 2017), Kosovo (Krasniqi 2019; Van der Borgh 2012), Taiwan (Corcuff 2012; Friedman 2021) or Hong Kong

(Yep 2013); insurgent groups that demand reunification with a neighbouring state, as in Northern Ireland (Aretxaga 1997; Little 2014); or separatist movements as in Catalonia (Achniotis 2021; Bárcena 2020; Enguix Grau 2021), Kurdistan (Gunes 2012; Watts 2010), northeast India (Baruah 2007) and Myanmar (Brenner 2017) – and, as discussed in this book, in northeastern Sri Lanka.

By challenging the foundational premises of state sovereignty, these movements unsettle the self-referential cycle of analytical and normative claims that undergird the notion of legitimate state sovereignty. Once that cycle is interrupted, the established moral yardsticks for political order – what historical precedents impart, what the law prescribes, what the nation consents to – offer us little recourse because each of these categories is itself implicated by the prevalent conception of a particular state. Separatism thus confronts us with a combined normative and analytical problem. I will posit that the literature on performative politics lends us a helpful lens to navigate this problem. This enables us to approach the institutional framework established by an insurgent movement as a contingent sovereign experiment. Rather than placing upfront the prevalent criteria of validity and legitimacy (this is or is not a sovereign state, because ...), this directs our attention to the way political assertions are put to practice in pursuit of sovereignty, what kind of de facto realities ensue, the spectacle and uncertainty around them, and how these interact with the question of normative status.

The second half of this chapter discusses the historical trajectory of Tamil nationalism and that of the Sri Lankan state and its failed attempts at sovereign power-sharing. While the basic tenets of this history will be familiar to many South Asianists, the perspective of performative contestation over sovereign claims places some elements of Sri Lanka's ethno-political conflict in a new light.

Sovereignty

The term 'sovereignty' is slippery because it means so many different things at once. It may denote a national right (self-determination), the status of a recognised state (state sovereignty), a violent potency (sovereign power), an individual with regal attributes (the sovereign) or the capacity to suspend the law (sovereign exception), to name the most salient examples – and these conceptions then yield more derivatives and combinations. I discuss a conceptualisation of sovereignty that draws on several of these meanings in relation to the phenomenon of a separatist insurgency. First, however, it is instructive to take a step back and consider the historical luggage vested in the modern discourse of sovereignty as the bedrock of the international order of legitimate states.

The institutional jungle of Sri Lanka's civil war may seem like an anomaly, but if we broaden our view – in both spatial and temporal terms – and place the political landscape of the Tamil insurgency in the context of South Asia throughout the twentieth century, this convoluted landscape is no longer so exceptional. Constellations with competing claimants to sovereign authority, convoluted layers of rule, permeable boundaries and fragmentary legal regimes look rather less exceptional. And more significantly, the conception of sovereignty – as a deceptive benchmark of legitimate statehood – itself emerges as a product of the colonial past.

Notwithstanding its rampant violence, colonial rule did not comprise an all-encompassing imposition, a European blanket of legal-political ordering that was rolled out through imperial conquest. The notion of colonial sovereignty as a systemic form of rule over people and territory was 'a performative ideal', Hansen (2021: 41) argues.[1] In practice, this historical process was characterised by contingencies, rough administrative edges, legal ambiguity, institutional competition, and continuous interaction between attempts at governance, push-back, unintended consequences and ground realities that kept shifting beyond the clasp of policy. The mercurial nature of colonial law stems from the unremitting challenge of having different kinds of law for different kinds of people and territory (Benton 2002, 2009; Chatterjee 1993). This multiplicity yielded ambiguity and friction because these differences were never watertight: human affinities and relationships blurred racial distinctions; human bodies, claims and entitlements crossed territorial divides (Benton 1999; Cooper 2014; Lombard 2020; Mongia 2018; B. Rutherford 2004). As a result, colonial rule (and postcolonial transition) offered an incessant flow of hazards and opportunities around the tensions and niches of legal pluralism. Customary authorities sought formal recognition and exploited legal ambiguities to redefine laws in their favour (Moore 1978). Overlapping forms of jurisdiction between the legal frameworks of the state, customary tradition and religion resulted in both forum-shopping and shopping forums (Von Benda-Beckmann 1981).

The so-called Westphalian notion of sovereignty did not simply come of age in Europe to then be imposed on colonies; it was itself shaped by the colonial encounter (Anghie 1999; Cooper 2014; Hansen 2021; Scott 1995). Colonial rule was propelled by sovereign experimentation, resulting in forms of order that were incomplete and subject to attempts at encroachment and adaptation. Empires comprised inconsistent, incomplete and indirect rule resulting from détentes and treaties with sultans, kings, religious jurisdictions, tribal councils or other forms of authority. India's 'princely states' within the British Raj were a salient example (Beverley 2013, 2020b; Gilmartin, Price and Ruud 2020; Purushotham 2015). Colonial administrations were riven by the divergent trajectories of different tentacles of government, which prompted tensions and scuffles, for example, between the executive and the judiciary or between capitals and delegated authority. Colonialism was thus characterised by multiple, competing sources of legal authority, implicating the legal politics of colonisers and colonised alike (Benton 2002; Beverley 2020a; Cooper 2014; Mongia 2007, 2018; Mukherjee 2010).

The process of decolonisation harboured a similar set of tensions (Chatterjee 2005; Sherman, Gould and Ansari 2011). The formative moment of independence tends to feature in historical canons as a grand unifying struggle against European domination; at closer scrutiny, it was almost invariably shaped by conflictual encounters between competing aspirations of sovereignty and ruptures around the demarcation of a national *demos*. It was fragmented, and the resulting nations were composed of diverse fragments (Chatterjee 1993). Purushotham's (2021) recent effort to reinterpret India's transition 'from raj to republic' illustrates that the violent rearticulation of boundaries was not confined to the geopolitical strokes of independence and the partition. It also comprised intense struggles over ethnic, religious, ideological and patriarchal claims to authority, both within and across these national demarcations. Sovereign violence and sovereign exceptions abounded, not only in the encounter with colonial authority but also in subjugating the unresolved contradictions and unruly potentials within.[2] Purushotham illustrates that India's discourse of popular sovereignty and civic nationalism, enshrined in a federal democracy, emerged out of the violent conflicts inside the anti-colonial struggle. The competing imaginations of sovereignty were brought in line with violent impositions, and as such, 'India's liberal democracy was grafted onto an authoritarian state' (Purushotham 2021: 251). The foundations and demarcations of the political system were established through sovereign violence, which carved out space for a proud national tradition of democracy and the rule of law (Chatterjee 1986; Jalal 1995). Challenges to these sovereign delineations were placed out of bounds. Struggles about the nature of the state (for example, the Naxalite movement: Kunnath [2012]; Parashar [2019]; Shah [2013]; Suykens [2010]) and its territorial demarcation (for example, across India's borderlands: Baruah [2007]; Duschinski et al. [2018]; Shani [2007]; Vandekerckhove [2011]) persisted, but they were banished to extra-democratic spaces and dealt with accordingly – a dynamic that is also observed in other South Asian states (Chowdhury 2003; Gardezi and Rashid 1983; Gellner 2007; Jalal 1990; Lecomte-Tilouine 2013; Malik 2018).

The postcolonial moment marked a historical watershed where a particular sovereign constellation prevailed over its alternatives. Apart from establishing national boundaries, this juncture solidified the national foundation of law and concurrent delimitations of the sphere of legitimate politics. Yet it would be misleading to present this watershed simply as the historical transit point between imposed colonial order and postcolonial self-rule, where European concepts of state sovereignty and national self-determination were imparted to the rest of the world (Anghie 1999; Beverley 2020a; Chatterjee 1993; Cooper 2002; Hansen 2021). This view would oversimplify the multifarious and splintered nature of colonial rule before independence; it would elevate a specific mode of government, steeped in a specifically European experience of national sovereignty, to become a general interpretative norm; and it would relegate the fractured and contentious nature of postcolonial sovereignty to the background. Postcolonial scholarship helpfully offsets the idealised image of the modern European state as the inevitable master frame of our analysis. Questions of sovereignty and sovereign power abound in this literature, but rather than validating the vestiges of the state, these terms denote unresolved tensions and contradictions. This contradictory character of sovereignty is no figment of the past or a watermark of political immaturity in the global periphery. It is inherent to sovereignty.

Defining sovereignty thus becomes an onerous endeavour. An initial definition would be the supreme right and ability to govern over people and territory without yielding to a purportedly higher external force. As such, sovereignty operates on the interstices of power (the supreme *ability* to govern) and legitimacy (the perceived *right* to do so). The heart of the problem, Gilmartin (2020) holds, is that worldly power cannot legitimise itself. It must source its moral authority from beyond the political community to which it pertains, often by alluding to transcendental or mythical registers. As a result, sovereignty is simultaneously conceptualised as an integral part of the society it claims authority over *and* as a register of power and legitimacy that stands apart from society. This dual quality of being both within and outside society generates a relentless contradiction, Gilmartin argues – not a contraction that is difficult to resolve but rather one that *cannot* be resolved.

At first sight, this conceptualisation appears at odds with a Wilsonian understanding of sovereignty, a term premised on the national right to self-determination. After all, this right is purportedly sourced from within. From this perspective, and its codification in international law (most obviously the 1933 Montevideo convention[3]), a nation's entitlement to self-rule, free from colonial occupation, derives from its internal character in terms of language, territory and political history. But this supposed internality is part of nationalism's fiction. Nations are political constructs that emerge from violent histories of nationalist contestation and state formation, *not* immanent political communities that offer a clear popular foundation for the state. A body politic may be depicted as an extension of kinship, where family serves as a trope for the nation. The definition of that family – its character, its internal composition and its demarcations – is inherently contested. It consists of diverse human bodies that are categorised with ascriptions of race, purity (for example, in relation to caste) and sexuality. The historical emergence of a national community, with distinct cultural customs and virtues, thus pertains to the intimate sphere of kinship, sexuality, gendered bodies and kinship. The nation is an inherently gendered construct (Barker 2006; Chatterjee 1993; Cooper 2014; Jayawardena 1986; Parashar 2018; Spivak 1988). It is steeped in masculine and feminine renditions of origin, reproduction, guardianship, modernity and destiny. It is premised on differential forms of gendered subjectivity, where women adopt secondary roles. And as such, it is subject to tussles over the way gendered conduct is practised, depicted and policed (Chatterjee 1993; Parashar 2018; True 2018; Sylvester 2011; Yuval-Davis 1997).

As discussed in the context of the British Raj earlier, the discourse of self-determination offered no fitting template for the multifarious landscape of a colonial empire in demise with fierce and violent competition between monarchic traditions, the awakening of ethnic, religious, or linguistic communities, peasant uprisings, leftist mobilisation and nascent forms of civic nationalism (Chatterjee 1993; Purushotham 2021). The notion of sovereignty that the discourse of self-determination propels is thus not simply sourced from within, as a derivative of a community's national qualities. It is subject to a relational history between that community and its supposed others. National sovereignty invariably emerges from a genealogy of mixture and dissociation, settlement and mobility, autonomous authority and occupation, internal violence and external violence, because claims to self-determination are rarely singular. The reflexive prefix – self – tends to be subject to competing political interpretations of collective selfhood (G. Simpson 1996).

Democratic theory has difficulty adjudicating competing claims to self-determination. If the national demarcation of democracy, the *demos*, is contested, democratic principles offer no firm redress. A democratic system cannot resolve disagreements over its own boundaries, Whelan (1983) famously posited, because it is itself a function of that demarcation. After all, if one were to subject the demarcation of the people to a vote, who would be entitled to vote on it, and which majority would count? A referendum on the bounds of the people would itself require bounds. Moreover, every boundary has two sides, so those excluded from a particular rendering of the people should be entitled to have a say on it too.[4] A related theoretical reflection in legal scholarship may be found in Brilmayer's (1989) claim that the legitimate origins of law inevitably involve 'bootstrapping': law circularly reasons itself into being.[5] Sovereignty is ultimately a self-referential concept, Hansen and Stepputat (2005, 2006) underline. It is presented as the self-evident foundation of state power and legitimacy but ultimately has recourse only onto itself. Seen in this light, the assertion of national sovereignty may be depicted as the original sin of the moral framework of constitutional democracy. It celebrates itself as a legal-political order beyond violence but originates from (and continues to be anchored in) the violent and illiberal crafting of its own prerequisites: the definition of a national community (and its internal norms and hierarchies), the demarcation of territory, the foundation of law and the state's mandate to govern.

The provenance of most sovereign states, including the European ones that are often held up as the implied model, is therefore caught up with sovereign power. In the European tradition, the referent of such sovereign power has historically migrated from god to king, to parliament and finally to the nation at large (Bartelson 1995; Kantorowicz 1997 [1957]). Similar, but different, sovereign genealogies may be found in South Asia (Gilmartin 2015, 2020; Heesterman 1985). Sovereign power is not simply supreme legal authority but the ability to bring legal authority into being or to take it away. Given that this is not just about the rules of political conduct but about the ability to change the rules or to declare exceptions (Agamben 2005; Schmitt 2005 [1922]), sovereign power is inherently caught up with violence: not only the predictable violence of the legal procedures of discipline but also the sublime violence of disregard for human life if it so pleases the sovereign (Hansen 2001). It is capricious. There are rules and rights. But they can change.

This was perhaps more visible during feudal or colonial times, when sovereign power was dispersed among a raft of lords, suzerainties, companies and private armies, which subjected populations and extracted economic value with a large degree of impunity. But arguably, many of these 'de facto sovereigns' are still with us, in the form of offshore border patrols and incarceration systems (Bilgiç 2018; Little, Suliman and Wake 2023; Mountz 2011), assemblages of remote warfare (Akhter 2019; Demmers, Gould and Snetselaar 2020; Hayat 2020), militias (A. Sen 2007; Verkaaik 2004), quasi courts (Buur 2005; Malik 2018) or political strongmen (Michelutti et al. 2018; Piliavsky 2014a). Hansen and Stepputat (2006: 269) define 'de facto sovereignty' as the ability to exercise 'discipline with impunity'. Phrased with a bit more detail: the ability to initiate rules and enforce them, if need be, with lethal violence (exercise 'discipline'), without yielding to a more powerful governing force ('with impunity').

Insurgent groups that supplant existing state institutions with their own, impose rules, enforce loyalty, levy tax, recruit cadres and foster legitimacy with minimal forms of service provision (Arjona, Kasfir and Mampilly 2015; Caspersen 2012; Klem and Maunaguru 2017; Mampilly 2011; Staniland 2012, 2014) may thus be categorised as de facto sovereign. Yet applying this term to a separatist insurgency gives the discussion an additional twist, because such movements differ from most of the political actors that feature in discussions on de facto sovereignty. First, the narrative of sovereignty as self-determination comes back in. The de facto sovereignty of insurgent movements may have much in common with political strongmen or private companies, but it is embedded in a more encompassing aspiration of sovereign power and legitimacy – one that is not merely 'de facto'. Second, more thoroughgoing insurgent movements like the Liberation Tigers of Tamil Eelam (LTTE) blur the implied distinction between de facto and de jure sovereignty because they establish legal foundations in pursuit of a separate state. Even if these foundations are not recognised as official law, this arguably makes such movements de facto de jure sovereign as well.

To sum up, the apparent simplicity of defining sovereignty as the supreme right and ability to govern over people and territory succumbs to foundational complications around the meaning of the words 'right' and 'ability'. The sovereign *right* to govern is often encoded in a discourse of national self-determination, but rather than providing a firm conceptual basis, 'the nation' confronts us with contested interpretations, murky boundaries and gendered categories, violent genealogies, and recourse to the legitimating aura of gods, kings and other intractable figures. The conception that sovereignty offers a stable bedrock for the modern order of states is itself a product of a long history of conflict and occupation. There is no escape from the fact that the legitimating logic of sovereignty is ultimately self-referential. The sovereign *ability* to govern spawns similarly complicated queries. State capacity is typically conjugated with other forms of authority, and its supposed monopoly of violence often rests on more fragmented patterns of delegation and the countenance of de facto sovereign entities within its realm. Rather than simply denoting the authority to set the rules, sovereignty ultimately entails the ability to establish rule-setting authority. By implication, sovereign power also comprises the capricious ability to exempt, break or rewrite the rules.

Performative politics

Rather than seeking (or pretending) to resolve the tensions around the term 'sovereignty', this book endeavours to keep them intact by placing unsettling questions about the contested, self-referential nature of sovereignty at the heart of the analysis. The perspective of performative politics is helpful in navigating these questions. As a preliminary point, this approach requires a conception of politics that is not confined to the official trappings of elections, parliament and government policy. My understanding of politics is mediated by political anthropology (Banerjee 2014; Bertrand et al. 2007; Geertz 1980; Hansen 2001; Michelutti et al. 2018; Paley 2008; Ruud 2009) and the work of Spencer (2003, 2007, 2008, 2012) in particular. This scholarship takes an expansive view of politics that traverses the broad canvas of the state, the nation, sovereignty and political potency, and the way these interacting notions are constructed, experienced and contested. Seen this way, politics involves antagonism and feuding, the moral drama of electoral dramaturgy, normative transgressions and violence, as well as humour, humiliation and awe. The realm of 'the political' encompasses carnivalesque rituals, drunken victory parties on election night, the thuggery of political big men, and the cults of sacrifice and martyrdom among armed insurgents. It involves contentions over honour, morality, pride and shame, and as such, it encompasses projections of masculinity and femininity.[6]

One of the foundational contentions in political anthropology is that this pastiche of practices across the permeable bounds of the political arena is no antithesis to Western modernity – to its bureaucratic rationality, its discrete institutional architecture or its preoccupation with secularism. Amalgamations of modern politics with religious or cultural repertoires may be found across the globe: the cult of adulation around the king in modern Thailand (Stengs 2008), the political energy of Indian deities (Singh 2012), the religious aura of the French president exhibited during rituals of inauguration and pilgrimage (Abeles 1988) or the public veneration of Lady Di after her fatal car crash (Watson 1997). All of these examples encompass potent political performance. The formal legal and political premises of these phenomena tell us little about what is going on and what it means politically. Without considering the performative aspects – the staged conduct, the customary scripts, the symbolic references, the interaction with the audience – they do not make sense.

The academic origins of performative thought lie with research on everyday social interaction. Goffman's (1959) classic analysis used dramaturgical metaphors to describe how people adhere to the unwritten strictures of cultural expectation when they present and comport themselves in front of others. In its original form, this approach implies a clear distinction between the personal identity of social beings and the way they conduct themselves in public: 'behind Goffman's analyses of interaction lies an active, prior, conscious, and performing self' (Gregson and Rose 2000: 433). The influences of post-foundational thought (Featherstone 2008; Marttila 2016) and feminist scholarship (Butler 1990; Cockburn and Omrod 1993) have obscured this distinction. Men and women do not merely perform predefined scripts of masculinity and femininity; they continuously shape that script. The social routines and strictures of traditionally dominant cis-hetero schemata are challenged and rearticulated by people with identities that diverge from these trappings, be it through their everyday conduct, or in more expressly political ways (Aretxaga 1997; Bosia 2018; Haraway 1997; Leigh and Weber 2018).

Through these performative practices, the supposed character that people perform blurs with who they are, or who they consider themselves to be. There is – to borrow Butler's well-known paraphrasation of Nietzsche – no doer behind the deed. An intersubjective understanding of the social world unmoors the notion of fixed identities and deliberate conduct: rather than a distinct agentic self and performative practice, both are reproduced through performativity. This complicates questions of performative veracity and authenticity – rather than simply shrugging aspirational political conduct aside as fake (Chandler 2000), it warrants more fundamental reflection. Performative action may comprise elements that are clearly and deliberately fictional or truthful, but the boundary between the two remains contingent, opaque or subject to slippage. Absurd imitations may become accurate when social reality evolves and starts matching this absurdity. Authentic performative conduct can become farcical when the political setting changes. The distinction between actor and character becomes equally blurry, when performative acts implicate the self-perception and social position of the person acting: actor and character converge, masks become faces, an imaginary script becomes a lived habitus.

A performative perspective has intuitive relevance to studying politics and state conduct. Public authority – as a relational form of legitimate power – may in part be derived from official mandates, but it becomes manifest in the way it is practiced (Klem and Suykens 2018). Institutional frameworks are shaped by a continuous interaction between formalised foundations and enactment in practice. Institutions are no hostage to their statutes. Their role, ability, legitimacy, reach and perceived significance derive in part from how they feature in everyday life. This may take shape at the level of routine institutional practices (for example, the reproduction of authority in the bureaucracy: Hull [2012a]; Jeffrey [2013]; Mathur [2015]), and it can assume the form of a spectacularly staged performance (for example, an election rally, inauguration ceremony, staged political visits to symbolic places: Bertrand, Briquet and Pels [2007]; Hansen [1999]; Kuttig and Suykens [2020]; Paley [2008]; Spencer [2007]; Strauss and O'Brien [2007]).

The contingency around these institutional practices and performances opens up intellectual space to explore how the perceived nature of an institution can change over time, even when its formal structures remain in place. Moreover, institutions continuously interact, and this creates new opportunities for redefining their role. Their significance and legitimacy can expand or demise. They are subject to 'institutional bricolage' (Cleaver 2012; Douglas 1987), and they may function like 'twilight institutions' (Lund 2006). In a similar vein, political performativity can enable an institution, ideology or person to change vessel – to become unhinged from one arena and be embedded in another. For example, it has the capacity to enact a repertoire as explicitly political, and as such it can add gravity to societal symbols of class, ethnicity, locality or religion. It may elevate a leadership figure to become a person who commands state potency. Conversely, political performativity may propagate a repertoire of 'anti-politics' (Hansen 1999; Spencer 2008), by seeking a puritan dissociation from the dirty tricks, underhand deals and scolding of the political arena. Such discursive framing commonly serves to construct a platform in the name of 'the people', 'the nation' or a particular cultural or religious orientation as 'anti-political'. Inevitably, this involves the ironic double bind that any claim to *not* be political is itself political. After all, the repertoires of anti-politics lend themselves for highly political ends (Spencer 2007).

Political repertoires are never invented completely anew. For audiences to recognise the staging of might, mischief, disruption or solemnity, it needs to look sufficiently like the repertoires people are familiar with. In fact, sometimes the script of a political action is driven by the expectations of the spectators, rather than by the intent of the political protagonist. Danilyn Rutherford (2012: 7–10) beautifully illustrates this point in her book on sovereignty and audience in West Papua with a George Orwell fragment about a colonial police officer in British Burma who is called in to take care of a marauding elephant. He is determined to let the poor animal be but feels obliged to shoot it once faced with the large crowd waiting for the spectacle to happen. In other words, the scripts of performative politics – and the stage, the symbols, the props – are steeped in public consciousness. Performative politics may be understood as an exercise in citational practice (Weber 1995, 1998). It hinges on references to earlier political activity, and it often comprises elements of mimicry (Bhabha 1994). It evolves through repetition, but such repetition creates scope for slippage and mutation. Citational practice reiterates prior conduct but places it in a new context, thus shifting its meaning and opening space for deliberately ambiguous references or dog whistles. Mimicry, similarly, is a performative act that yields a 'duplicate but not quite', and as a result, the character and impact of political mimicry can be slippery: the lines between docility, compliance, camouflage and mockery may be thin (Bhabha 1994: 85–92; see also Klem and Maunaguru 2017: 632–633). Wedeen's (1999) work on the personality cult around Syria's Hafez al-Assad illustrates this well. She describes how citizens practice camouflaged repertoires of compliance, despite their scepticism of the president's supposed stature, omniscience and benevolence. They engage in 'as-if politics' to show their colours to a political repertoire that is effectively a state religion, but rather than merely a charade, this repertoire is a crucial part of the way Syrians navigate and reproduce their own society.

In a different context, such performative pretence can assume a subaltern meaning. State propaganda can be undermined with humour or satire (Bhungalia 2020; Fluri 2019; Sörensen 2016), and the notion of 'as-if politics' can be turned on its head. By staging a political outlook that is suppressed or criminalised, make-belief repertoires can take an aspirational form and make the unimaginable thinkable (Navaro-Yashin 2012; Watts 2010). Performative bodily conduct or protest may challenge or ridicule prevalent gender norms (Haraway 1997; Leigh and Weber 2018). The malignity and malfunction of migration management policies can be exposed by staging refugee bodies and through performative activism, as we saw in Australia and elsewhere (Hodge 2018; Little, Suliman and Wake 2023). And state denial of a separatist national community can be unsettled by staging that national community in a self-declared referendum, as in Catalonia (Achniotis 2021; Enguix Grau 2021).

The perspective of performative politics offers a helpful conceptual vantage point to understand the liminalities of governments in exile (McConnell 2016; Alice Wilson 2016), militant democratic parties (Watts 2010) and unrecognised states (Bobick 2017; Bryant and Hatay 2020; Dimova and Cojocaru 2013). As I will illustrate in the chapters to come, it helps us come to terms with the tensions and frictions around the term 'sovereignty', and it lends us an analytical idiom to describe a nationalist movement that is defined by being both similar to and different from a recognised state. Instead of assessing reality in terms of implied norms – seeking to adjudicate the Tamil right to self-determination or the legitimacy of the Tamil insurgency – a performative perspective directs our attention to the way normative eligibility and entitlement are contested on the ground through the experimentation with institutional form.

The terminology that I use in this book thus steers clear of depicting sovereignty as a status or condition and instead comprises concepts that denote an activity, a process, a yearning or an ambition. I use the term *sovereign aspirations* to connote a collective desire and a claimed entitlement to be recognised as an independent state, a claim that is typically legitimised with reference to the right to self-determination. The pursuit of such aspirations may encompass a fake-it-till-you-make-it approach, whereby sovereign aspirants engage in *sovereign performance*: practices that emulate those of recognised states to assert an implied form of the supreme right and ability to govern. This may include violent conduct (disciplining subjects, eliminating traitors, warding off contenders), institutional practices and the deliberate performative staging of political authority, judiciary power, celebration or commemoration. One may distinguish between the performance of internal sovereignty (aimed at supposed subjects of rule) and external sovereignty (valorising performative conduct towards states, including the 'mother' state, a 'patron' state, other 'third' states or other sovereign aspirants) – though the two are arguably never completely detached.

When these practices and performance comprise a sustained and accumulative effort, as was the case with the LTTE in the 1990s and 2000s,

I refer to them as a *sovereign experiment*. This term highlights the provisional and probationary character of insurgent performativity. Improvised institutional conduct serves to test boundaries and explore possibilities, to find out what works and what one might get away with, which then offers a basis to gradually solidify a governing apparatus in pursuit of sovereign aspirations. Such an experiment does not only involve the staging of institutional autonomy and territorial dissociation but also *sovereign encroachment*: the practice of gradually percolating and co-opting previously existing institutions, such as the government bureaucracy, rather than opposing and supplanting them. This engenders deliberate blurring and tactical restraint, but ultimately sovereign experiments are necessarily backed up by the ability to deploy violence and coercion to impose authority and stand one's ground. Here I draw on Hansen and Stepputat's (2005, 2006) term 'de facto sovereignty' to describe the ability and self-claimed right to enforce discipline among a subject population without yielding to a higher or external force. Finally, I refer to the defeat of the LTTE's sovereign experiment and the wrecking of its symbols, institutions and territorial markers as *sovereign erasure*.

Tamil nationalism in Sri Lanka

As we move from the first half of this chapter to the second, we change tack. The broad canvas of the conceptual discussions makes way for the specificities of the Sri Lankan context (readers less familiar with Sri Lanka will find more detail in elaborate endnotes to the second half of this chapter). As I attend to particulars of Sri Lanka's history of ethno-political conflict, I will highlight the performative politics of citational practice, mimicry and institutional bricolage. While this does not overhaul the existing scholarship on Sri Lanka, it does intervene in established historiography by placing different accents and highlighting citational cadences that cut across phases and realms that are normally kept separate. As a result, the emphasis and narrative sequencing differ from much of the existing scholarship (though see Sumathy [2001] and Thangarajah [2012], who both develop a line of thought that resonates with mine). For one thing, it is less conventional to start with Tamil nationalism, rather than with, say, the overall character of the Sri Lankan state, but in view of the aforementioned reflections, I believe this is a useful analytical gesture.

In its contemporary form, Tamil nationalism is premised on a Wilsonian conception of sovereignty, which conceives of the Tamils as a nation endowed with the right to self-determination by virtue of it being a political community with distinct linguistic and cultural characteristics and a territorially delineated historical homeland in the northeast of the island. This view aligns broadly with the criteria defined at the 1933 Montevideo conference, the central reference point for declarative interpretations of state sovereignty in international law (though it would clearly fail the 'saltwater test'[7]). From this perspective, the assertion of Sri Lankan sovereignty comprises the foundational problem of Sri Lanka's constitutional order. In short, the Sri Lankan government cannot reject Tamil separatism on the count that it lacks democratic legitimacy and violates the law because both these moral yardsticks of the Sri Lankan state must derive their validity from the popular consent of the Tamil people, which is historically lacking (Guruparan 2016; A. J. Wilson 1994b; for further discussion, see Edrisinha et al. 2008). This political stance centres on 'the Tamil people' as a self-evident national reference point. However, defining and demarcating this community as a national *demos* raises a raft of ambiguities and contentions, which have significantly shifted over time. As a twentieth-century phenomenon, the discourse of Tamil nationalism projects firm claims about racial, linguistic and territorial distinction and pegs these to modern conceptions of the state. Yet that discourse is itself a consequence of Sri Lanka's embattled political history, and it bears influences from concurrent struggles elsewhere.

Tamil identity politics has a long and turbulent history – what it means to be Tamil and what that implies in terms of collective political aspirations has changed significantly in the course of history. Some of the key antecedents of Tamil political history date back to the Nallur kingdom on the northern Jaffna peninsula (thirteenth–seventeenth centuries), a region that continued to be ruled as a distinct entity under Portuguese and Dutch rule, even after the kingdom had succumbed to colonial occupation. Although their exact nature and significance is debated, the emergence of Tamil administrative practices and customary law (especially the northern *thesavamalai*) stand out as important historical precedents for the Tamil nationalist discourse (Gunasingam 2016; Guruparan 2016; Hellmann-Rajanayagam 1994a; Wickramasinghe 2006). Under British colonial rule, the concentration of missionary schools in the north turned Jaffna into an educational powerhouse bolstering both Tamil literary culture and white-collar employment (Arasaratnam 1994; Sitrampalam 2005). The concurrent awakening of Tamil identity in the mid-nineteenth century was premised on caste, religion and language. A movement pioneered by the Hindu revivalist Arumuga Navalar propagated a Tamil version of Hinduism, countering the influence of both colonial Christianity and India's 'Brahmanical' Hinduism. Within this *saiva siddhantam* (Saivite philosophy), a prominent place was reserved for the Jaffna Vellalas (the dominant caste of land-owning cultivators). Being Tamil was thus premised on a caste position (Vellala), religious orthodoxy (Saivism), patriarchy, and language (Tamil) – not (yet) on being part of an ethnic group or a nation (Cheran 2009; Gunasingam 2016; Hellmann-Rajanayagam 1994b;

Sitralega Maunaguru 1995; Rogers 1994; Wickramasinghe 2006; A. J. Wilson 2000). Later incarnations of Tamil identity politics explicitly challenged the Vellala-dominated caste hierarchy, most obviously in the campaign against 'low' caste exclusion from 'high' caste Jaffna temples in the 1960s (Pfaffenberger 1990; see also Jayaweera 2014: 139–150), but also through opposition to gerontocratic hierarchies and gendered strictures. The associated tensions within Tamil nationalism – whether to eschew internal difference or take issue with it – would continue to stir emotions in years to come. Until today (as discussed in Chapter 4), we can discern a conservative strand of Tamil nationalism (premising Tamil nationalism on the preservation of tradition and social hierarchy) and an emancipatory strand (combining Tamil national liberation with the ambition of liberating society from intra-Tamil forms of discrimination) – and lots of hedging in between.

When a political campaign for the advancement of Tamil rights and aspirations gathered pace in late colonial and early postcolonial times, the political demarcation of the Tamil community remained contentious (Cheran 2009; Sumathy 2001; Vaitheespara 2009; Wickramasinghe 2006). At its narrowest, it effectively catered to the upper-class Vellala elite in Jaffna and Colombo, even if it paid tribute to the Tamil masses in legitimating its claims; at its broadest it encompassed not only the category now known as Sri Lankan Tamils (with all its sub-categories of class, caste, religion and region) but also all Tamil-speaking populations, thus including the Muslims ('Islamic Tamils') and *malaiyaha* Tamils ('Indian Tamils').[8] A related distinction concerns the regional divergence between the north ('Jaffna Tamils') and the east ('Batticaloa Tamils'), which embody distinct histories, dialects, caste delineations and cultural practices. The north, which has always had an overwhelming majority Tamil population, has been the main locus of Tamil nationalism; the east, which has a multi-ethnic composition (see Map 2.1), has by and large been placed in a subservient role.

In sum, the emergence of Tamil nationalism was initially quite far removed from a campaign for sovereign self-determination, but through the experience of escalating conflict over the past hundred years, the politics around Tamil identity itself transformed. Rather than an assertion that accrued from historical criteria around homeland, culture, race and language, the Tamil claim to self-determination came of age through the interaction with Sri Lanka's process of state formation.[9] This deserves some emphasis because it relates to the central focus of this book. The diverse performative politics of Tamil nationalism are not competing renditions of an inert mother script of Tamil nationalism that is staged and projected in different ways. Rather, the dynamics around this long history of competing renditions have transformed the tenets of Tamil nationalism and the lived experience of being Tamil. The cornerstones of

Tamil identity have shifted through the encounter with nineteenth-century Hindu revivalism, the global circulation of nationalist ideas, the birth of the postcolonial state and, perhaps most of all, the intensification of the ethno-political conflict and the 2009 defeat of the LTTE (Cheran 2009; Sumathy 2001; S. Thiranagama 2011; Wickramasinghe 2006).

These historical transformations of the Tamil nationalist script co-evolved with – to stick with the theatrical idiom – changes in the performative cast. I will briefly elaborate on this: apart from illustrating this point, it will offer readers less familiar with Sri Lanka a simplified aide-memoire with key names and acronyms of the Tamil nationalist movement. In the nineteenth century, the key protagonist (Arumuga Navalar) may perhaps best be categorised as a public intellectual who staged lectures and wrote scholarly texts and pamphlets. In the late colonial era, the key characters comprised an elite of English educated lawyer-politicians from affluent high-caste backgrounds, who worked from within Sri Lanka's national parties. Around the turn of independence, these gentlemen politicians established their own political vehicles. Key acronyms to remember are ACTC (the first Tamil party, founded in 1944), ITAK (which became the foremost Tamil party, founded in 1949), the TULF (the joint platform of Tamil nationalist parties, founded in 1976) and the TNA (a political reincarnation of the TULF, created in 2001, arguably in the service of the LTTE).[10] Parliament was the primary arena for all these parties, but they also performed non-violent protest campaigns and advocated during court proceedings.

These parliamentary voices were relegated backstage when Tamil youth militants assumed a dominant role in the 1970s and 1980s. Constitutional bargaining and political rallies made way for hit-and-run attacks in the northeast. These youths represented diverse social backgrounds, and their mobilisation instigated a welter of armed groups, which were prone to rifts and rivalry, yielding a concurrent alphabet soup of names, including TELO, EROS, LTTE, EPRLF, PLOTE.[11] In the mid-1980s, the LTTE annihilated its rival militants and declared itself the sole protagonist. As discussed in the chapters to follow, subtle shifts took place in the 1990s and 2000s, when the movement countenanced docile fellow protagonists, both in parliament and within the state bureaucracy, as extensions of its sovereign experiment. These actors then assumed new roles in articulating the Tamil nationalist script with the military defeat of LTTE in 2009.

My nutshell historiography of Tamil nationalism is inevitably truncated. To summarise the historical background of the ethno-national conflict on Sri Lanka is to traverse a discursive battlefield where rival canons of grievance, valour and legitimation beckon the author to adopt their preferred diagnoses, chronologies and terminology. To describe a conflict is to intervene in it.

Accrediting all alternative renditions of Sri Lanka's modern or ancient history is neither feasible nor helpful, but two critical counter-narratives must be acknowledged, because they have intimately affected the Tamil social and political arena: the first concerns the Muslim community, the second a feminist critique of Tamil nationalist thought.

Sri Lanka's Muslim community, and the Muslims of the northeast in particular, has much in common with the Tamil community. Their language, cultural practices, kinship structures and the history of minority grievances are similar, and even if religion is their primary distinctive marker, Islamic practices in Sri Lanka have historically been shaped by their interactions with the island's other religions (DeMunck 1998; Klem 2011; McGilvray 2008; Nuhman 2002; Spencer et al. 2015). As a discrete ethnic category, rather than a religious sub-group of Islamic Tamils (alongside Hindu and Christian Tamils), the Muslim community is an anomaly, and this anomaly is itself a product of Sri Lanka's history of ethno-political conflict. While the Muslim community has a distinct genealogy in the arrival of Arab (and South and Southeast Asian) traders, their self-identification as a separate ethnic group gained currency in response to the hardening of Sinhala and Tamil ethno-nationalism in the 1970s and 1980s, with 1990 as the definitive breakpoint. In that year, the LTTE purged the entire Muslim community from the north. In the east, praying Muslims were gunned down in a sequence of mosque attacks (Hasbullah 2001; S. Thiranagama 2011: 106–182).

The emergence of a distinctive Muslim politics and the rise of the Sri Lanka Muslim Congress (SLMC) as the premier Muslim party were directly connected to the escalating civil war (Ameerdeen 2006; Ismail 1995; Johansson 2019; Knoerzer 1998; Nuhman 2002). This violent dynamic gave buoyancy to the eastern Muslim community (previously a peasant hinterland to the Muslim elite in Colombo and Kandy) as a central locus of Muslim aspirations, and it yielded increased contentions over gendered practices, orthodoxies of piety and religious sites (Haniffa 2008; Hasbullah and Geiser 2019; Heslop 2014; Klem 2011, 2014; Mihlar 2019; Spencer et al. 2015). The ascendency of a Muslim discourse of collective rights, autonomy and even self-determination – which reached its apex during the Norwegian-facilitated peace process of the early 2000s – has implicated the narrative and bargaining position of the Tamil nationalist movement (Lewer and Ismail 2011; McGilvray and Raheem 2007; Schonthal 2016b). A Tamil nationalism without Muslims makes no territorial sense (see Map 2.1).

The feminist critique of Tamil nationalist thought unearths the (often implicit) gendered premises underpinning the historiography of the Tamil nationalist movement that I have summarised earlier. From Arumuga Navalar's Hindu revivalism of the mid-nineteenth century through to the caste contentions over temple entry, the post-independence grievances over franchise, land ownership, university quotas and employment opportunities, the growing preoccupation with Tamil cultural purity, the staging of political protest and the escalation of violent militancy – gender politics is present every step along the way (Coomaraswamy and Perera-Rajasingham 2009; De Alwis 2002; De Mel 2001; Sitralega Maunaguru 1995; Satkunanathan 2012; Sumathy 2016b). The inherent tension within Tamil nationalism between cultural preservation and liberation comes out in stark relief here. On the one hand, the Tamil leadership has historically professed a conservative stance on Tamil cultural traditions and patriarchal views on the role of women in Tamil nationalism (Coomaraswamy and Perera-Rajasingham 2009; Satkunanathan 2012). From this perspective, women are essential for the reproduction of the values, customs and purity of the Tamil nation, and they are considered innately connected to land and soil. On the other hand, a discourse of ethnic liberation cascaded into other emancipatory agendas, where liberation from caste oppression, class inequality and gender discrimination converges with national liberation. This opened space for new forms of female leadership, and it gave rise to the martial femininity of women warriors, whose perceived feminine virtues yielded a distinct military prowess (De Mel 2004; Sitralega Maunaguru 1995; Samuel 2003; Sumathy 2016b).

The escalation of violent conflict in the 1970s and 1980s added new gravitas to female sexuality, and it gave new impetus to (attempts to) control it, be it through scorning of ethnic mixture, the cultural policing of female dress and conduct, the enforced celibacy of (male and female) cadres and social consequences of wartime rape (De Mel 2007; Hyndman and De Alwis 2004; Satkunanathan 2012; Sumathy 2016a). Let me close with two examples that illustrate the important dimensions that feminist scholarship adds to the established junctures of Tamil nationalist historiography. The first concerns the Muslim Eviction from the north in 1990. This violent act of purported purification also affected Tamils who were seen to deviate from cultural custom, such as transgenders (Sumathy 2016b). Subsequent killings under LTTE rule and postwar tussles over sexual practices may be considered in a similar light. The second concerns the 1991 assassination of former Indian prime minister Rajiv Gandhi, widely considered an LTTE reprisal for India's brutal counterinsurgency on the movement. A feminist reading of this attack highlights that the suicide bomber who self-detonated on Gandhi's body was herself a rape victim of Indian soldiers and may thus be understood as a woman who not only revenged herself and her nation but also purified her supposedly polluted body by turning it into a weapon that simultaneously killed and self-sacrificed (Sitralega Maunaguru 1995: 170–171).

Map 2.1 Sri Lanka's ethnic and political geography

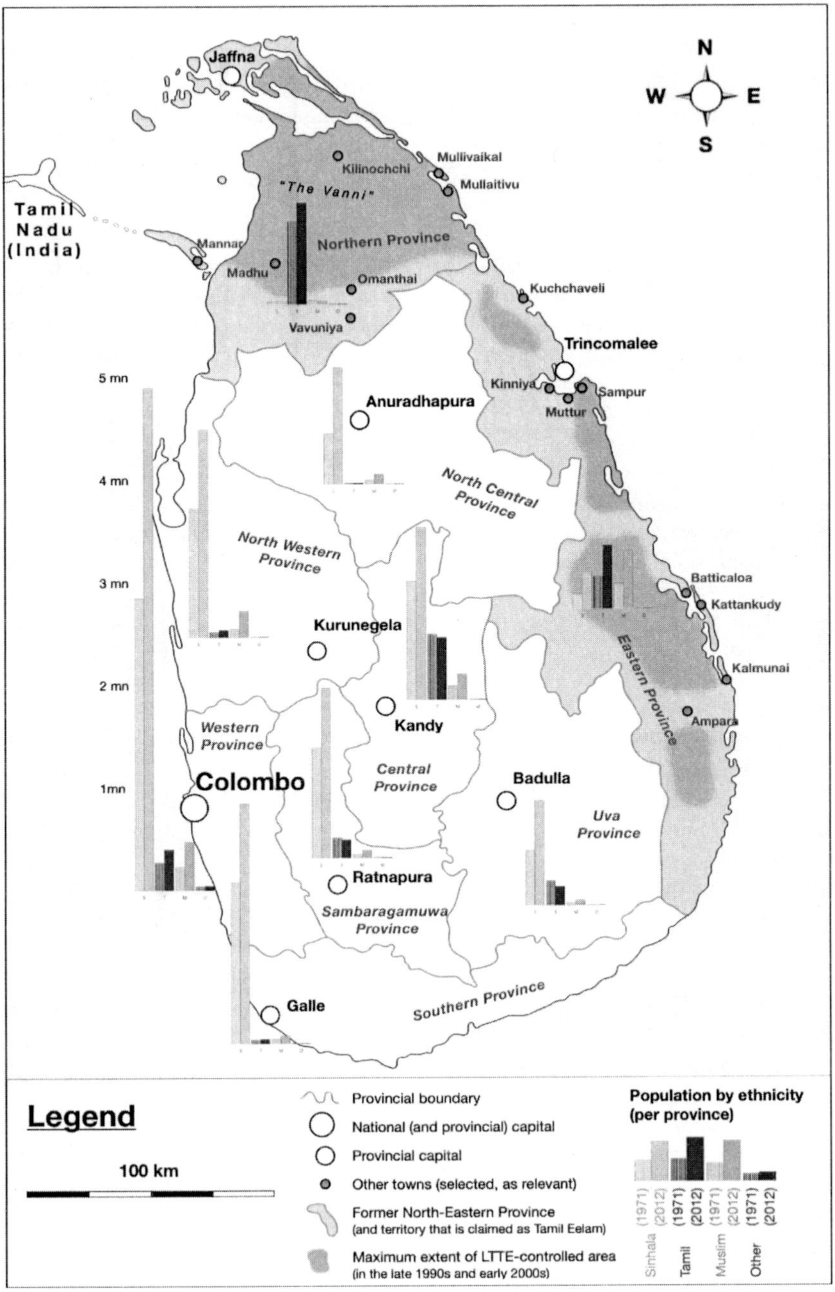

Source: Map by author based on Sri Lankan government censuses (1971 and 2012) and field observation (LTTE area).

(*Contd*)

Map 2.1 (*Contd*)

Notes: Maps are spatial representations. They embody political choices and have political consequences. Map 2.1 serves to give readers a basic impression of Sri Lanka's ethnic and political geography, but through its selection of data and categories, it inevitably intervenes in the core analytical and normative concerns of this book: the territorial demarcation of political order and the spatialisation of national and/or ethnic communities.

To depict the ethnic composition per province, I have used data from two censuses, one before the war (1971) and one after the war (2012), to capture both an overall picture and a sense of change over time. The wartime censuses were all incomplete. I have simplified the ethnic categories used in these censuses (which are in turn based on self-identification). More specifically, I have collated low-country Sinhalese and Kandyan Sinhalese (a distinction still made in the 1971 census) as simply Sinhalese; Sri Lankan Tamil and Indian Tamil as Tamil; Sri Lankan Moor, Indian Moor and Malay as Muslim; and Burghers, Veddahs, Chetties and several smaller communities as Other.

Politically significant cartographic choices relate to historical delineation (adding an older census would, for example, show the relative increase of Sinhalese in the Eastern Province as part of government-sponsored irrigation schemes; Manogaran [1994]) and the politics of scale: it makes a political difference whether we aggregate data at a national-, provincial-, district- or ward-level basis. I have chosen to highlight the provincial level, given that the provincial council system is one of this book's central concerns. Also, it helpfully reveals the divergent composition of the (Tamil-dominated) north versus the (multi-ethnic) east versus the (Sinhala-dominated) rest of the country. However, as a result of this, the Muslim community is rendered inconspicuous because it mostly lives in concentrated localities and has no provincial majority anywhere. A ward-level overview would, for example, highlight some very clear green pockets, especially in towns along the east coast.

I have depicted all nine provinces and coloured the merged North-Eastern Province, which existed from 1987 to 2006. This area then broadly converges with the claim to a Tamil homeland and the aspired territory of an independent Tamil Eelam (occasionally Puttalam District, the western coast between Mannar and Colombo, is included as well), though it is clearly peculiar for a separatist claim to premise itself on the administrative boundaries of the state it rebels against. As a result, ironically, some areas that the government had earlier added to the Eastern Province (like the excision of Dehiattakandiya, west of Batticaloa) to thwart Tamil separatism by artificially increasing the Sinhala presence in this minority-dominated region thus became a part of Tamil separatist claims.

The delineation of LTTE-controlled areas is based on my own observations across the span of my fieldwork in the 2000s. This raises political questions about lending credit to insurgent claims (cf. Sarvananthan 2007) by depicting the lay of the land at what was arguably the height of the LTTE's power (late 1990s and early 2000s), though this results in the exclusion of Jaffna (which was LTTE controlled in the early 1990s). It also raises interpretative questions: On what basis do we colour an area as LTTE controlled when clear boundary demarcations are lacking? If the movement operates in a forested area without significant settlements, what does control imply? I have therefore chosen to blend these areas in by using blurry delineations.

Sri Lanka's tribulations with shared sovereignty

The life cycle of Tamil nationalism cannot be understood in isolation from the evolution of the Sri Lankan state. The attrition of Sri Lanka's constitutional settlement and the majoritarian forcefields of its democratic framework spurred the transformation of the Tamil nationalist movement from a moderate democratic body with an agenda of power-sharing and minority rights protection into a violent insurgency demanding a separate state. There is a formidable tradition of scholarship on Sri Lanka's history of ethno-political conflict, covering the history of the constitutional framework (Amarasinghe et al. 2019; Bastian 1994; Coomaraswamy 2003; Schonthal 2016a; Welikala 2012a; Wickramaratne 2014: 137–250), the majoritarian government policies in the fields of language, education, religion, employment and land allocation (De Silva 2005; DeVotta 2004; Harris 2018; Herring 2001; Jayasundara-Smits 2022; Korf 2006, 2009; Peebles 2006; Rasaratnam 2016; Uyangoda 2007; Venugopal 2018; Wickramasinghe 2006) and the failures of successive pacts with the Tamil leadership (Edrisinha et al. 2008; Sampanthan 2012; A. J. Wilson 1994b, 2000).

Rather than rehearsing this well-established history, I will review these dynamics through the prism of sharing and contesting sovereign power. Doing so places the inherent contradictions of shared sovereignty at the heart of the analysis. This is a controversial conceptual angle in Sri Lanka,[12] but I posit it is warranted. Much of the scholarly debate has focused on the distribution of power within the Sri Lankan state – mainly through the so-called devolution of power from centre to peripheries – without confronting the contested sovereign foundations of the postcolonial state at large. This has propelled a focus on institutional design, federalism, decentralisation, regional autonomy and electoral systems (Amarasinghe et al. 2019; Bastian 1994; Coomaraswamy 2003; ICES 1996; Rupesinghe 2006; Thiruchelvam 2000; Welikala 2012a, 2016; Wickramaratne 2014: 137–250) – as well as meticulous debate on the many forms devolution could take.[13] Such a focus sits uneasily with the transgressive nature of Sri Lankan politics. Studying the island's tryst with power-sharing from a purely legalistic perspective misses the point. After all, we have defined sovereignty as the power to invoke or suspend law and authority over people and territory, a form of power that does not yield to outside interference and is ultimately steeped in violence. How to draw up the rules for sharing a kind of power that is defined as the ability to (violently) change the rules? It follows that shared sovereignty is not simply about the constitutional distribution of sovereign powers but about the full range of political instruments used to effect sovereign power. To understand how such power is distributed, it does not suffice to analyse the constitutional settlement. We must also contend with all means available to amend, override, twist, reinterpret or simply break the official rules.[14] In other words, the political trick book cannot be shrugged aside from the analysis as improper political practice – these are the means through which sovereign power is shared, distributed, wrested or fragmented.

The performative perspective advanced in this book expands our focus from formal attempts of sharing state power to the way such power is distributed in practice, through validating repertoires, political trickery, twisted idioms and violent contestation. This is important because it places wartime institutional transgressions and experiments in a historical perspective. There were precedents of institutional transgression to the LTTE's experiment of inventing, reorienting and co-opting legal and political institutions (described in Chapter 3). The movement's self-declared courts and departments may be understood as a radical iteration of older repertoires of changing and bending the law through institutional practice and performance. The competing forms of sovereign experimentation during the war years have subtle precursors in the transgressions of the pre-war decades. To study the history of Sri Lanka's conflict as an escalating dynamic of contesting, enacting and wresting sovereignty requires us to blend the realms of constitutional law, politics, governance and armed conflict, which are normally kept separate. After all, the analytical and normative distinctions between these spheres are themselves a function of the contestation that we seek to understand.

Contentions over the accommodation of ethnic minorities – and the Sri Lankan Tamil community in particular – date back to the very origins of Sri Lanka's history as a constitutional democracy. The overall trend from 1931 (Donoughmore constitution, the advent of democratic politics), to 1947 (Soulbury constitution, which marked Sri Lanka's independence) to 1957 (pact between Prime Minister Bandaranaike and Tamil leader Chelvanayakam) to 1965 (Senanayake–Chelvanayakam pact) is one of attrition. In terms of power-sharing and minority rights, the proposed compromises became ever more watered down. Section 29 of the Soulbury constitution encoded minority protection but offered a feeble defence against majoritarian politics; the pacts of 1957 and 1965 eschewed fundamental issues and remained unimplemented.

The constitutional reforms of the early 1970s comprised a decisive turning point in Sri Lanka's trajectory of ethno-political conflict.[15] The 1972 republican constitution marked the completion of Sri Lanka's decolonisation process. It was drafted alongside the first uprising of the Sinhala leftist revolutionary movement (the Janatha Vimukthi Peramuna [JVP]), and it enshrined Sinhala-Buddhist nationalism and linguistic chauvinism.[16] As such, it sparked the transformation of Tamil nationalist politics into violent separatism and ensnared the constitution itself at the heart of the conflict dynamic. Transgression followed on transgression, and foundational logics of legality and political legitimacy were turned on their head. The 1972 constitution was promulgated with some convocational creativity. Having secured a landslide victory with the United Front (a coalition around the Sri Lanka Freedom Party [SLFP]) in 1970, Prime Minister Srimavo Bandaranaike confronted the bootstrapping problems of constitutional authorship by declaring parliament a constituent assembly mandated with drafting a new, autochthonous constitution to free the country from remaining colonial entanglements (Edrisinha et al. 2008: 232–253; Welikala 2012b), thus violating constitutional safeguards against majoritarian law-making.[17]

In response to this experiment in unilateral constitution-making, we see the first signs of a state-like posture by the Tamil leadership, an incipient kind of sovereign mimicry.[18] The main Tamil party, ITAK, abandoned the constituent assembly in protest and rejected the resulting constitution. ITAK leader Chelvanayakam demonstratively resigned his seat in the new parliament (premised on the new constitution) and declared the subsequent by-election for his electorate a referendum on the new constitution (Sampanthan 2012; A. J. Wilson 1994b: 123–125). In parallel, the Tamil leadership shifted from advocating federalism to demanding a separate state, based on the Tamil homeland and the right to self-determination (A. J. Wilson 2000: 101–110). In 1976, the Tamil political parties established a joint platform (the TULF) to propagate their stance in the so-called Vaddukoddai resolution, which promulgated more legal manoeuvring and a fascinating court case. The government had outlawed opposition to the constitution and in effect criminalised the dissemination of the Vaddukoddai resolution (Edrisinha et al. 2008: 261). The main Tamil leader A. Amirthalingam[19] was arrested on this ground and prosecuted for sedition in a special tribunal mandated by the emergency provisions of the 1972 constitution. However, Amirthalingam's defence used the tribunal as an elevated public stage to publicly amplify Tamil dissent – the very act for which Amirthalingam was on trial – by challenging the legal validity of the constitution on the count that it lacked the consent of the Tamil nation. Given that the tribunal derived its mandate from an invalid constitution, it was itself a nullity, Amirthalingam's counsel claimed (Edrisinha et al. 2008: 261–262).[20] This subaltern politics from within the state's own arena continued during the 1977 parliamentary elections, where the TULF campaigned with an explicit agenda of seeking plebiscitary endorsement from the Tamil people for the Vaddukoddai resolution. The landslide victory in all Tamil-dominated electorates of the northeast (and 18 out 168 parliamentary seats) was held up as popular affirmation of its separatist course.

These transgressions heralded more trickery. The unilateral constitutional reset of 1972 was replicated when the rival United National Party (UNP) regained power and instated its own constitution (1978) with an all-powerful president and more red tape around separatist politics.[21] Upon expiry of its electoral mandate, the UNP extended its super majority with an extra six years by holding an election in the shape of referendum.[22] In short, the 1970s and early 1980s witnessed a definitive escalation of the stand-off between the Sinhala-dominated government and the Tamil political leadership into no-holds-barred confrontation. The deliberation of constitutional bounds and political antagonism in the democratic arena of the 1950s and 1960s transformed into a dynamic of legal skulduggery and transgressive political performativity. Parliament, an institution mandated by the constitution, declared itself an institution authorised to rewrite the constitution; elections were performed as national referendums; a referendum was held in lieu of elections; new powers and tribunals were established as exceptions; and a court against separatism was performatively turned into a platform to advocate it.

These chains of transgressive citational practice continued in a more violent and rupturing manner in the 1980s. This was the decade where political antagonism transformed into a full-blown, internationalised armed conflict that ravaged Sri Lankan society. In the context of the deepening political crisis, the Tamil political leadership was relegated to the margins by a raft of proliferating Tamil youth militias. The traumatic watershed of 'Black July' 1983, where the government condoned anti-Tamil pogroms, sparked further escalation and prompted the Indian polity in Chennai (Tamil Nadu) and Delhi to adopt a more interventionist stance. India's involvement, which was riddled by divergent interests (Krishna 1999), comprised a two-pronged strategy: covert support for Tamil militants to thwart an overly assertive Sri Lankan government[23] and a diplomatic process aimed at negotiating a moderate political compromise on the ethnic minority issue. Both interventions initiated long parallel chains of consequences, with blowback effects that harmed all players involved. Political negotiations and military escalations alternated in rapid succession in the mid-1980s, with the so-called All Party Conference in 1984, the Thimpu talks in 1985 and backchannel diplomacy in 1986 culminating in the 1987 Indo-Lankan Accord.[24] In parallel to this turbulent sequence of negotiations, the LTTE responded to India's divide-and-rule tactics towards the diverse Tamil militant groups by attacking and eradicating its rivals and declaring itself the sole voice of the Tamils – a violent turning point with enduring consequences for the Tamil nationalist movement (Bose 2002; Hellmann-Rajanayagam 1994b; Rajan Hoole 2001; S. Thiranagama 2010, 2011; A. J. Wilson 2000).

The 1987 Indo-Lankan Accord arguably comprises the historical counter-cadence of the 1972 and 1978 constitutions. In the 1970s, the Sri Lankan government had used its legal and political dominance to unilaterally shape a unitary state architecture. In the 1980s, the Indian government used its military dominance to impose a constitutional framework of shared sovereignty in all but name. The Indo-Lankan Accord aimed to settle the Tamil question with a compromise solution of regional autonomy – the provincial council system. The north and east were merged to create the NEPC, thus establishing a degree of regional autonomy for an area that effectively matched the homeland aspired by Tamil nationalists (see Map 2.1). The Indian Peacekeeping Force (IPKF) was deployed to safeguard the new constellation and disarm the Tamil militants, but it was soon drawn into an unsuccessful counter-insurgency campaign against the LTTE.

The Indo-Lankan Accord implanted an institutional fix that met some important Tamil demands (a degree of self-rule for the northeast), but one that was embedded within Sri Lanka's sovereign framework. The thirteenth amendment, the constitutional ratification of the accord, inserted a layer of quasi-autonomous provincial governance into a constitution that was characterised by an enormous central concentration of executive power within a unitary state.[25] The resulting constitutional settlement was rife with ambiguities and subject to divergent expectations. It had been presented to Tamil nationalists as a form of shared sovereignty, or at least a stepping stone towards it (Balasingham 2004: 97–110), but that was clearly not what the Sri Lankan government signed up to, and the actual accord text steered well clear of that terminology. The insertion of provincial devolution into an otherwise unitary constitution yielded so many tensions and paradoxes that the framework became legally schizophrenic, and provincial autonomy was compromised from its inception.[26] The constitutional settlement of devolved governance that the Indian government thrust on Sri Lanka with military might was subsequently scuttled by legal and administrative pushback. What started with a show of force by the Indian military was neutralised by minute insertions in the law books and the slow grind of bureaucratic procedure.

The Indo-Lankan Accord did not yield one experiment in performing government but several competing ones. Before the violent escalation of the 1980s, Sri Lanka had experienced a spiral of legal trickery and transgressive politics from within the democratic arena. What ensued after India's intervention was a veritable onslaught between three competing projects of statecraft, based on divergent interpretations of sovereignty. The Sri Lankan government (which was simultaneously threatened by the second revolt of the Sinhala leftist JVP) strove to repair Sri Lanka's singular sovereignty of a unitary state by curtailing the NEPC and undermining the IPKF (to then fight the LTTE afterwards). The Indian government propped up the NEPC to boost its performative effort as a 'Tamil Provincial Government' (Dixit 2003: 283–284) for the northeast, thus effecting a maximal form of shared sovereignty within the existing legal constraints.[27] The LTTE rejected the NEPC altogether and started fielding its own institutional apparatus as a separate state premised on Tamil sovereignty. Going by the formal standards of Sri Lankan law, the first effort was the norm, the second was dubious and the third was illegal, but that tells us little about the actual governing capacities of these competing institutional forms or about the understandings and perceptions of legitimacy among the people governed by them.

Conclusion

Sri Lanka's history of contestation over political identity and power-sharing cannot be understood from a purely constitutional or institutional perspective. The infringement on legal frameworks and institutional mandates is central to the phenomena we seek to understand. The country's tribulations with ethnic power-sharing are embedded in a more fundamental set of questions about how sovereignty is defined and how the nation (and the *demos*) is demarcated. In line with the literature on the self-referential underpinnings of legitimate government (Beverley 2020a; Gilmartin, Price and Ruud 2020; Hansen 2021; Hansen and Stepputat 2006; Spencer 2012), a political compromise on the ethno-nationalist conflict raises questions about the validity and provenance of the constitutional foundations of the Sri Lankan state and about whether or not the Tamils are defined as a distinct nation. As a result, it becomes difficult to clearly delineate legitimate and illegitimate forms of political contestation. After all, the foundations on which such delineations are based are themselves core elements of the conflict.

A performative perspective – drawn from authors like Bertrand, Briquet and Pels (2007), McConnell (2016), D. Rutherford (2012), Spencer (2007), Weber (1998) and Wedeen (1999) – helps expand our focus from the distribution of powers in the constitutional architecture to the way such power is distributed in actual practice. These practices include the full repertoire of the political trick book, including political deception, legal skulduggery, twisted idioms, administrative subversion, transgressive institutional bricolage and the deployment of violence. Competing efforts to shape Sri Lanka's political landscape have shifted vessel over time. The realms of law, politics, bureaucracy and violence became entangled, and in the process the dynamics and protagonists changed. What started as a consultative debate on constitutional design in the late British era yielded a cycle of legal hoodwinking in the 1970s and then escalated into armed insurgency and international military intervention, which then circled back to the constitutional settlement.

With the 1987 Indo-Lankan Accord, India forced a corrective implant into Sri Lanka's constitution, spearheaded by a compromised form of shared sovereignty through the provincial apparatus of the NEPC. The escalation of Sri Lanka's ethno-political conflict thus comprises a history of contesting, enacting and wresting sovereignty, which eventually resulted in violently competing forms of sovereign experimentation in the late 1980s and early 1990s. The rise and fall of the LTTE's de facto state institutions (discussed in Chapters 3 and 4) must be seen in this light. The provincial apparatus of the NEPC (discussed in Chapters 5 and 6) may seem marginal and obscure, but it derives significance from the fact that it embodies the crumble zone between these rivalrous forms of statecraft.

Notes

1   This performative ideal engendered 'an aspiration toward effective on-the-ground authority, ownership (whether legal or symbolic), and de facto impunity that states, private corporations, rulers, private armies, and many other "de facto sovereigns" strive to project and maintain' (Hansen 2021: 41). The presumed contrast between precolonial traditions of authority relying on theatrical conduct and modern states relying on a bureaucratic apparatus disguises the fact that performativity was a crucial aspect of the colonial endeavour too (Bertrand, Briquet and Pels 2007; Hansen 2021; S. Sen 2002).

2   Purushotham (2021) reviews the profound contestation around Hyderabad, the foremost 'princely state' within the British Raj and a monarchical, Islamic space at the heart of Indian territory, which was eventually reined in with large-scale militarised violence. He highlights the ambiguities and interstitial spaces resulting from the division of Punjab. And he points to the peasant uprising of Telangana as a contrarian effort delineating the populace and their cause – one articulated with a global class struggle rather than the ethno-religious composition of the nation – which was violently crushed.

3   Self-determination has been codified in international law on the basis of empirical characteristics: a defined territory, a permanent population, a government and a capacity to enter into relations with other states. These four criteria form the heart of the 1933 Montevideo conference, which is the central reference point for *declarative* interpretations of state sovereignty in international law. The alternative, *constitutive* interpretation of state sovereignty centres on recognition by other sovereign states.

4   Contemporary scholars (Arrhenius 2005; Bloemraad 2018; Little 2008; Ochoa Espejo 2020) have adopted less rigid approaches to the 'democratic boundary problem' – in a hybrid, mobile and globally interconnected society, demarcations are never static and never final: a *demos* may transform and *demoi* may overlap. However, contestations over these transformations and overlaps have yielded precisely the dynamics that the postcolonial literature describes.

5   As a critic of consent-based theories of law, Brilmayer argued that the juridical authority of the state over its people cannot originate from consent, because such consent presumes the existence of the state to which one can consent. For more recent reflections on concurrent interpretative dilemmas, see Barnett (2004); Michelman (1998); Zurn (2010).

6   Claims to political legitimacy often draw on tropes of protective, virile men and chaste, caring mothers, daughters and wives. Conservative renditions of gendered morality may then invoke a counter-politics that exposes the hypocrisies and silences (Aretxaga 1997; Coomaraswamy and Perera-Rajasingham 2009; Enguix Grau 2021; Parashar 2019; Satkunanathan 2012; True 2018).

7   The dominant reading of UN General Assembly resolutions in relation to the Montevideo Convention restricts the right to self-determination to the decolonisation of overseas territories of former European empires, though this saltwater test is increasingly criticised (G. Simpson 1996).

8   'Tamils of recent Indian origin' is arguably the best term. The alternatives could be seen as pejorative ('plantation Tamils'), too geographically limited ('upcountry' or *malaiyaha* Tamils) or misleading ('Indian Tamils', since the long history of the 'Sri Lankan Tamils' is traceable back to India as well; moreover, these supposedly 'Indian' Tamils are now Sri Lankan citizens).

9   In this connection, Tamil nationalism has been denoted as a 'defensive nationalism' (Nithiyanandan 1987). However, to depict Tamil nationalism as merely a response to a Sinhala majoritarian state would be to underestimate the political agency and energy vested in the insurgent movement (cf. Wickramasinghe 2006: 253).

10   In full: All Ceylon Tamil Congress (ACTC), Ilankai Tamil Arasu Kadchi or Federal Party (ITAK), Tamil United Liberation Front (TULF) and Tamil National Alliance (TNA).

11   The key groups in the 1970s were the Tamil Eelam Liberation Organisation (TELO), the Eelam Revolutionary Organisation of Students (EROS) and the LTTE, with two additional factions emerging in the early 1980s: Eelam People's Revolutionary Liberation Front (EPRLF, split from EROS) and People's Liberation Organisation of Tamil Eelam (PLOTE, split from LTTE).

12   The dominant legal and political understanding, certainly among Sinhala nationalists but also among constitutional scholars, is that Sri Lankan sovereignty is indivisible. However, from a Tamil nationalist perspective, the principle of

devolution only has merit if it comprises the devolution of *sovereign* power. This disagreement conjures up the demarcation problems and bootstrapping dilemmas that have riddled political and legal theorists, as discussed in the first half of this chapter.

13 Sri Lanka's devolution debate has mainly revolved around three sets of issues. First, the parameters of devolution, which include the unit of devolution (the whole northeast or smaller, less politically significant entities), the degree of devolution (emulating regional self-government or merely distributing public services and resources) and the question of symmetry (a uniform system for the whole country or a special arrangement for the regions of ethnic minorities, most obviously the Tamils). One can set these three parameters in such a way to let devolution fulfil Tamil nationalist aspirations (a powerful arrangement for the whole northeast) or to effectively frustrate or thwart them (with a country-wide system of district-level bodies that serve as extension schemes for centrally controlled state largesse).

The second key aspect of devolution concerns the legal status of a power-sharing arrangement: an interim arrangement, an act of parliament, a constitutional amendment or something else. This determines the robustness of a devolved system of government against attempts to stifle or overturn it with executive orders, new legislation, constitutional reform, emergency powers, budget cuts, political trickery or extra-constitutional measures. A third important aspect of Sri Lanka's devolution lexicon concerns the language and performative dimensions of devolution. As we will see, devolved units may be aggrandised with the terminology of government or trivialised with more technical-sounding terms, and they can be granted the potency of patronage or starved into political impotence.

14 One significant exception, which *does* think in a direction that resonates with the perspective taken here, is the collection edited by Jayadeva Uyangoda and Neloufer de Mel (2012), especially the chapter on the poetics of state government in eastern Sri Lanka by Yuvi Thangarajah (2012). For a related line of reasoning, more squarely focused on constitutional law, see Schonthal's notion 'pyrrhic constitutionalism' (2016a).

15 Arguably, this historical juncture is cognate to the multifarious struggles around India's constitutional settlement in the 1940s, though the scale and the levels of violence are evidently different.

16 The 1972 'republican' constitution apportioned a 'foremost place' to Buddhism, despite also alluding to secularism (Coomaraswamy 2012; Schonthal 2016a), and it introduced several Sinhala nationalist measures like a Sinhala language policy and the name Sri Lanka. Perhaps most significantly, it bolstered the executive by weakening checks and balances and enabling wide-ranging emergency powers (Edrisinha et al. 2008: 232–253).

17 More specifically, the SLFP-dominated assembly brushed aside the protections against majoritarian law-making in section 29 of the Soulbury constitution (Ludsin 2012; Sampanthan 2012; Wickramaratne 2014: 75–95; A. J. Wilson 2000: 104).

18 Arguably, V. Navaratnam's 'Thamil Suya Aadchi Kadchi' in the late 1960s was a precursor to this, given its insistence on a sovereign Tamil stance. Navaratnam was a founding member and theoretician of ITAK but fell out with the party over its decision to join the 1965 Senanayake government (A. J. Wilson 2000: 95).

19 Amirthalingam had been an ITAK member from the start, initially as its youth wing leader. At his 1976 arrest at the Jaffna bus stand (along with three other Tamil front men), he was the secretary-general of the newly founded TULF. After Chelvanayakam's death in 1977, Amirthalingam became the ITAK/TULF leader.

20 This claim confronted the court, in a very direct and concrete way, with the complicated legal conundrum of navigating the bootstrapping problem of law: asserting the legal authority to assess its own legality would result in circular reasoning. The court eschewed a verdict on the constitution as a political matter and referred the question of its own validity to the Supreme Court. These legal proceedings were overtaken by events: the government decided to abandon the case, as it had itself become a platform for advocating separatism (Edrisinha et al. 2008: 261–262).

21 Reminiscent of the dynamics around Amirthalingam's trial, and in the immediate aftermath of Black July in 1983, the Jayawardena government pushed through a constitutional amendment to outlaw separatism by forcing parliamentarians to swear an oath of allegiance. Tamil parliamentarians forfeited their seats in protest.

22 The UNP held a parliamentary majority that was so vast that new elections could only lower his numbers. When parliament's term expired, President Jayawardena held a plebiscite on extending that term by another six years (Spencer 2007: 72–95). This enabled him to preserve an 83 per cent majority (the composition of Parliament) with only 55 per cent of the votes (the result of the referendum). In formal terms, this was a popular referendum, but in terms of its political significance one could just as well argue that it functioned like a parliamentary election with very skewed math, or – more to the point – a political scam.

23 This covert support programme was complicated by internal differences: the secret service mainly supported non-LTTE groups, which then prompted Tamil Nadu Chief Minister M. G. Ramachandran to bankroll the LTTE (Balasingham 2004: 62).

24 The initial mediation attempt (Annexure C, 1983–1984) comprised an expansion of previous deals: like the 1965 DC Pact and the district development councils created in 1981, it took districts as a point of departure but empowered them to be amalgamated into larger regions. The next iteration of Indian mediation (the December 1986 proposals) scaled up to provinces as the unit of devolution, but it tried to tinker with the delineation of provincial boundaries, mainly by taking Sinhala-dominated areas out of the Eastern Province (Balasingham 2004: 49–54; Dixit 2003: 22–23; Edrisinha et al. 2008; Loganathan 2006; TULF 1988: 50–141). During this poorly publicised phase, detailed negotiations over power-sharing and regional autonomy through a revised constitution took place between the Jayawardena government and TULF, the joint platform of

Tamil political parties (TULF 1988: 83–146). This resulted in what has been referred to as the 'December 19 proposals' (1986), which carved out a middle ground between secession and unitarism by devolving power to the provinces, a solution modelled on India's own state structure (Bose 1994; Dixit 2003: 41–65; Loganathan 2006). The proposal was arguably the inverse of an accord: the text was not made public, and none of the parties embraced it. But interestingly, it had a lasting impact – in hindsight, Sri Lanka's present system of devolved governance stems from this proposal. The final package (the Indo-Lankan Accord of 1987) further upgraded this model by warranting the provisional merger of the Northern and Eastern Provinces, a unit of devolution that matched the aspired Tamil homeland, though this was an interim measure subject to a future referendum in the Eastern Province.

25 This was a feat in itself: a blockage of the thirteenth amendment on the grounds that it violated the unitary character of the state and the indivisible nature of parliamentary sovereignty was narrowly averted in the Supreme Court with a vote of five to four (Thiruchelvam 2000: 206; Wickramaratne 2019: 1–12).

26 First, the thirteenth amendment constrained provincial competencies by adding annexes with special provisions and a blanket stipulation that 'national policy' on devolved subjects remained with the centre, thus opening an administrative Pandora's box. The centre also retained control over the civil service (in terms of hiring, training, pay, promotion, discipline). Key gatekeeping power over provincial finance, staffing and legislation was given to a presidentially appointed governor. In addition, the thirteenth amendment left ample space for the centre to restrain the provinces through procedural stalemates and inaction: provincial land powers, for example, were contingent on the delineation of provincial lands by a commission that was never created (Coomaraswamy 1994; Shastri 1990; Thiruchelvam 2000; TULF 1988).

Second, the northeast merger (a cornerstone of the Indo-Lankan Accord) was created through the emergency powers of the public security ordinance, rather than a constitutional clause, which severely weakened its legal robustness and eventually resulted in the 2006 Supreme Court verdict to 'de-merge' the north and east (Wickramaratne 2019: 12).

Third, the provincial councils were outmanoeuvred by a whole suite of institutional tentacles drawing power back to the centre. Local government officers (divisional secretaries) were further empowered in a hierarchy that allowed them to bypass the provinces and an array of new authorities and presidential schemes also circumvented the provincial council system (Coomaraswamy 1994; Thiruchelvam 2000).

Provincial tax revenue, finally, was truncated to negligible proportions (Gunawardena 2019).

27 Neither the Indo-Lankan Accord nor the thirteenth amendment use the language of shared sovereignty, but they work to assuage Tamil secessionism with a compromise in that direction.

3 Performing an Insurgent Sovereign Experiment*

This chapter discusses the rise of the Liberation Tigers of Tamil Eelam's (LTTE) de facto state after the retreat of the Indian military in 1990, when the movement firmly asserted itself as the sole voice of Tamil nationalism, and its climax during the internationalised peace process of the 2000s. The subsequent LTTE defeat and its aftermath are discussed in Chapter 4. Like other insurgent movements and unrecognised forms of government (Arjona, Kasfir and Mampilly 2015; Caspersen 2012; Corcuff 2012; Kyris 2022; Mampilly and Stewart 2021; Staniland 2014; Alice Wilson 2016), the LTTE operated in the conviction that *acting like* a state may lead to *being seen as* a state, which may lead to implied forms of acceptance and a better prospect of *becoming* a state. The movement set out to normalise and stabilise control over people and territory with an array of governing institutions, thus probing its trajectory towards more established institutions and implied forms of recognition. Other authors have described the probationary character of such an unfinished aspirational trajectory as a 'dress rehearsal' (McConnell [2016] in relation to Tibet) or an 'aporetic state' (Bryant and Hatay [2020] in relation to north Cyprus). I will describe the evolution of the LTTE's institutional framework as a sovereign experiment, an exploratory pursuit that comprises sovereign mimicry and sovereign encroachment.

---

* Parts of the first half of this chapter build directly on my joint work with Sidharthan Maunaguru (Klem and Maunaguru 2017, 2018). Some quotations I use and observations I make have previously appeared in these texts or in my work on wartime civil servants (Klem 2012). The second half of the chapter draws on material from confidential Norwegian archives and interviews with key figures, which were part of an official evaluation of the peace process, commissioned by the Norwegian government, co-authored by Jonathan Goodhand, Gunnar Sørbø and me (Goodhand, Klem and Sørbø 2011). In a slight stylistic break with other chapters, I will reference evidence taken from the Norwegian foreign ministry archives in the notes.

Sovereign mimicry is a form of citational practice (Weber 1998) whereby insurgencies replicate prior institutions, rules, buildings, uniforms, emblems and flags but make small adjustments. Like any other form of mimicry, this yields outcomes that seem like duplicates of the state but are in fact slightly different, and herein lies their unsettling potential (Bhabha 1994; see also Klem and Maunaguru 2017, 2018). Sovereign encroachment entails a practice of tacit restraint towards the purportedly hostile institutions of the Sri Lankan state and deliberate attempts at percolating and co-opting these institutions – a form of bricolage in support of insurgent assertions of rule. Crucially, the performative efforts of insurgent movements like the LTTE are undergirded by the capacity for violence, of both a disciplinary and a spectacular kind. The de facto sovereign ability (Hansen and Stepputat 2005) to enforce rules, impose punishments, control territory or recruit cadres adds gravity to insurgent institutional practices and enables them to hold their ground.

The blurry lines of sovereign encroachment, the tentative character of sovereign mimicry and the uncertainties around battlefield accomplishments yield an inherent indeterminacy. There is a fine line between mimicry and mockery, between looking authoritative and looking foolish, between percolating an institution and being sucked in. Performative efforts can be interrupted or reversed, and their credibility remains contingent. How do people respond to the proverbial clothes that the self-declared emperor has borrowed? Will the self-proclaimed rulers get away with their performance, or will someone pull out the rug from under them? The performative angle that I adopt mitigates the inclination to try and adjudicate whether the enacted institution is what it purports to be and instead underlines that one can never quite be sure about such judgements. In fact, to some degree this uncertainty is the point. Rebel rule tends to be accompanied by excitement, anxiety and anticipation *because* of this uncertainty, not despite of it.

Though much has been written about the LTTE, there are only few detailed empirical accounts, and there has been little systematic conceptual reflection on the movement's sovereign experiment. Initially known as the Tamil New Tigers (founded in 1972), the group renamed itself as the LTTE in 1976 (Balasingham 2004: 25). The emergence and evolution of the movement and its ideology have been well documented (Cheran 2009; Hellmann-Rajayanagam 1994b; Hoole et al. 1992; Schalk 1997a; Sumathy 2001; Thangarajah 2012). In the 1970s and early 1980s it was one of a whole raft of proliferating Tamil militias. With its origins on the Jaffna peninsula, the group had a strong northern signature and would only gain foothold in the east in the late 1980s. Though the LTTE embraced an agenda of social revolution alongside Tamil nationalism, it professed less of a leftist ideology than did other groups. The Tigers stood out for their ruthless deployment of violence, especially when challenged from within (the group suffered two significant internal rifts) or from rival Tamil groups (it decimated the other Tamil militias in the mid-1980s). In the late 1980s, the LTTE became the dominant force of Tamil nationalism and arrogated itself the privilege of being the sole voice of the Sri Lankan Tamil community.

Scholarship has documented the movement's coercive violence (Hoole et al. 1992; Rajan Hoole 2001), its gender dynamics of combined emancipation-subjugation (Sitralega Maunaguru 1995; Satkunanathan 2012; Sumathy 2016a) and its interlinkages with the large Tamil diaspora community (Fuglerud 2009; Laffey and Nadarajah 2016; Orjuela 2008). The first detailed academic study of the ground realities of the LTTE's state-like institutions was Trawick's (1997, 2007) ethnography of the eastern town Kokkadichcholai, later followed by Stokke's (2006) article on the sprawling of LTTE institutions after the 2002 ceasefire. Both of these contributions, and Stokke's in particular, have received criticism for too readily adopting the benign self-image projected by the LTTE (Sarvananthan 2007; see Stokke [2007] for a rebuttal) – an attestation of the embattled problems of interpretation that this book is concerned with. Other authors have focused on specific aspects of the LTTE's institutional framework, including its Women's Wing (Brun 2008; De Mel 2007), courts (Provost 2021), cemeteries (Natali 2008), symbolic repertoires (Terpstra and Frerks 2018) and subtle regional differences in the movement's conduct (Thangarajah 2012). Sharika Thiranagama's (2011) ethnography of Tamil militancy and everyday life during the Sri Lankan civil war discusses the articulation of different kinds of life and death under the LTTE and the pervasive impact of the movement's surveillance regime, but it deliberately displaces the LTTE as the central force.

This chapter complements the scholarship on the LTTE by considering it in terms of institutional mimicry and encroachment and disciplinary and spectacular violence. Rather than classifying these efforts as state or non-state, real or pseudo, the chapter highlights the many inherent tensions of the LTTE experiment. The movement became a de facto sovereign formation in the sense that it ruled people and territory in an unchallenged manner. But at the same time, its rule was enacted through the convoluted practices of encroachment: blurry lines, institutional overlap and tactical restraint. As a result of these contradictions and overlaps, the institutions of the LTTE's sovereign experiment were simultaneously normal and stunning, worldly and divine, orderly and capricious. These contradictions were no sign of incompleteness, a leftover tension that was yet to be resolved; rather, they stood at the heart of LTTE sovereignty.

Sovereign aspirations and disregard for human life

My discussion of the LTTE's sovereign experiment starts where it began for me: in Sampur, a small rural town on Sri Lanka's east coast. It was 2000, and I was a master's student collecting material for my research thesis. Much of what I am about to write was not clear to me at the time. I will introduce Sampur in some detail, as we will return to this locality in later chapters.

Sampur is located on the southern mouth of the Koddiyar Bay, across from Trincomalee's adulated natural harbour (see Map 2.1). It is a settlement of Vellala cultivators, who are considered to be a high caste, and it is home to a well-known Hindu temple with a history predating the arrival of colonial powers. Situated in one of Sri Lanka's most ethnically mixed districts, Sampur is known for being an exclusively Tamil space, surrounded by Muslim-dominated towns like Muttur and Tophur and the Sinhala settlement colonies around Seruwila, which were erected from the 1950s onwards (Gaasbeek 2010: 80–82). It was plausibly for this reason of being a 'pure Tamil space', along with its strategic location opposite Trincomalee's navy harbour, that Sampur became a regional hub and model village for the LTTE in the 1990s, much like Kokkadichcholai further south (Trawick 2007).

When I first visited Sampur in 2000, getting there required a visit to the army's civil affairs office at the Monkey Bridge camp before passing the government military checkpoint at the eastern outskirts of Muttur. After the barrier at the Muttur checkpoint was a dirt road that crossed an arm of the lagoon at a small, run-down viaduct, locally known as Majeed's Bridge.[1] This was the point where de facto Tamil Eelam began, the illustrious territory ruled by the LTTE as a Tamil state in the making. There was no checkpoint or visible surveillance – everyone knew the movement did not need such clumsy measures to monitor everyday life.

Strangers (like me) had to report to the local LTTE compound in Sampur. The small town was home to several LTTE institutions. There was an LTTE office and an LTTE bank, talk of LTTE armed positions and a secret medical surgery theatre, and an LTTE cemetery which showcased neat lines of impressive tombstones for fallen cadres. The impeccable state of the graves contrasted with Sampur's general run-down condition. Roads were in an even poorer state than in government-controlled rural areas – even at slow speed, traversing all the potholes was an arduous undertaking. Many buildings were ruined or poorly maintained, and there was no public electricity (Photo 3.1).

Photograph 3.1 Traveling to Sampur

Source: Photograph by author.

Note: One of three ramshackle cable ferries on the bumpy dirt track along the Koddiyar Bay, the access to and from Sampur, in 2010. Soon after, a brand-new major road with bridges would open – one of the many hallmarks of the postwar government's vision on developmental take-off (and of the foreign debts that would trouble Sri Lanka in years to follow).

But apart from that, Sampur looked a lot like other rural Sri Lankan towns. It was only on special occasions like the annual commemoration of LTTE martyrs (*Maaveerar Naal* on 27 November) that Sampur's status as a model village of Tamil Eelam became visible. I happened to drive across Sampur the day before the celebration in 2000. We had to abort our trip and turn around when we came to a small bridge that had been converted into a triumphal arch with such an abundance of garlanding, flags and flowers that no car could pass. The plaque at the heart of it depicted cadres who had died for the cause. The next day, we were told, there would be parades, speeches and public ceremonies. Buses would be chartered. The whole community would join martyr families to visit the LTTE cemetery and pay respect to those who had sacrificed their life. The highlight of the day, not least for Tamils living elsewhere in the world, was something like an Eelam version of the State of the Nation: the live broadcast of the annual speech of LTTE leader Vellupillai Prabhakaran in which he would reflect on the past year and foreshadow what was to come.

The office of Sampur's LTTE commander, which I visited several times in this period, was in a converted residence with a few armed guards in the centre of town across from the main school, the only multi-storey building in Sampur. I vividly remember one encounter with him in late 2000. I had come to ask permission to conduct field research in a neighbouring LTTE-controlled village with a Tamil man from Trincomalee who translated for me. All three of us were in our early twenties. The meeting was brief – he saw no problem with our work. As we got up to leave the house, the LTTE commander engaged in what seemed like small talk with my companion, but when we were out on the road and took our moped off its stand, I saw his hands shaking and fear in his eyes. The commander had casually asked him what his name was and where he lived. Upon hearing the answer, he had paused to think and then said something to the effect of: 'Ah yes, it is at the end of that alley, right? With that particular tree in the garden.' The commander then casually inquired after his parents and sister, using their intimate names normally reserved for the inner family, and he referred to things in their living room. It is not hard to see how one could come by such information. But to a young Tamil man of recruitable age standing face-to-face with a commander who pretends to simply recall these intimate details from memory, this was an intimidating way of 'being known', an invasive kind of surveillance that made government checkpoints with uninterested soldiers glancing over identification papers while asking routine questions look amateurishly ineffective.[2]

The ability of the LTTE commander to instil fear and docility with a few well-posed questions was a testament to the movement's infamous reputation. The LTTE's assertion of power rested squarely on the movement's capacity for violence. Like any other Sri Lankan, my companion knew full well how the LTTE dealt with anyone resisting orders. The liquidation of supposed traitors and the LTTE's brutal massacre of other militant groups in the 1980s loomed large in the collective memory. The systematic assassination of more moderate, non-violent advocates of Tamil nationalism – politicians, peace activists, human rights defenders – had closed all space for dissent (Bose 2002; Hellmann-Rajanayagam 1994b; Hoole et al. 1992; S. Thiranagama 2010, 2011). A mere recital of those who were killed would suffice to delineate the discursive dead zone of Tamil public consciousness under the LTTE: Amir (Amirthalingam, the Ilankai Tamil Arasu Kadchi [ITAK] leader), Rajani (Thiranagama, academic and human rights activist), Neelan (Thiruchelvam, constitutional lawyer and peace architect), Ketesh (Loganathan, former militant and peace advocate), and so on. Like any other Tamil inhabitant of the northeast, my companion had memories of young children being dragged out of their house to be forcibly conscripted as cadres. New recruits unable to execute the training drills were beaten and mistreated. There were harsh punishments for failure to pay taxes, the consumption of alcohol or extra-marital sex (Hoole et al. 1992; Rajan Hoole 2015; Sumathy 2016a; Thamizhini 2021; Thangarajah 2012). Some of these punishments were meted out in public. It was dangerous to say anything that could be construed as questioning or criticising the movement. 'We only open our mouth to eat', people would tell me.

The ubiquitous fear of the movement's violent capacities was matched by widespread support and admiration. The extent of this support was difficult to verify, but there was no doubt that large numbers of Tamils sympathised with the national cause and shared a sense of awe and respect for the movement's prowess and determination. The hardship endured by LTTE cadres, their perseverance against the odds, the courage they mustered to take on a better-equipped army and the fact that they seemed incorruptible all endowed the LTTE with an enigmatic reputation.

The LTTE's repertoire of violent sacrifice and sacralised devotion had a rich but discordant pedigree. It was influenced by the martial idioms of India's independence movement, most obviously the Nazi-inspired anti-imperialism of Subhas Chandra Bose. At the same time, it adopted specifically Tamil forms of warrior adulation and martyrdom from the Dravidian movement (in turn inspired by Hindu rites of the precolonial Bhakti movement), which pitted itself in direct opposition to the Brahmin domination and pan-Indian nationalism associated with Bose and his ilk (Roberts 2014; Schalk 1997a, 1997b; Trawick 2007). More concretely, LTTE cadres were known to have a necklace with a cyanide pill to avoid being captured alive. This became a symbol of their selfless dedication to the cause. Martyrs were referred to as *tiyaki* – literally, those who had 'voluntarily abandoned life' (Fuglerud 2009; Schalk 1997a, 1997b; S. Thiranagama 2011). Chief among these were the so-called black tigers, a suicide squad that became a significant military instrument, mainly for the assassination of high-profile public figures. But suicide attacks were not just an effective military tactic; they also projected a cult of LTTE dedication and shrewdness, celebrating how Tamil youth used their own lives as a weapon against the enemy. A special place was reserved for them in martyr cemeteries, where they were venerated in the absence of a grave as superhuman figures: the *kaval theivankal*, or protective gods of Eelam (Klem and Maunaguru 2017).

Prabhakaran, the movement's supreme commander, epitomised this mixture of nationalist ideology, violent determination and divine resonance. As the founder of the movement, he remained the unquestioned leader until the very end. He outmanoeuvred and outlived many of his enemies, including the Sri Lankan president Premadasa and former Indian prime minister Rajiv Gandhi, to name two famous opponents who were killed in suicide attacks.

Prabhakaran also outlived his fellow militants: leaders of other groups had died or were forced to turn to the government, and most other Tigers from the early days had died in the war. LTTE cadres replaced their birth name with a nom de guerre, but not Prabhakaran.[3] He was simply referred to as *talaivar* (leader) or *anna* (older brother). In LTTE propaganda, he was also referred to as the sun god (*suriya thevan*), a divine figure with superhuman qualities of foresight and omniscience and a perplexing ability to escape death – a figure who, like the gods, was capable of unleashing sublime violence when enraged. As illustrated in diaries kept by cadres (Thamizhini 2021), he was a man who was rarely sighted but whose presence was often felt. Meeting Prabhakaran was seen as a scarce privilege, reserved for a very small selection of cadres and visitors. Suicide cadres had a last meal with him before they were deployed on their fatal mission.

These theological dimensions of LTTE rule illustrate that there is more at stake here than drafting regulations and enforcing them. Sovereign power does not only encompass the measured trappings of discipline but also a ruthless ability to strike with a spectacular show of violent force. Like deities, sovereign rulers have both a benign side and a violent face. They have the potency to unleash sublime violence when their authority is challenged, and they need to set the record straight. The LTTE's ritualisation of martyrdom, its repertoire of violent sacrifice, the harsh punishments for treason and the cult around Prabhakaran resonate well with this conceptualisation of divine kingship.

Prabhakaran pervaded the entire LTTE repertoire of sacrifice, struggle and authorised force. It is perhaps no coincidence that the word *talaivar* translates into German as *Führer*. As pointed out by Agamben (2005), the notion of *Führertum* positions the leader as the sovereign referent, the embodiment of the cause and the foundation of law – not simply an authority but the one authorised to bestow authority.[4] All the chains of self-referential authorisation – including the authority to establish rules and institutions and the subsequent ability to impose exceptions to them – ultimately derived from Prabhakaran, without whom the entire effort would be unsettled.[5]

This cult of an unchallengeable commander resonated throughout the Tamil community. And in this sense, Prabhakaran himself became the sovereign referent not just of the LTTE but also of Tamil nationalism more widely, even if there were many who opposed or detested him. Let me illustrate this with a quotation from a senior Tamil civil servant in Trincomalee who was well into retirement age and had all the qualities of a bureaucratic habitus: the dress, the diction, the predilection for text, procedure and paperwork, and an archival memory for political history. He was, in other words, the opposite of a youth militant, but, like so many Tamils, he confessed that he could but admire their dedication and sacrifice. 'I never joined a militant group', he told me.

> I don't like violence.... Non-violent struggle is more powerful. If both parties have a stick, the people think both must be guilty. Think of [the LTTE cadre] Thileepan, who died of a hunger strike in 1987. Still people talk about him. Why? Because his non-violence is so powerful. I respect [former ITAK leader] Chelvanayakam, but he was a man of compromise.

He paused for a minute and closed his eyes and then said with a concentrated emphasis: 'Prabhakaran's beauty was: if he does anything, he will do it perfectly. He would tell his people to do something: do it or die.' He almost seemed in trance for a moment. When he opened his eyes, he stared at me intently. The line between violence and non-violence is evidently quite thin here, but what runs across it is a reverence for unconditional dedication matched with a disregard of human life, be it one's own or someone else's.

The blurred boundaries of sovereign encroachment

The paradox within the LTTE sovereign experiment and the emergence of a de facto state of Tamil Eelam in the 1990s and 2000s is that it presented LTTE rule both as a visible display of systematic order (with institutions, offices, uniforms and codified rules) and simultaneously as an intractable violent force. Much of the power of the LTTE was derived from the fact that one could never be sure of what the LTTE was up to, what it was able to see and hear, what military capacities it had in store and where it would strike next. My Tamil companion's encounter with the LTTE commander in Sampur was suggestive of this capricious potential. Similarly, the *talaivar* Prabhakaran was ungraspable. He did not reside in a palace where one could request an audience. His whereabouts were subject to continuous speculation; like the gods, he would reveal himself.

This tension between the orderly and the capricious must inform our understanding of the LTTE's unfolding institutional landscape. First, it is intuitive to assume that rules and institutions are somehow foundational to governmental conduct. But what the evolvement of the de facto sovereign framework of the LTTE shows is that the practices, violent coercion and compliance regimes came first, and the institutional shells were added later. The movement's violent capacities and capricious ability to strike never actually disappeared. Yes, there were institutions and rules, but the rules could change, and not all violent conduct was bound by them. Notably, as Sharika Thiranagama (2011: 215) points out, the two most significant kinds of death, the sacrifice of the martyr and the obliteration of the traitor, were exceptional – neither involved the measured trappings of discipline. Second, it is intuitive to interpret institutions as a form of rendering natural: when offices and courts are stabilised, they gain legitimacy and respect, and people will abide by their rules. This may be so, but a crucial element of people's awe and amazement for the various LTTE offices was that the LTTE's institutional efforts were in fact not natural at all. There was a widespread amazement for the boldness, creativity and perseverance of the LTTE in creating what had long been unthinkable: a Tamil state ruling Tamil people in Tamil territory. A group that had started with youngsters on bicycles, commonly referred to as 'our boys' (*namada podiyankal*), had started running something resembling a government – and they pulled it off!

To understand the significance of the LTTE's sovereign experiment, we thus need to consider how the experiment originated. I encountered the LTTE in 2000 when it was acting like a state, fighting a near-symmetrical war with the government and controlling significant territories (see Map 2.1): the culmination of a long historical process since the movement's creation in the 1970s. Some qualities of the LTTE were relatively constant throughout its history, most obviously its staunch Tamil nationalist outlook, its preoccupation with Tamil grievances and its bold conviction that these injustices could only be redressed by an uncompromising violent insurgency. Other elements of its agenda proved more pliable, most obviously its commitment to social emancipation. The LTTE transformed gerontocratic hierarchies and gender roles. It was ruled by youngsters, and it adopted from other Tamil groups the practice of recruiting female cadres (after having initially belittled the Eelam People's Revolutionary Liberation Front [EPRLF] and the People's Liberation Organisation of Tamil Eelam [PLOTE] for recruiting women; Satkunanathan 2012: 31). These young women displayed non-traditional roles of authority and had distinct outfits of boots, belts and braids (Sitralega Maunaguru 1995; Thamizhini 2021; R. Thiranagama 1992). Female suicide bombers made an enormous impression. Sympathisers glorified LTTE girls and women as self-assertive agents of liberation (Ann 1993; Schalk 1994). Other authors underlined that the LTTE's concern with women's social advancement was always subservient to the armed quest of Tamil nationalism (Coomaraswamy 1996). In short, Coomaraswamy and Perera-Rajasingham (2009: 132) posit: 'Women must [be] and are controlled by the LTTE to be armed virgins before marriage and allowed sexual relations only once they have accepted the institutions of marriage'. Yet the movement's law-and-order feminism had profound intended and unintended ramifications on Tamil society (Alison 2003; De Alwis 2002; De Mel 2001, 2004; Gowrinathan 2017; Sitralega Maunaguru 1995; Satkunanathan 2012; S. Thiranagama 2011). The LTTE commitment to eradicating caste hierarchies and other anti-revolutionary cultural traditions yielded similarly ambivalent outcomes (Bose 1994; Bremner 2013; Klem and Maunaguru 2018). Many of the traditional norms that contravened the LTTE's revolutionary outlook continued to prevail in subdued form, only to come back out into the open after the war (see Chapter 4).

Most significantly for this chapter's line of argument, the LTTE's strategy of adopting a sovereign state-like posture evolved over time, gradually yielding a structure embedded in Tamil society but also set aside from it. In the early 1980s, the movement staged hit-and-run attacks, ambushes, bank robberies and prison breaks. In this period, cadres maintained close ties with their families. The affectionate reference to the movement as 'our boys' was reflective of the intimate relations between many Tamil families and a movement comprised of their kin (Klem and Maunaguru 2017; S. Thiranagama 2011). Though that masculine familial trope continued to be used, the proximity between the cadres and Tamil society changed in the late 1980s. The LTTE transformed through India's attempt to impose a peace settlement. It was against the background of New Delhi trying to outmanoeuvre the LTTE by offering other groups diplomatic and military support that the movement crushed rival Tamil militants, leaving deep scars within Tamil society. In the process, the LTTE declared itself the sole voice of the Tamils, thus narrowing the diverse arena of Tamil nationalism into a coercively singular landscape. Moreover, the LTTE cult of self-sacrifice matured against the Indian military,[6] and the movement derived an enigma of invincibility by successfully taking standing up against the regional hegemon.

In the early 1990s, the movement controlled small swathes of territory and started burying its cadres in venerated graves, inscribing their sacrifice in the land (Schalk 1997a). Furthermore, it sought to ethnically 'purify' its territories by violently driving out the Muslims (S. Thiranagama 2011: ch. 3; Hasbullah 2001) as well as people who were considered deviant, such as transgenders (Sumathy 2016b), a purge known as the Eviction. The LTTE started to develop a more methodical administration on the Jaffna Peninsula, not only to systematically enforce recruitment and taxation but also to deal with myriad local issues in need of adjudication. The movement was driven out of Jaffna in the mid-1990s and took its subject population with it in retreat: the so-called Exodus (S. Thiranagama 2011: 67–73). By consequence, its sovereign efforts came of age in what had always been a marginal part of the Tamil homeland: the rural scrublands of the Vanni region.

In sum, the LTTE's institutional landscape that we know from the late 1990s and early 2000s evolved from the gradual systematisation of this sequence of impromptu governing practices. The traces of this gradual process were still discernible in 2000, when I first encountered the LTTE in Sampur. Sovereignty is associated with supreme power, a totalising ability to enforce rules. But rather than a straightforward sovereign imposition, the evolution of the LTTE de facto state was characterised by a process of sovereign encroachment. It involved blurry lines, deliberate ambiguities and overlaps, and forms of tactical restraint and connivance. It did not simply erase the prior institutional landscape but gradually pervaded it by co-opting, inverting, redirecting or tweaking the existing institutions.

This blurriness first became clear to me in the weeks after the aforementioned meeting with the LTTE commander in Sampur. We had visited him because I wanted to conduct a study of a small income generation project run by a Dutch NGO in a village that I have called Adivasipuram elsewhere (Klem and Maunaguru 2018[7]). Adivasipuram is not far from Sampur, about an hour's cycle on a dirt track (today a mere 10 minutes on a motorcycle), but the socio-economic differences are striking. Its inhabitants belong to the indigenous Veddah community,[8] and most of them lived in *cadjan* (palm leaf) huts; others had built rudimentary brick walls with asbestos roofs. The local Hindu temple had a tiny shrine, and the village had but one small shop that sold basic household items, agrarian implements and – if one was lucky – a few soft drinks and biscuits. Adivasipuram's inhabitants struggled to make ends meet with agrarian labour, hunting, collecting forest products and fishing. The livelihood project I had come to study comprised a micro-credit scheme offering revolving loans to rear goats or chickens or engage in 'home-gardening' (growing vegetables for sale). It operated through the local community platform that one finds in virtually every rural Sri Lankan village: the Rural Development Society, or RDS.

I never saw a single LTTE cadre in Adivasipuram, but it soon dawned on me that LTTE oversight did not require visible patrols. My interviews with the RDS leaders tended to result in evasive answers, and as a novice to fieldwork it took me some time to understand what their equivocation was signalling. I was initially frustrated by their inability to provide me with such basic things as a list of beneficiaries and a financial overview, but with time I surmised they themselves had neither of these things. They would cycle back and forth to the LTTE office in Sampur to obtain instructions and get the project funds which had been deposited in an LTTE bank.

Meanwhile, in my household interviews, I learned more about the activities of the RDS. In the past, the RDS had organised *shramadana*s, or collective community work to clean up, clear bushes, level tracks: a common occurrence in rural Sri Lanka. But when I was told about youngsters with spades putting their labour to public service, it occurred to me that a small adjustment could completely change the picture – what if the spades became rifles? It was only a small step from this kind of mobilisation to full-fledged recruitment for the cause of national liberation. This idea took firmer root when I heard that the same group of people had been involved in enforcing particular rules (such as banning alcohol), a common practice throughout LTTE territory. Punishments could be crude: some people recounted the use of physical force and people being placed in a plot surrounded by barbed wire. People's recollection of these practices revealed slippage between the RDS and the LTTE. This confused me, as they were two different entities in my mind. But perhaps this ambiguity was the point, I realised, when I learnt that almost all of the youngsters who had participated in the social work of the RDS were no longer in the village. They had joined the battle, and most of them never returned. I had been studying what I thought was a village development institution, but I slowly came to realise that I was exploring a tentacle of the insurgency that policed the community and recruited cadres by proxy.

RDSs were originally a government invention. They exist across rural Sri Lanka and often function as a clearing house between state entities or specific politicians and the respective community (Brow 1996). The basic concept of village development societies being used for political penetration of rural areas was thus not something the LTTE came up with; they just reoriented it as a contrarian state project. Interestingly, these ties to Sri Lankan state entities were not completely severed when the LTTE brought RDSs like the one in Adivasipuram into its orbit. The lowest rungs of the government bureaucracy – *grama niladaris* (village- or ward-level officers) – continued to interact with the RDS as a representation of the people. Through such connections, a small trickle of government welfare benefits (mainly *samurdhi* poverty relief) continued to flow into LTTE-controlled areas, and the movement made no effort to block this. It would not have been difficult for the movement to force the RDS to shun any ties with the Sri Lankan government and demand complete and exclusive loyalty, but the LTTE evidently preferred an approach of tactical restraint and ambiguity, at least for the time being.

A more significant form of LTTE restraint could be found in the heart of Sampur, at the Sri Paththirakaali *kovil*, a major Hindu temple. Like virtually any other social institution in the territories under its control, the LTTE attempted to regulate temples as part of its sovereign project. The need to do so was prompted by the social divisions and hierarchies of temple affairs. Like so many other temples, the Sri Paththirakaali temple was subject to fiercely contested hierarchies of caste and intra-caste *kudis* (clans), which became manifest in the temple board and at the temple festival. This particular temple was controlled by a subset of *kudis* from the local Vellala caste while other *kudis* (as well as other castes) were excluded. Such intra-Tamil discrimination and discord was at odds with the LTTE's outlook of a national liberation movement. In the 1990s, the local commander therefore decreed that the excluded *kudi*s be incorporated in the ritual festivities of the annual temple festivals. Much in line with observations in other LTTE-controlled areas (Klem and Maunaguru 2018; Sidharthan Maunaguru 2021; Maunaguru and Spencer 2013), this invoked resistance, a member from one of the leading temple families told me. In protest to the LTTE's intrusion in Hindu affairs, the temple management called off the annual festival altogether – a major affront – and the LTTE commander caved in.[9] There is no question that the movement had the coercive power to enforce its rules, but the cost of alienating a significant Tamil community made a position of tactical restraint and ambiguity preferable, lest it be seen attacking the people, places and traditions that it claimed to be fighting for.

Performing sovereignty on an international stage

Not long after my stay in Sampur and Adivasipuram, the LTTE's sovereign experiment took a quantum leap. The Norwegian-facilitated peace process took off, after a long and troublesome run-on.[10] As in other conflict hotspots, Norway presented itself as a peace broker, offering soft-power mediation – while boosting its own reputation, relevance and access on the global stage. This period comprised the climax of the LTTE sovereign experiment, where it expanded its performances of statehood to the international arena in pursuit of recognition. Much in line with my analysis earlier, this engendered a convoluted process of gradual expansion and encroachment, where the LTTE leapfrogged marginal opportunity spaces and tacit forms of implied acknowledgement. As we know from other cases, international acceptance may be highly variegated, and rifts between official recognition and actual treatment may conjure up both challenges and possibilities – ask the governments of Somaliland, North Cyprus, Kosovo, Taiwan or any other partly recognised state (Caspersen 2012; Jeffrey, McConnell and Wilson 2015; Krasniqi 2019; Kyris 2022; Pegg and Kolstø 2015; Thompson 2006).

   Of central importance to the LTTE's separatist outlook was the conversion of de facto military parity with the Sri Lankan government into de facto political parity, which the LTTE aspired to ultimately convert into de jure recognition. In that sense, the ceasefire marked a moment of triumph and anticipation. It was not a truce that the movement had been forced into.[11] The LTTE had successfully deterred the government military and rapidly regained large swaths of territory (even if its attempt to reconquer Jaffna had failed). It had started running a de facto sovereign administration in its territory, which the government had been unable to stop. It had provoked the government by declaring a sequence of monthly unilateral ceasefires in late 2000 and early 2001. And it subsequently outmanoeuvred President Kumaratunga (Sri Lanka Freedom Party, or SLFP) by striking a bargain with her United National Party (UNP) arch-rival, the newly elected prime minister Wickremesinghe, with whom the movement signed an official, internationally monitored ceasefire on 22 February 2002. In the subsequent year, the delegation of LTTE negotiator Anton Balasingham was flown around the world to negotiate with the government. 'The boys' were clearly no longer just boys. They were treated like diplomats in foreign embassies; they sat on the stage as a party equal to the government; and the world media queued up to take pictures and interview them at press conferences. The performative benefits were enormous. From a Tamil nationalist perspective, this comprised an endorsement of the movement's military accomplishments and its emerging de facto state. And it offered a vantage point for converting these de facto realities into something official.

The LTTE used the relative calm of the ceasefire to bolster its own institutions. The Vanni became a showcase region for LTTE governance. Having consolidated its territory in the Vanni, the LTTE moved its administrative hub in Mallavi (a small village where international humanitarian agencies had established themselves to coordinate their Vanni operations) to the town of Kilinochchi, which emerged as the de facto capital of Tamil Eelam. A growing palette of LTTE departments popped up along the town's main road, each with impressive office buildings surrounded by gardens, official signposts, flags and a modest fleet of official vehicles: the Political Wing, the Peace Secretariat, the Planning and Development Secretariat, the Department of Education, the Tamil Eelam Police headquarters, different kinds of courts, a human rights secretariat and more. Some of these institutions were new inventions; others had existed in some form and were now further officialised. Letterheads, visiting cards and uniforms proliferated.

Much in sync with this rapid expansion of the LTTE's institutional dramaturgy, major changes took place at the front line. The entry to the Vanni had long had an LTTE checkpoint (unlike in Sampur), but of a functional, military kind. With the ceasefire, it was moved from a jungle track near Madhu to the main road in Omanthai, and it was transformed into an elaborate gateway to Tamil Eelam. A new customs service was created with a new uniform. Visitors had to fill out various kinds of paperwork, answer questions, pay import taxes and submit their vehicles to checks. The procedures were all friendly and professional, especially to international visitors – this was not the kind of checkpoint where one would worry about being harassed or where the half-baked questioning by poorly motivated soldiers seemed like a pointless nuisance. Everything about the conduct of the LTTE customs officers service suggested they were adamant about performing the quintessentially sovereign task of marking a border, not just by mimicking the Sri Lankan government but by enacting a superior version. Significantly, the staged gateway to Tamil Eelam enjoyed implicit international endorsement: the government allowed it to exist, the Norwegian-brokered ceasefire agreement provided written acknowledgement of LTTE-controlled territory (further bolstered by the International Committee of the Red Cross monitors occupying a post between the government and LTTE checkpoints) and international visitors queued up to join the show and see Tamil Eelam for themselves.

Having cleared customs, most visitors would proceed on the A9, a rudimentary gravel road which was soon to be asphalted. Large billboards had been placed along the road, informing visitors about life in Tamil Eelam, glorifying the work of various LTTE-associated organisations and applauding their dedication to the cause and their loyalty to the leader. Upon arrival in Kilinochchi, most visitors could not resist taking snapshots of the various signs and buildings of the unfolding LTTE state before joining the performative action inside. Journalists and academics conducted official interviews, aid workers coordinated their projects, diplomats engaged with political officers. More photos were taken, including by LTTE communication officers who would post them on their various websites. The more prestigious visitors would be offered an official lunch, or – if they stayed the night – accommodation in the official LTTE hotel, where two enormous pictures of *talaivar* Prabhakaran decorated the stairwell. Like the LTTE lunch, the LTTE rooms were decent but not exorbitant, as if to signal the movement was serious but moderated.

The LTTE Political Wing reciprocated these visits and travelled to remote places like Oslo, Berlin and other European capitals. As mentioned at the very outset of this book, I was a junior researcher at the Clingendael Institute in The Hague at the time. I vividly remember the visit of the LTTE Political Wing leader S. P. Tamilselvan (a suave senior cadre who walked with a cane), his elderly translator George, the head of the LTTE Peace Secretariat S. Pulitheevan, and a handful of male and female representatives of various other LTTE departments, typically in their twenties. It was clear that some of them were still getting used to wearing blazers and loafers and casually walking around in seventeenth-century manors.

It was as exciting for us as it was for them. One does not host the delegation of an aspiring sovereign state every day. It had long been virtually impossible to meet any senior LTTE officer, and now they were right there in the meeting room down the hall. I could not help feeling that we needed to act the part: that is, to host them as what they were trying to be, with a discursive language that matched theirs. So there we were, talking about the prospects and challenges of a sovereign Tamil state, occasionally hinting at critical issues but never offending our guests outright. Figureheads like Tamilselvan and Pulitheevan were the talk of the Colombo expat circuits in those years. Diplomats, advisors and aid workers exchanged observations, interpretations and gossip, and they came up with creative workarounds to grapple with this unusual situation.[12]

For both domestic and international audiences, there was something exciting about the evolution of the LTTE's sovereign experiment. All the acting normal was matched with the realisation that this was, in fact, extraordinary. LTTE institutions were headed by people who had been jungle child soldiers just a few years ago and were now advancing on the world stage. It was an improvised performance from all ends. Of course, all forms of protocol and diplomatic exchange have theatrical qualities, but this was an unusually exciting kind of theatre, an unbounded, experimental kind of theatre – there was no telling when the curtains would fall, what the stage would look like when they did and which protagonists would still be standing. Notwithstanding the cordial exchanges, the movement's violent track record was obvious, and it continued to be banned as a terrorist group in powerful countries like India and the United States. The movement's leader Prabhakaran insulated himself from all these interactions, and there was no way to predict his next moves. Despite the mushrooming of bureaucratic institutions along the Kilinochchi main road, the capricious potential of the movement never lifted.

Showdown of asymmetry

The Norwegian-facilitated peace process offered the LTTE an international stage, but this proved to be a perilous podium for the insurgents. The expeditious take-off of the peace process had been precipitated by a shallow convergence of interest between the UNP government, the LTTE and the Norwegian foreign ministry, each of which sought to marginalise President Kumaratunga (SLFP), but for very different reasons. The Norwegian mediators had internally formulated a peace strategy,[13] but the ink was barely dry when they fell out with the president.[14] Their plan lay in shambles, and they needed a face-saving exit. The newly elected UNP, locked in a life-long rivalry with the SLFP, needed a quick win to wrest the political initiative from their political arch-rival Kumaratunga. Only two years prior, the same UNP had derailed Kumaratunga's attempt to initiate peace talks (demonstratively burning the substantive core of her peace plan: the so-called devolution package), but now the tables had turned, and the Norwegian peace effort offered a means to outmanoeuvre her. The LTTE despised Kumaratunga for the violence she had inflicted on them in the late 1990s, and they rejected the conditions she had posed for the signing of a ceasefire or the commencement of formal talks. The UNP offered them an opportunity to embark on a peace process without such requirements.

The divergence underlying this shallow convergence were exposed when core political issues were tabled at the Oslo talks of December 2002. After that meeting, the Norwegian government issued a press release stating that both sides had agreed to 'explore a solution founded on the principle of internal self-determination in areas of historical habitation of the Tamil-speaking peoples, based on a federal structure within a united Sri Lanka'.[15] The ambiguity of combining Tamil nationalist lingo (internal self-determination) with Sinhala nationalist lingo (united Sri Lanka) under the rubric of a term that neither side embraced (federalism) provoked knee-jerk reactions in both the Tamil and Sinhala camp. Instead of jointly exploring constitutional reform and federal power-sharing, subsequent talks were about damage control. The Muslim community, in turn, was alarmed by the suggestion of a federal arrangement, fearing a scenario where the northeastern Muslim community would be sacrificed as a small ethnic minority in a Tamil-dominated region. This gave new impetus to Muslim youth protests, demands for safeguards and protections and propositions for self-government in a non-contiguous Muslim region (Lewer and Ismail 2011; Mohideen 2006). As the peace talks stalled and distrust grew, ground-level realities in the northeast continued to yield instability with regular ceasefire violations, gross human right abuses and unclaimed killings.

To equip the peace process with shock breakers, backchannels and consultation mechanisms, a whole architecture of ceasefire monitors, peace process co-chairs, sub-committees, development donor facilities and civil society initiatives had been set up.[16] Central to the whole design was Norway's self-presentation as a non-coercive mediator with an even-handed, consensual approach towards the government and the LTTE. This attempt to sidestep the question of sovereignty and the associated conundrums of (a)symmetry soon emerged as the cardinal problem in managing the peace process. By enacting the peace process as one of two equal sides, fundamental disagreement on this issue had been deferred to a later date. When that date came, the process unravelled. As described earlier, the LTTE entered the peace process from a position of military strength. It had successfully insisted on a state mediator (and ceasefire monitors) to counter-leverage Sri Lanka's privileged position as a state,[17] and it had outmanoeuvred President Kumaratunga by negotiating with Prime Minister Wickremesinghe instead. The prime minister went along with the premise of parity in the signing of the ceasefire and the format of the talks. But given his weak position (stuck in a cohabitation arrangement with arch-rival Kumaratunga and mustering only a slim simple majority in parliament), any compromise Wickremesinghe's negotiators could offer would have to stick to the bounds of the constitution, parliamentary endorsement and presidential approval – the very premises that the LTTE, and the Tamil nationalist movement more broadly, had long fulminated against.

The Norwegian team similarly deferred the question of asymmetry. From the moment overtures to the LTTE were made, the foreign ministry worried about being seen as too 'LTTE-friendly'.[18] The Norwegians nevertheless embarked on an even-handed peace process between two asymmetrical political entities. This process had the appearance of parity between the parties, but it took place in a regional and international context that offered very little scope to treat the LTTE like a state. The Norwegian government was not equipped to redress the fundamental asymmetries at stake, and when these came to the fore, the process derailed.

The LTTE suspended its participation because of its concern with the asymmetries of the international constellation around the peace process. The movement's leadership knew that the implied political parity of the peace process could be undone with a stroke of the pen. The government was hedging its inability to make constitutional compromises.[19] Meanwhile, the ceasefire placed no restrictions on the government procuring arms or recruiting troops, while the LTTE received continuous flack for smuggling and forced recruitment (and child recruitment in particular).

In a letter to the prime minister on 21 April 2003, lead negotiator Balasingham announced the suspension of LTTE participation in the peace negotiations. Key reasons cited included a preliminary donor conference in Washington, DC (which the LTTE could not attend as a proscribed organisation under US law), the unaddressed military occupation of public and private Tamil property in the northeast and the tendency of the Wickremesinghe government to subsume welfare conditions in the northeast under a general vision of economic growth, rather than identifying the political causes underpinning the Tamil plight.[20]

Balasingham's demonstrative protest has been well publicised. Less is known about what happened backstage at this important juncture. Our perusal of the confidential archives of the foreign ministry in Oslo[21] suggests that the Norwegian team misread the LTTE's determination. The subsequent email from special envoy Solheim to Balasingham implies that the LTTE's stance was interpreted as tactical opposition that could be redressed with some extra measures. It starts with an upbeat 'Bala!' and then reads:

> We have as you will know, studied your letter to the prime minister....
> In your letter you are demanding that the [Sri Lankan] government

should do much more on implementation when it comes to resettlement of internally displaced and refugees, reconstruction of the Tamil areas and normalcy for the inhabitants of the north and east. The government recognise that a lot more should be done. They are not satisfied with the progress but want to enter into a dialogue, listening to your suggestions, before making new important decisions.[22]

The email goes on to discuss the travel plans of government negotiator G. L. Peiris and Norwegian (deputy) ministers Vidar Helgesen and Jan Petersen to suggest tagging on a discussion with the LTTE. Balasingham's response three days later was curt:

Mr P [Prabhakaran] is firmly determined that the [Sri Lankan] government should take action to fulfil the obligation of the CFA [ceasefire agreement]. We are awaiting the Prime Minister Mr Ranil Wickramasinghe's reply to our letter.[23]

If this was not clear to begin with, Balasingham's email to Solheim six weeks later left no space for doubt:

As you are aware, we are not very happy over the approaches and methods undertaken by the facilitators [the Norwegian team] to satisfy the expectations and interests of the international donor community thereby ignoring the complexity of the ground reality. Priority was given to human values, principles, guidelines, milestones and roadmaps to an imaginary final settlement in an unknown future rather than offering concrete solutions to concrete problems. The peace process was further complicated by intense internationalisation that effected a serious imbalance in partnership placing us at a serious disadvantageous position. As a state Sri Lanka was given all privileges and encouragements whereas the LTTE, even in its absence, was treated shabbily with warnings and threats that eroded our self-confidence. As you know, intense pressure will make the LTTE intransigent.[24]

The underlying tensions of Norway's even-handedness were starting to become painfully apparent. The Norwegian team had engaged with the LTTE as a state-like actor without challenging its sovereign aspirations, but simultaneously it had assured the government that a separate Tamil state was 'out of the question'.[25] This ambiguity could not last. The Norwegians had designed a process that appeared to tilt in the LTTE's favour: the ceasefire enabled the movement to consolidate its control and they gained enormous political capital from their international performance as a state-like actor. But the process was embedded in a regional and global context that was dominated by the deep-seated state bias of the international system. The Indian government firmly opposed the LTTE being legitimised as part of any solution. More generally, the pro-state reflexes of both Asian and Western governments were compounded by the anti-terrorist discourse that swept across the globe after the September 11 attacks in 2001 (directly in parallel to the peace talks). Even supposed soft powers like the European Union and Canada officially proscribed the LTTE as a terrorist organisation in 2006. In the early days of the ceasefire, the Norwegian experiment of parity was tolerated, but when the peace process lost momentum, it offered the LTTE no defence against regional and global pressures.

The movement continued presenting itself as a state in the making, but without the entourage of a promising international peace process these performative efforts lost credibility among its international audience. Half a year after suspending its participation in the talks, the LTTE unilaterally presented the contours of a transitional political framework, which clearly transgressed the bounds and biases of the international system: the proposal for an Interim Self-Governing Authority (ISGA), a five-year transitional arrangement for the northeast with a governance structure that bordered on independence.[26] This document may be seen as the political terminus of Sri Lankan Tamil nationalism. It embodied the legal conversion of the LTTE's de facto sovereign rule over people and territory into a formal and recognised form of self-government, and it marked the rejoining of the LTTE's trajectory of armed militancy with the older political trajectory of democratic campaigning and constitutional bargaining. As such, it comprised the culmination of the long history of wrecked power-sharing arrangements, Tamil nationalist contentions with the Sri Lankan constitution and violent insurgency. The ISGA was also a terminus of Tamil nationalist politics in the sense that it was a dead end. It did not result in any negotiations, let alone an agreement. The proposal sparked a political crisis, and the peace process, which had already been in dire straits for nearly a year by now, unravelled definitively.

The crisis over the ISGA proposal had rupturing consequences in all camps. For the UNP government of Prime Minister Wickremesinghe it was a political bombshell. And for the Norwegian government, it precipitated a crisis that spun beyond its mediation capacities. The release of the ISGA proposal prompted President Kumaratunga to declare a state of emergency and assume control over three key ministries, thus exploiting Wickremesinghe's feeble political position and effectively rendering his government impotent. Public dismay over the Norwegian-facilitated peace process gave Sinhala-Buddhist nationalism a firm electoral tail wind, which brought a hardline nationalist to power: Mahinda Rajapaksa (SLFP) was elected president.[27] His rise to power would fracture the traditional elites of both mainstream parties and would mark Sri Lanka's political trajectory for seventeen years to come. The LTTE also experienced the rupturing effects of the peace process when it suffered an unprecedented split. In March 2004, the LTTE's eastern commander Karuna defected from the northern-dominated movement. This drastic move, he claimed, was driven by a difference of strategic perception between him and LTTE leader Prabhakaran (Sánchez-Meertens 2013). The Karuna split was quickly defeated by the LTTE, but it left the movement both weakened and emboldened in its military course.

Insurgent sovereign experiments that have successfully converted themselves into relatively stable (if largely unrecognised) states almost invariably enjoy the support of a powerful patron state, typically a regional hegemon. Examples include the republics in the former Soviet fringe (South Ossetia, Abkhazia, Transnistria – all backed by Russia) and North Cyprus (backed by Turkey) (Caspersen 2012). The LTTE lacked such a patron. India had played this role in the 1980s for the Tamil militancy more widely, but after the LTTE turned its guns on the Indian military and killed Rajiv Gandhi, such recourse was permanently disabled. The Norwegian government presented itself as an honest, even-handed broker, but it was neither capable nor willing to counter-leverage the Sri Lankan state in order to preserve symmetry. The LTTE was remarkably effective in using the ceasefire to roll out an elaborate institutional architecture reminiscent of a state. It skilfully developed a level of international goodwill, and it had drafted a radical but credible proposal for political transition. These were necessary accomplishments for the LTTE in anticipation of a more recognised form of self-rule, but they were no defence when the process collapsed.

In fact, they arguably provoked additional concern, not least for the Indian government. India never openly opposed the peace effort, but the apparent appeasement of the LTTE raised alarm, our interviews in Delhi confirmed. 'Norway gave the LTTE a certain legitimacy. We found that very uncomfortable,' a former Indian foreign secretary told us. 'The perception was that the Norwegians were becoming apologists for the LTTE' – not because of personal sympathies but because of the approach of treating both sides even-handedly. The 2004 Lok Sabha elections compounded the Indian position. They brought Congress, the party of the Gandhis, back to power, cementing Delhi's willingness to side with the Sri Lankan government. And it gave the main party of Tamil Nadu – the Dravida Munnetra Kazhagam (DMK), a Congress ally – a stake in tempering controversy over Sri Lanka. When the war resumed in 2006, India firmly sided with the Sri Lankan government with support to naval operations, radar capacities and intelligence (Hariharan 2010).

Conclusion

The LTTE manifested itself as a de facto sovereign by exercising 'discipline with impunity' (Hansen and Stepputat 2005, 2006). It established a regime of discipline and a chain of authority over people and territory that did not yield to the Sri Lankan state. It also coerced the multifarious movement of

Tamil nationalism into a singular effort, with the movement as the 'sole voice' and its *talaivar* Prabhakaran as the ultimate sovereign referent. An array of LTTE departments popped up, each with their own offices, uniforms and letterheads. These institutions by and large resembled their analogues in the Sri Lankan state apparatus. As such, I have argued, they can be understood as sovereign mimicry (Bhabha 1994; Klem and Maunaguru 2017). The sovereign performance of the LTTE yielded institutions that were similar to those of its adversary, thus making them easily recognisable as the apparatus of government but also slightly different. The movement aspired to an institutional order that was no mere replica of the state but a superior version, a dress rehearsal (McConnell 2016) for a new glorified state to come.

This chapter also observed that there was a significant paradox in the LTTE's sovereign experiment. On the one hand, the movement went to great lengths to present its rule as orderly and institutionalised, but on the other hand, it derived much of its power and enigma from being unpredictable and unknowable. The performative practices of governance did not cull its capricious potential. Alongside the bureaucratic trappings and codifications, the movement nurtured a powerful cult of violent dedication, sacrifice and martyrdom. One could never quite know what the LTTE was up to or what it was able to do. It had an elaborate system of regulations, but – much in line with the literature on sovereign violence (Gilmartin 2020; Hansen 2001; Klem and Maunaguru 2017; Spencer 2007) – LTTE rules could change, and the potential for violence never waned.

I have argued that the LTTE's sovereign experiment in the 1990s and early 2000s did not comprise a clear-cut imposition of rule and a delineation of people and territory that severed all ties with the institutional landscape of the Sri Lankan state. On the contrary, it unfolded through fuzzy boundaries, institutional overlap and tactical restraint. Rather than enforcing exclusive loyalty and crisply demarcated boundaries, this process was characterised by the ambiguity of institutional bricolage, first within its own territory and then, with the ceasefire, in the international arena. The LTTE gradually co-opted institutions, and it connived the continued functioning of Sri Lankan government entities on its turf in overlap with the creation of its own state institutions.

This process of sovereign encroachment was manifest at the village level in Adivasipuram, where the RDS (originally a government rural outreach mechanism) was brought into the orbit of LTTE rule, while interactions with government officers and services also continued. In Sampur, the movement did not coerce the Vellala-dominated Hindu temple to abandon its strict caste and *kudi* hierarchies when the temple board demonstratively called off the annual temple festival. The LTTE exercised a similar form of restraint towards government officers, most obviously the ward-level *grama niladaris* in LTTE-controlled areas, who continued to function as part of the government institutional hierarchy, with information, documents, decisions and a trickle of resources going back and forth across the front line. The LTTE's strategy of sovereign encroachment served a long-term objective of carving out a path towards an effective and recognised government: to gradually transform itself from an insurgency with some de facto institutions into a de facto state, then graduate into a state with de facto recognition and ultimately seek formal recognition. The Norwegian-facilitated peace process and the 2002 ceasefire agreement offered the LTTE an opportunity to convert its military parity with the government to an implied form of political parity and showcase its state-like posture.

Norway's even-handed, consensual approach to the 2000s peace process created the pretence of parity between the LTTE and the government. The Norwegians were prepared to facilitate the LTTE in consolidating its performance of sovereign mimicry and expanding this repertoire on the international stage. For the LTTE this was the crown on many years of gradual maturation as a de facto sovereign political structure. LTTE-controlled territory was formally acknowledged with a ceasefire agreement, and the governing institutions of Tamil Eelam were sprawling along the Kilinochchi main road. Meanwhile, LTTE negotiators travelled the globe in an official capacity and thrived on the implied endorsement of photoshoots, protocol and diplomatic networking.

International actors were no passive audience to the LTTE's conduct; they were part of the performative action. During the peace process, diplomats, aid workers and other foreign visitors, like me, were acting the part when they engaged with the unusual phenomenon of an insurgent state in the making, to see where the plot would take them. After the core political issues of the peace talks were tabled at the December 2002 Oslo meeting, the illusion of symmetry fizzled out, and when the movement unilaterally presented its own vision of a transitional political framework – the ISGA proposal – the underlying tensions and contradictions of the process were exposed. The legitimating teleology of an insurgency transforming itself into a peaceful political actor crumbled, and the LTTE's posturing could no longer mitigate the perception that they were violent insurgents, if not terrorists. Rather than dazzling international audiences with its sovereign performance, the LTTE had alarmed them. Re-assembling the repertoires of the Tamil nationalist movement, the LTTE set out to advance a comprehensive enactment of Tamil sovereignty, steeped in a Tamil *demos* and homeland, and a legal framework premised on the national right to self-determination. But political performativity, however vivacious, can unravel or assume different connotations when the setting or the audience changes.

The line between validating performance and farce became thin for the LTTE's sovereign experiment when the peace talks petered out. The movement had no recourse to the counter-leverage of a patron state. The Norwegians had been prepared to artificially level the playing field for talks, but they were neither willing nor able to neutralise the growing international pressure on the LTTE.

Notes

1   Named after the political patron who enabled its construction, the renowned Muslim leader Abdul Majeed from neighbouring Kinniya (a member of parliament on an SLFP ticket from 1960 to 1977).

2   For a detailed discussion about the significance of knowledge and intimacy around LTTE surveillance, the sense of belonging instilled by 'being in the know', and the preoccupation with traitors, see S. Thiranagama (2010).

3   Other exceptions were S. P. Tamilselvan (who headed the Political Wing in the 2000s and used to have a nom de guerre earlier: Dinesh) and Anton Balasingham (the LTTE 'ideologue' and negotiator).

4   Agamben (2005) raises the German term *Führertum* in his discussion of the paradox between two forms of authority in Roman law: *potestas* (legal authority) and *auctoritas* (the more fundamental capacity of conferring such legal authority: the authority to generate legal validity). *Auctoritas* thus resembles the ability to bootstrap the law into being (Brilmayer 1989), and as such, it is closely related to the sovereign capacity of suspending or (re-)enacting law, including the ability to place a person within or outside of the law. The two forms of authority are a binary pair, Agamben observes, but they may converge in one institution or person as is the case with the notion *Führertum*, a concept associated with the Nazi adulation of Adolf Hitler, as the ultimate sovereign referent. When the state of exception that binds *potestas* and *auctoritas* together becomes the norm, Agamben posits, the juridico-political system effectively becomes 'a killing machine' (Agamben 2005: 86).

5   There are fascinating parallels here to Abimael Guzmán, the former leader of Sendero Luminoso (the Communist Party of Peru – Shining Path). Degregori (2012) conceptualises Guzmán as a 'cosmocrat', a figure that mixes the repertoires of science, Catholicism, communism and fuses the qualities of an oracle and a martial leader capable of inflicting violence.

6   This violence arguably targeted the more intimate figure of a guardian that betrays its duties, a view that resonates with Thiranagama's argument that the figure of the traitor is defined by intimacy: it is intimate knowledge that spells danger, so the reneging of intimate actors is seen to warrant especially violent measures (S. Thiranagama 2010).

7   A small fragment of the material used in Klem and Maunaguru (2018) informs this section as well. The two paragraphs 'I never saw ... recruit cadres by proxy' comprise an edited version of the corresponding paragraphs in Klem and Maunaguru (2018: 797).

8   Though the Veddahs are classified as a very small separate ethnic group, they were considered Tamil in Adivasipuram. Brow (1996) argues that Veddahs are best referred to as a *variga* (kind), somewhere between a caste group and an ethnic group at the fringes of both the Tamil and the Sinhala community.

9   Some *kudis* were added in subsequent years, but resistance remains.

10 Norwegian involvement has a much longer history than is generally assumed. It in fact dates back to the immediate aftermath of India's military and diplomatic withdrawal. First Norwegian overtures occurred when a well-connected Norwegian and long-time resident of Sri Lanka by the name of Arne Fjørtoft sent out feelers, partly inspired by Norway's growing peace activism in other parts of the world. The Norwegian government first offered its services to help facilitate peace on 22 January 1991 (MFA archives Oslo: 307. 30/442, 1996/01182, 55–72, Letter from foreign minister Godal to Solheim, 3 June 1996). During the peace talks of the mid-1990s, the conflict parties agreed on an international monitoring mission of which Norway was a part, but the process collapsed before the mission was fielded. The Norwegian government continued to make overtures, and the embassy in Colombo was given a more active role – a departure from Norway's standard approach of using proxies. Norwegian diplomats held exploratory meetings with government and opposition in Colombo, but felt they lacked a 'real contact' point with the LTTE (MFA archives Oslo: MFA. 302. 77 [1998/04913-4], Colombo to Oslo, 21 September 1998). In May 1999, Kumaratunga officially issued a secret request to the Norwegian government inviting them to facilitate a peace process.

11 It has been argued that the LTTE made a strategic shift due to the drastic changes in global security dynamics (Gunaratna 2003; Saravanamuttu 2003), and it is true that the truce followed shortly after the 11 September 2001 Al Qaida attacks and the declaration of the so-called global war on terror. However, the LTTE's positioning in relation to the peace process predated this shift.

12 For example, foreign donors seeking to work in LTTE-controlled areas without formally supporting the LTTE found a convenient go-between in the bodies of the state that continued to function in LTTE areas, including the provincial council. In a similar vein, they engaged with the Tamils Rehabilitation Organisation, an outfit of the Tamil diaspora (though they eschewed direct funding). Officially an international NGO like so many others, it was well known that the organisation was in fact a diaspora-associated appendage of the LTTE. By not openly claiming control over the organisation, the LTTE was not only able to attract benefits for the population but also lent credence to the fact that it was tolerant enough to have something resembling a civil society in Tamil Eelam.

13 This confidential Norwegian document of 2000 envisaged a sequence starting with a ceasefire to establish stability, followed by normalisation, aid programmes and interim measures to bolster confidence, to then finally establish a conducive constellation for an overall peace agreement. This confidential plan envisioned monthly meetings between the parties, which would be underpinned by a ceasefire and bolstered by an international group of friends whose development aid would lubricate the process. Within six months, the parties would present a proposal for an interim solution and a timeline for future negotiations (MFA archives Oslo: 307.3 [2000/00522-36], MFA to Colombo, 20 September 2000). The 2002–2003 process (after circumventing President Kumaratunga) adhered to this game plan almost literally – except it did not end as planned.

14 When Kumaratunga's peace overtures balked – with the LTTE attacking her with a suicide bomber (1999) and regaining territory (2000), the UNP scuttling her devolution proposal (2000) and her losing control of parliament (2001) – Norwegian special envoy Erik Solheim zealously tried to break the gridlock by reaching out to the opposition and international actors. This elicited major irritation from Kumaratunga – especially his plea to the US government to pressure the Sri Lankan government to de-proscribe the LTTE (MFA archives Oslo: 307. 3 [2001/00612-51], Minutes from meeting between Solheim, Westborg, Tromsdal, Kumaratunga and Kadirgamar, 30 April 2001). When we interviewed Kumaratunga (London, 5 June 2011), she commented 'Solheim was ambitious and he made some mistakes.... A negotiator should melt into the walls. Disappear when the parties come to an agreement. He was not like that. He always had a one-upmanship.... He always wanted to be one up to the government.' In response to this perceived over-assertiveness, Kumaratunga called on the Norwegian government to remove Solheim from his role. He stayed on board, but the Norwegians were forced to reshuffle their team.

15 Full text available in Edrisinha et al. (2008: 646–648) and on many online repositories. See also Balasingham (2004: 405).

16 The academic work on the peace process and its architecture is formidable (Goodhand, Korf and Spencer 2011; Rupesinghe 2006; Stokke 2010; Stokke and Uyangoda 2011; Venugopal 2018; Wickramasinghe 2006; Winslow and Woost 2004). There is an even larger body of applied research in connection to the process (including reports by Centre for Policy Alternatives, Foundation for Coexistence, Berghof Foundation, International Crisis Group, as well as many donor-funded consultancy reports) and a small collection of memoirs (Balasingham 2004; Fernando 2008; Gooneratne 2007; Thamizhini 2021; Weerakoon 2004).

17 There had in fact been some 'mediator shopping'. In the late 1990s onwards, Canada, the Netherlands, the UK, the Commonwealth, the Catholic Church, civil society organisations and several other actors had been offering their services in one way or the other – in Kumaratunga's words, 'they were falling over each

other' (interview in London, 5 June 2011). The Norwegian government was agreeable to both sides as a state actor (considered essential by the LTTE) but not a major power with a direct stake in Sri Lanka (unlike India) and not a power with leverage against the government (a condition for the Kumaratunga administration). After correspondence with the LTTE, Kumaratunga covertly invited the Norwegian government to facilitate a peace process.

18   MFA archives in Oslo: 307. 30/1997/02601, 1–15, 5, Memo, 3 July 1997.

19   In follow-up to the discussions on federalism at the Oslo meeting, the government proposed a provincial administrative council, as an interim arrangement towards constitutional power-sharing and alongside the existing provincial council (North-Eastern Provincial Council, or NEPC). While this setup would give the LTTE seats without having to stand for elections, the legal status of the proposed council was unclear, and its mandate excluded security, policing, land, tax revenue and law-making capacity (Edrisinha et al. 2008: 650–661). In parallel, there had been several initiatives towards informal forms of collaboration on humanitarian and rehabilitation issues (and more were to follow after the December 2004 tsunami), but the funding for such mechanisms flowed through channels in Colombo and could thus be turned off like a tap.

20   Letter from Balasingham to Wickremesinghe, cited in full in Balasingham (2004: 434–439).

21   As mentioned in the first note of the chapter, this archival research was part of a commissioned evaluation of Norwegian peace efforts. One member of our team, Ada Nissen, studied these archives, made summaries and detailed translations of key fragments. The quotations used in this chapter are taken from these excerpts and translations.

22   MFA archives in Oslo: 307. 3 (2003/00027-218), Solheim to Balasingham, 23 April 2003.

23   MFA archives in Oslo: 307. 3 (2003/00027-218), Balasingham to Solheim, 26 April 2003.

24   MFA archives in Oslo: 307. 3 (2003/00027.221), Balasingham to Solheim, 16 June 2003.

25   One of Norway's most senior diplomats gave the Sri Lankan minister of foreign affairs Kadirgamar this assurance during their first encounters in 1998–1999 (interview, 9 December 2010).

26   The text of this document is widely available (see https://en.wikipedia.org/wiki/Interim_Self_Governing_Authority [accessed 6 December 2023]). For an LTTE perspective on this, see Balasingham (2004: 450–465). For a critical constitutional appraisal, see Edrisinha and Welikala (2008). The ISGA was to have 'plenary power' over northeastern Sri Lanka, including over revenue, budgetary authority (and the ability to attract donors, investors and lenders), law and order, and control over land as well as marine and offshore resources.

LTTE representatives would have an absolute majority until the interim period expired and elections were to be held. The proposal was notably mute on the relationship with the legal, political and administrative structure of the rest of Sri Lanka. There was no mention of power-sharing or a federal framework. Instead, the proposal underlined the 'parity of status' between the LTTE and the Sri Lankan government and envisioned a tribunal to settle disputes, with a composition that would ultimately be adjudicated by the International Court of Justice (Edrisinha and Welikala 2008; Edrisinha et al. 2008: 662–675).

27 While this electoral backlash to the peace process was evident, it may be argued that Mahinda's election was also precipitated by an LTTE-enforced Tamil boycott of the polls.

4 Reconstituting 'Pure Tamil Space' after Sovereign Erasure

The May 2009 defeat of the LTTE was a watershed moment in modern Sri Lankan history. In the final year of intense fighting, the insurgency was gradually pushed back into an ever-smaller swath of the northern Vanni. With hundreds of thousands of civilians trapped between the battle lines, the humanitarian situation became more acute by the day. There was frantic speculation about an LTTE comeback, a final trick or a last-minute international intervention. And then the LTTE sovereign experiment disintegrated. Scores of battered survivors poured out of the last rebel stronghold in Mullivaikal, a sliver of northeastern coastline squashed between the lagoon, the sea and the advancing government forces (see Map 2.1). The remaining LTTE leaders were killed, including, in the final hours, the movement's illustrious commander Prabhakaran. The news of his death, supported by graphic pictures, conveyed the definitive defeat of the LTTE and resounded throughout the global expanse of the Sri Lankan community. This changed everything.

Earlier phases of the war had been defined by violent turning points that left scars of irreversible societal rupture: Black July in 1983, the Eviction in 1990 and the Exodus in 1995. 'The End' in 2009 (Seoighe 2017; S. Thiranagama 2013) surpassed these junctures. In terms of historical significance, it arguably even surpassed Sri Lanka's independence, which had after all been a relatively smooth, non-violent recalibration of the sovereign arrangement under the British crown. The 2009 military victory marked the singular sovereign assertion of the Sri Lankan government. It elevated President Rajapaksa to the level of a mythical and unquestionable father of the nation, at least initially. And it marked the perishing of LTTE sovereignty, voiding its moral and legal referents – acts committed in its name had now become baseless.

The pictures of Prabhakaran's corpse did not just display a fallen military commander. They showed the slain embodiment of the LTTE struggle, revered like a divine figure and the ultimate referent of the movement's sovereign power. His death had profound consequences for the Tamil nationalist movement at large. The collective trauma of the wholesale killing of civilians in the run-up to the LTTE defeat, widely considered genocide in Tamil circles, left deep imprints in Tamil political consciousness. But deprived of recourse to an insurgent military force, the Tamil polity was to abide by the government's rules of the game, a sovereign arrangement that was ultimately underpinned by the very violence of the End.

The LTTE defeat, the death of Prabhakaran and the military seizure of what had been de facto Tamil Eelam in the making comprised a process of sovereign erasure. The movement's performative repertoires and institutional apparatus were undone. By reflecting on this moment of defeat and the political landscape that emerged in its wake, we embark on an exploration of postwar transition as a process of continued and retrospective struggle. The present chapter focuses on the authority and cultural hierarchies associated with caste and clan strictures. We will later turn to the apparatus of the provincial civil service (Chapter 5) and the electoral politics of Tamil nationalist parties (Chapter 6). Each of these arenas was conjugated with (and implicated by) the LTTE sovereign experiment but never fully subjugated to it. And after the LTTE defeat, they were shaped by the renewed opening of public space and a concurrent sense of disorientation. The dominant narrative about postwar Tamil politics is preoccupied with the interaction between the Sri Lankan government, the Tamil leadership and international actors. It foregrounds the standoff at the United Nations Human Rights Council over the violent acts in the last phase of the war; the militarised and authoritarian conduct of the Rajapaksa government after its victory; Tamil demands for solutions; skirmishes over land, shrines and claims to sacred space; and revived attempts at a negotiated outcome and constitutional reform after the Sirisena government came to power in 2015 (Goodhand 2010; Harris 2018, 2019; Höglund and Orjuela 2012, 2013; International Crisis Group 2017; Rasaratnam and Malagodi 2012; Seoighe 2016a, 2016b; Stokke and Uyangoda 2011; Wickramasinghe 2009). While these are indeed the main contours of the political process, such a reading may easily skim over the broad and diverse arena that Tamil politics once more came to be after the LTTE defeat.

In this chapter, I will therefore take a perspective that deliberately avoids placing the Tamil leadership, its positions and its strategies at the heart of the equation. Rather than centring my discussion on elections, manifestos, coalitions and elite bargaining, I will start my discussion of postwar Tamil politics by looking at the everyday struggles and contentions that unfold in the aftermath of sovereign erasure. This directs us to the troubled reconstitution of a postwar Tamil community and the resulting scuffles over designations of pure Tamil space and Tamil cultural stratification. In order to grapple with these questions of gendered subjectivity, social boundaries, hierarchies and antagonism within the Tamil community, I will draw on Sharika Thiranagama's (2011) work on the rearticulation of Tamil subjectivity and Spencer's (2003) essay on the politics of purification.

Rather than treating mundane social divisions and contested purities as cultural phenomena detached from politics, this chapter puts them upfront. The 2009 defeat did not only mark the termination of the LTTE sovereign experiment. The collective audience of Tamil nationalist performance – the Tamil community from which any Tamil political claim ultimately derives its meaning and legitimacy – was itself in complete disarray. The defeat of the movement, the unspeakable losses, the military seizure of Tamil land and the dashed prospects for nationalist aspirations left the Tamil community in a disoriented state. This gave renewed buoyancy to several long-standing identity struggles within the Tamil community. The fragments of the Tamil nation, to borrow Chatterjee's (1993) phrase, comprise of social delineations and hierarchies of caste, clan, class, generation, religion, region and gender. Each of these categories had been used for mobilisation and agitation, yielding a diverse spectrum of political repertoires, particularly in the 1970s and 1980s. These were then silenced, co-opted or suppressed when the LTTE imposed its dominance, but now that the movement was defeated, these contentions came back out in the open, and this severely complicated the plight of Tamil nationalist politics. On the one hand, the arena of Tamil politics was severely constrained by the end of the war (due to a triumphant government setting the terms), but on the other hand, it radically opened up to become a pluriform arena for political mobilisation around *intra*-Tamil issues.

This chapter takes a specific Tamil community in eastern Sri Lanka as the point of departure to explore the simultaneous curtailment of Tamil nationalist politics and the invocation of renewed intra-Tamil antagonism. As such, it sets the stage for the remainder of this book. For reasons discussed in some detail ahead, the chapter is mainly focused on Sampur, rather than Mullivaikal, as the empirical site for studying the consequences and aftermath of sovereign erasure. The chapter starts out with a discussion of why Mullivaikal – the location of the war's final battles and the focal point of a highly staked discursive struggle – is such a difficult place to write about. It then turns our gaze to Sampur (which we encountered in Chapter 3), the place where the End arguably began. The government military campaign started with the capture and erasure of Sampur in 2006. In hindsight, the nature and ramifications of this conquest were a harbinger of the turn of events to come. And in terms of postwar dynamics – Sampur was finally resettled in 2015 – it offers a crucible of what was at stake in the postwar Tamil community.

Writing the End

The Norwegian-brokered peace process had been moribund for some time but eventually collapsed in August 2006, when the government started full-scale military operations. Its first territorial gain was Sampur, one of the LTTE's two eastern hubs. From there on, the movement lost ground rapidly, and a year later, in July 2007, the government declared to have liberated the east. This then cleared the way for a full-scale offensive on the LTTE's main territory, the northern Vanni. A string of defeats and tactical retreats followed, each time condensing the LTTE and a large population under its control onto a smaller piece of land. This had been the case in earlier phases of the war and was generally seen as LTTE strategy: pull back to force the enemy to spread thinly, use the outcry about humanitarian crisis to deter attacks, dissolve cadres into the human and natural terrain, to then strike back with full vigour, force the enemy on the run, rapidly retake territory and negotiate from a position of strength. That is what had preceded the 2000s peace process when the LTTE had pushed President Kumaratunga on the back foot, and it is what pundits were reckoning with this time around. But with the fall of the main LTTE town Kilinochchi in January 2009, more heavily embattled LTTE retreats and the Rajapaksa government defying international pressure, the window for a retreat-and-strike-back strategy was closing. Government firepower had massively grown, and the military started beating the LTTE at its own game with effective adaptation of guerrilla tactics (De Silva-Ranasinghe 2010; Hariharan 2010; Hashim 2013). Weakened by the legacies of the Karuna split and the complete disappearance of a front in the east, the LTTE was pushed back further. It continued to fight a near-symmetrical war – apparently it was unable or unwilling to abandon its own sovereign self-image and revert to guerrilla tactics. What ensued was a sequence of beleaguerments and the delineation of so-called no fire zones followed by more bombardments, finally culminating in the LTTE defeat at Mullivaikal in May 2009.

The government victory profoundly changed Sri Lanka's political landscape, and it endowed President Rajapaksa with unprecedented political capital. Upon seizing his victory, he held a triumphant address to parliament, where he famously declared:

We have removed the word minorities from our vocabulary.... No longer are the[re] Tamils, Muslims, Burghers, Malays and any other minorities. There are only two peoples in this country. One is the peoples who love this country. The other comprises the small groups that have no love for the land of their birth. (*Daily News*, 15 May 2009, adopted from Wickramasinghe [2009: 1046])

This perspective of what we may call a 'peace without ethnicities' denied the validity of minority grievances and the deep-seated perturbation about the final months of violence. What followed was a process of consolidating the government military victory in terms of electoral results (landslide wins in the presidential and parliamentary elections), the constitution (the eighteenth amendment further centralised power), the political economy (with highly militarised forms of development in the north and east, and an expansion of the military's role in government conduct more generally) and international alignment (attempts to solidify ties with China to offset pressures from either Western countries or India) (Goodhand 2010, 2012; Goodhand, Korf and Spencer 2011; Harris 2018, 2019; Jazeel and Ruwanpura 2009; Klem 2012; Rajamanoharan and Guruparan 2013; Sarvananthan 2016; Satkunanathan 2016; Seoighe 2016a, 2016b; Spencer 2016; S. Thiranagama 2013; Uyangoda 2011; Wickramasinghe 2014).

Hanging over this transition like the sword of Damocles was the interpretation of the military operations that culminated into Mullivaikal. In the government's view, the intense violence at the end of the war was foundational to a free sovereign order liberated from terrorism. But calls for accountability over that violence in the United Nations Human Rights Council and accusations of war crimes from Tamil diaspora networks did not let up despite deep-set government defiance. Civilians stood at the core of the disagreement, though calling them civilians already comprises a normative step into this embattled discursive terrain. Depending on the sources consulted, the fatalities at the end of the war were the result of people being held against their will by the LTTE (the position of then defence secretary Gotabaya Rajapaksa, Government of Sri Lanka [2009]), unfortunate collateral damage of a counter-insurgency campaign (the position among government proponents, depending on the occasion, Jayatilleka [2013]), victims of gross violations of International Humanitarian Law (civil society activists like Harrison [2012]; Human Rights Watch [2009]; Weiss [2011]) or deliberate targets of government-sanctioned genocide (Tamil nationalists, including diaspora platforms like Tamils Against Genocide, now renamed Together Against Genocide [2015]).

In reference to such situational uncertainty on the battlefield, the Prussian military strategist Clausewitz coined the phrase *Nebel des Krieges* or 'fog of war' (Clausewitz 1976 [1834]: ch. 3), a term famously adopted in Robert

McNamara's account of his involvement in the US bombing of Japan (Blight and Lang 2005; Morris 2003). But the metaphor of fog offers an overly convenient moral no man's land. It obfuscates the fact that the precipitation that obscures our view does not just come out of thin air; it is a human creation. This is more about smoke machines than mist. Irrespective of the conflicted nature of the various accounts, there is overwhelming evidence for three crucial observations: (*a*) many thousands of Tamil people who were not active LTTE cadres (including young children, wounded and elderly people) were killed in the final months of the war; (*b*) the LTTE tactic of enforced mixture of civilian and military positions created a condition that was prone to humanitarian crisis; and (*c*) many of those killed were victims of government bombardments of locations that either had a known civilian presence or that the government had itself declared safe. It is also clear that accurate conclusions about responsibility and culpability would benefit from more detailed research, as has been called for internationally, and that government affiliates have actively frustrated such efforts, disposed of evidence and intimidated witnesses.

The forensic scrutiny needed to adjudicate between the conflicting accounts of the respective fog machines is different from the analytical perspective needed to understand the historical significance of Mullivaikal as a moment of sovereign erasure. Among the Tamil community, Mullivaikal has become a central reference point for all that has happened, a codified term for the unspeakable, the zero point of post-defeat Tamil life. In Tamil Nadu, an official Mullivaikal memorial was erected in 2013, and Mullivaikal is central to the collective memory of the global Tamil community. It is also an actual place, a Tamil village in a rural backwater of Sri Lanka. Driving across the causeway from the district capital Mullaitivu, the contours of the palm trees along the lagoon shoreline resemble those of so many villages along the east coast.

Together with my friend and academic companion Shahul Hasbullah, I passed Mullivaikal in 2013, and again in 2018. It lies adjacent to the newly asphalted Kilinochchi–Mullaitivu main road. I probably was not the only one who gazed intensely at the passing homesteads to try and discern something meaningful, a trace of the recent past, from the landscape. It felt counterintuitive to just pass, to not pay tribute, to not acknowledge – and to not stop and see for oneself. Staring at monumental human tragedy hiding in plain sight. Then again, just the thought of parking the car to walk about and do a spot interview with one of the inhabitants was unbearable. What to even ask in a place that commands solemn silence? And how to talk oneself out of the subsequent interception by security personnel that would undoubtedly follow?

I was immersed in these thoughts as Hasbullah drove on, leaving Mullivaikal behind us. Then he started talking, first in small fragments, as he so often did, extracting memories to formulate his thoughts and then gradually gathering speed. He had been here, he said, very soon after it all happened. Somebody he knew. Hasbullah's networks were boundless. Someone had brought him here well before it had all been cleaned up, navigating the ruined landscape, the checkpoints and all the security perimeters. The image that had stuck in his mind, he said, was what he saw when he passed the place we just passed. An enormous stockpile of vehicles: buses, lorries, trailers, cars, tractors, motorcycles, bullock carts, bicycles, wheelbarrows. Anything that could carry a load. Most of it ramshackle to begin with, then heavily worn by its last journey and finally shoved together by bulldozers in a grand graveyard of steel and rubber. The material terminus of a besieged society. Testimony to the story of a people on the run, settling in an ever more densely populated territory as they were forced to retract. And retract. And retract. Until there was no territory left, and those who survived were captured and housed in highly securitised camps, leaving behind the pile of vehicles that had amassed them here. The end point of an ever-more compressed space, collapsing into ever-greater density, Mullivaikal was akin to a black hole: a point of great density around which so many other matters revolve, matters kept in orbit by the pull of gravity, a pull from which no escape seems possible, a force so intense that it keeps us from seeing clearly what lies at its core.

Sovereign erasure, 'pure Tamil' space, 'Tamil-free' space

If Mullivaikal was the End, Sampur – in hindsight – was the Beginning of the End. The long string of military attacks that eventually crushed the LTTE's sovereign experiment in Mullivaikal in 2009 had started three years earlier in Sampur. When the Norwegian-brokered ceasefire unravelled, the first major offensives took place in Sampur. And the modus operandi was remarkably similar, even if the scale was smaller: the LTTE sought to hold its ground among the civilian population in Sampur; the government nonetheless subjected it to an overpowering barrage of rockets and aerial bombardment, literally razing the entire Sampur peninsula to the ground; international alarms sounded about the humanitarian consequences but did not turn the tide; the driving out of the LTTE promulgated an exodus of distraught civilians to positions further south, where a similar sequence of events was repeated; the displaced people were eventually housed in carefully monitored government camps; and the government firmly inscribed its victory in the landscape by declaring Sampur a depopulated military zone.

People refer to Sampur as a pure Tamil area. In its most straightforward usage, this phrase refers to the fact that it is an enclave exclusively inhabited by Tamils within the ethnic checkerboard geography of the east coast. The notion of pure Tamil space has a more encompassing set of meanings, however. One of the analytical threads of this chapter is to unravel and interrogate what these are, but in short, this notion of purity is also a signifier of caste positions, of Hindu space and of a broader cultural repertoire of purification aimed at preventing unwanted mixture – not just across the ethnic divide but also within the Tamil community.

Sampur lent itself to become a model village for the LTTE in the 1990s partly because of its reputation as a pure Tamil place but also because of its geographical location (see Map 2.1). As mentioned in Chapter 3, it is located right across from the Trincomalee port and thus offers an ideal vantage point for monitoring navy movements. In addition, it is part of the tenuous string of Tamil settlements along the coast that connect the predominantly Tamil areas to the north (Vanni) and south (Batticaloa). Sampur is not a well-known place in Sri Lanka, but it played a role in the heated disputation over the Norwegian-facilitated ceasefire in the 2000s, when the alleged placement of LTTE artillery in Sampur sparked a fierce argument.

It was also here that the ceasefire eventually collapsed. In 2006, the LTTE closed an irrigation sluice gate in neighbouring Mavil Aru, thus blocking the basic means of survival to riparian farmers, many of whom were Sinhalese. In doing so, it replicated the long-established government strategy of placing LTTE-controlled areas under embargo, but it also offered the government military a credible justification to break itself free from the ceasefire and openly start military operations. The Mavil Aru sluice gate scuffle ignited a rapid chain of events. The government captured the sluice structure. In response, the LTTE conquered the town Muttur. The government then recaptured it and initiated an all-out offensive with heavy bombing on Sampur. Using multi-barrel rocket launchers, the military razed the Sampur Peninsula to the ground. According to the exhibition of the naval base museum in Trincomalee, which gives a detailed if coloured overview, the military used 'approx. 30.000' rockets to seize the area. Given that the Sampur Peninsula is about 6 kilometres across, it is unsurprising that the people who saw the area afterwards described it as a desolate landscape of rubble – barely enough remained of the ruins to even see where the town had been.

What had been a 'pure Tamil space' in effect became a 'Tamil-free space' after 2006. With the whole population forced into displacement, the government declared the entire area around Sampur a high-security zone and established a large military base to secure the mouth of the Koddiyar Bay and safe passage to and from the Trincomalee harbour. The people of Sampur, whom I periodically interviewed over these years, were barred from returning. They were forced to stay in displacement camps in Batticaloa (see also Amirthalingam and Lakshman 2009, 2014). Some stayed with relatives; others took refuge in Tamil Nadu. What followed was a protracted legal-political struggle over Sampur. In 2008, while the war in the north was still raging, Sampur residents teamed up with Colombo lawyers to file a case with the Supreme Court opposing the high-security zone. This caused the government to reduce the size of the zone and to reconceptualise it as a special economic zone (Fonseka and Raheem 2009, 2010; Klem 2014).

What had been a key site of LTTE sovereign experimentation thus became a site of sovereign erasure by the government. Big fences were put up, and like my research participants, I could but stare through the barbed wire at the bulldozed flatlands, beyond which it was said lay military complexes and demarcations for a newly planned coal power plant and heavy industry zone. In 2009, the residents, who had been staying in Batticaloa, were transferred to new camps in the vicinity of the Sampur zone (near Kiliveddy and Thopur). At this point, the group split into four. One set of people was able to return to their lands because the special economic zone had shrunk. A small second group took up the government relocation offer and moved to the neighbouring village of Ralkuli. Most, however, rejected this proposition out of hand. A third group thus remained stuck in the camps, insistently waiting for their return. A fourth group, mostly comprised of the better-endowed families, decided that the camp was no place for them to live – for one thing, the quality of the water was poor – so they took their fate in their own hands and brokered a deal with their acquaintances in the newly released parts of the zone in Kaddaiparichchan. They set up their own camp to live among their own kind, have better facilities and be closer to their own homes and lands, even if most of those places remained off-limits. Among this latter group were the main leaders and activists from Sampur, who continued their campaign against the special zone to regain access to their lands.

There is more to this disaggregation of the Sampur community than meets the eye. When I interviewed people about their life in displacement, the relocation offer and their enduring struggle for return, they hinted at the notion of purity. For example, I asked one of the inhabitants of the Kiliveddy camp in 2011 about his refusal to relocate to Ralkuli. After all, he had lived in camps for six years, and the prospect of the Rajapaksa government releasing his land seemed remote at best. He said:

> We will not go to Ralkuli. Not even animals can live there. There is no water.... Sampur people won't go to the jungle. They are cultivators. [In Sampur] there are so many [irrigation] tanks. All have so many acres [of paddy land]. We want to go to our own place.

At one level, this quotation makes agricultural sense: the owner of fertile and well-irrigated land will not trade his property for a barren place with poor water access. But the quotation also invokes a common South Asian trope about separating the pure from the impure. Clean water is not just an everyday life necessity; it is also a signifier of caste purity. The jungle is not just a forested area unsuitable for cultivation; it is also a signifier for wilderness, an uncivilised place of danger where animals roam. And a cultivator is not just a term for people engaged in planting rice; it is also a signifier for a respected 'high' caste community, in this case the Vellala. They are, it is implied, the kind of people who have a long-term commitment to work good land with clean water, and whose orderly lives are defined in opposition to the laws of the jungle. Rejecting relocation in Ralkuli, a 'low' caste Tamil area, was as much about upholding a cultural position as it was about preserving an agrarian livelihood. The insistent demand to return to Sampur comprised not only an economic attachment to property, homesteads and rice fields but also a cultural attachment to caste-based purities.

The perseverance to litigate against a powerful government and spend a decade in poorly serviced camps waiting for an uncertain outcome also derived from a larger political struggle. Leading Tamil politicians, such as R. Sampanthan – the leader of the Tamil Nationalist Alliance (TNA), who is from Trincomalee – put their weight behind the issue. Colombo-based lawyers and activists like the Centre for Policy Alternatives reached out to lend support. Then chief minister of Tamil Nadu J. Jayalalithaa (AIADMK)[1] – under pressure from her constituency for having silently stood by in the final months of the war – publicly declared her opposition. And United Nations human rights commissioner Navi Pillai visited the camps to underline her concern. The tussle over Sampur properties was not an ordinary land dispute. It attracted high-level interest because of its significance in the Tamil cultural and political landscape.

Bulldozing Sampur and declaring it off-limits did not just shrug aside the local community. This attack on prized Tamil space assailed a much larger community. The Sampur Vellala elite considers itself on par with elites in Trincomalee, Batticaloa and Jaffna. Because both the town and the famous Hindu temple have a long and respected history, the creation of a special zone mobilised resistance from people who had never before been to Sampur and might never bother to visit but nonetheless pitted themselves against the government. The sustained displacement of Sampur mattered to the international human rights community as evidence for government misconduct and human rights violations after the war. And it mattered to the international Tamil nationalist community as encroachment on a strategic territory in a wider ethnic geography: an 'ancient' Tamil enclave in a multi-ethnic district and part of a sequence of strongholds that connects the Tamil regions in the north and the east.

The persistence of the displaced Sampur community paid off. Fearing a pro-government court ruling irrespective of legal merit, the lawyers of the Sampur community opted for a tactic of trying to delay rather than win (see also Fonseka and Raheem 2009, 2010). They managed to stall the case for several years and eventually outlasted the Rajapaksa government, which was defeated in successive presidential and parliamentary elections in 2015. The Sampur community, which had spent a decade in temporary shelters, thus managed to withstand the formidable powers of the Rajapaksa government and claim their right to return.

Reconstituting Tamil purity

The triumph of the Sampur returnees was a muted one, for their victory was suffused with loss. Reconstituting pure Tamil space after the erasure by government bulldozers demanded more than rehabilitating physical structures. The cultural character of everyday Tamil life had been affected.

Photograph 4.1 Returning to Sampur

Source: Photograph by author.

Note: Temporary shelter in Sampur, a settlement erased by bombardments and the imposition of a military zone. In 2016, return was in full swing (after 10 years of protest and litigation). The bulldozing had been so thorough that it was hard to identify and demarcate plots. Temporary huts emerged and were soon converted into houses. The major Hindu temple was reconstructed, wells were rebuilt and the first paddy fields started growing.

I was in Sampur in 2016 when the bustle of return was still in full swing. Plots were being demarcated. Temporary sheds and half-finished houses sprawled (Photograph 4.1). The first paddy fields were growing while others were still lying fallow. And navy personnel were idling in their sentry points, overlooking the land they had been forced to yield. One of the people I visited was the principal of a newly rebuilt school. We had finished the interview about rehabilitation issues when he sat back in his office chair to ponder for a minute and said, 'We fear that our culture will break.... There is a lack of guidance and leadership.... We can no longer really identify as Tamil.' I asked him what he meant. 'Tamils have this moustache. The women have a *pottu* [a coloured dot adorning the forehead], and a *thali* [a sacred thread] when they get married. Some Tamil gents used to have these earrings and a ponytail. We had our strength, our heroes, our warriors.' All that was disappearing. 'Now, we can only identify by our language'. When I asked him what was causing these changes, he said, 'There is no obedience. Not following our culture. Not loving each other. Some people now send their parents to an elderly home. We had a structure of extended families. Now we are singular.' There was something ironic about the anxious feeling of becoming singular due to the crumbling of a collective Tamil character. Thirty years of separatist war had been fought in defence of a Tamil way of life in a Tamil homeland. Ten years of legal petitioning while suffering in displacement camps had centred on a desire to return to the pure Tamil space of Sampur. But now that the war was finished and they had returned to their homes, the Tamil way of life appeared to be slipping through their fingers, not because an outside assailant was taking it from them but because it was eroding from within.

My interpretation of these postwar anxieties is mediated by the work of two authors: Sharika Thiranagama and Jonathan Spencer. Thiranagama's (2011) discussion of how Tamil (and Muslim) subjectivities were rearticulated through the experience of war is very much in sync with the multilayered identity struggles I encountered in post-return Sampur. Her ethnographic work illustrates how 'war grounds life even as it takes it away – producing new people, new possibilities of voice, forms of heroism' (S. Thiranagama 2011: 12). The Tamil militancy, she posits, was caught up with intra-Tamil struggles over generational hierarchies, suffocating kinship trappings and the inequalities of caste and class. The impetus among Tamil youngsters to transform these conservative structures was 'part of the struggle for this generation to produce a new sense of Tamilness' (S. Thiranagama 2011: 184). However, partly because the LTTE disavowed much of its emancipatory agenda, many of the oppressive social structures from which youngsters had sought to escape remained intact throughout the war years. At the same time, the war unsettled the possibilities of social identification, affecting the very idea of Tamilness and its constituent elements. War does not only happen to people; it makes them who they are. This chapter illustrates that the wartime processes that Thiranagama describes – the rearticulation of the many aspects that comprise the self and the multilayered struggles over social difference and hierarchy – did not stop with the end of the war.

Closely related to these contested social delineations is the idea of purity vis-a-vis the question of mixture, for which I turn to Spencer (2003). The 'work of purification', he posits, comprises the 'cultural work that goes into maintaining the fictive separation of nature and society' (2–3). Such attempts at purification pivot on the management of movement and fixity. Purity requires spatial fixture and boundaries. And conversely, Spencer observes, movement and mixture are understood as a source of impurity and moral disorder. Excessive mobility produces morally loose people. The work of purification – regulating movement, instilling fixity – is necessary to 'maintain the illusion that "the nation is the same people living in the same place"' (3). However, purity and coherent nationhood are unattainable. The moral panic about the inability to sustain the idea of a nation as 'the same people living in the same place' is intrinsic to the fiction of the nation-state (Spencer 2003). These observations – both the preoccupation with purity and its mismatch with the fractures and rough edges that characterise the nation – resonate well with postwar tensions and anxieties among the Tamil community.

Both authors offer ideas that shed light on the irony of postwar Sampur: the notion of pure Tamil space, which had inspired the arduous journey of the Sampur community through war and displacement, disintegrated upon return. The desire to reconstitute Tamil cultural purities opened up social divisions and contested hierarchies, which then defied the supposedly harmonious quality of that puritan order. These divisions concern both caste (an identity typically apportioned to villages as a whole) and *kudi* (intra-caste clan delineations that regulate leadership, status and ritual hierarchies within villages). Put simply, caste mainly played a major role before return, in the tussle over displacement and resettlement; *kudi* mainly cropped up after return, in the contestation over leadership and Hindu religiosity.

Caste was an issue in regard to relocation because settling people in a different place interferes with the micro-geographies of caste. Even if there are often some families from other groups, most villages have a clear caste signature: Sampur is a Vellala (cultivator) village; adjacent Kunithivu is Thaddar (goldsmith); the neighbouring cluster to the south (Chenaiyur, Kaddaiparichchan, Kadatkaraichchenai) is Kurukulak Karaiyar (teachers who are historically linked to the fishermen caste); Pallikudiyirippu, a bit further afield, is Thimilar (warriors who have a history of owning land and are therefore associated with cultivation[2]); Ralkuli, to the west, is mainly home to Paraiyars (ceremonial drummers), Nalavars (toddy tappers) and Dobi (washermen), groups that are understood as *panchamar* castes;[3] and the villages to the east (including Nallur, Paddalipuram, Veeramanagar) are inhabited by Adivasis (Sri Lanka's indigenous population, often referred to as Veddahs). People's caste associations may no longer match their actual livelihoods. For example, many Vellala cultivators from Sampur, particularly the economically less fortunate ones, have turned to fishery. This affects their social status, but it does not make them Karaiyar (members of the fishermen caste).

Hierarchy between castes is not always straightforward. While some groups and villages are firmly understood as low caste (Ralkuli's Paraiyars, Nalavars and Dobis) or high caste (Sampur's Vellalas), many other hierarchies are unclear or contested, and this is further complicated by intra-caste *kudi* hierarchies. For example, the Kurukulak Karaiyars and the Thimilars consider themselves on par with the Vellalas, but Vellalas eschew arranged marriage with these castes (though a love marriage would be condoned). Conversely, Thimilars from a prestigious *kudi* may in fact look down on a Vellala who is either from a low *kudi* or a poor fisherman's family. The Thaddars may concede having a slightly lower place in the cultural hierarchy than the Vellalas but still consider themselves a high caste.

When the government offered the people displaced by Sampur's special zone a relocation site in Ralkuli, it effectively proposed to mix up caste-based settlement patterns. The diverse responses to this were also understood in terms of caste. The group that was able to return home early on when part of the zone was released comprised either Veddahs (from Nallur and its environs) or Kurukulak Karaiyar (from Chenaiyur and its environs). The group that accepted the offer of relocating in 'low'-caste Ralkuli were said to be 'low' caste themselves. The people who refused (with reference the above-mentioned tropes of pure water versus impure jungle) by and large belonged to 'high'-caste groups.[4]

Most of Sampur's Vellala community refused to stay in the government-serviced camp and moved to their self-managed shelters in Kaddaiparichchan (which is Kurukulak Karaiyar, not Vellala, but considered a respectable caste). I met one of the leaders of this self-managed camp in January 2016; I will call her Suriyamoorthy. She was from a respected Vellala family with a significant plot of paddy land near Sampur, and the family was getting ready to return. Sampur people 'love their home', Suriyamoorthy reiterated. They 'will not go anywhere else. Even if they are offered a place in paradise!' She smiled. 'Sampur is a whole Tamil area. We are not ready to mix with other people. Our unity and our culture will collapse.' Another leader from the camp, whom I will call Gnanasundaram, was a man in his thirties, also from a well-established family: a highly privileged *kudi* of the Vellala caste with rights at the Koneshwaram temple in Trincomalee. People born on Sampur's soil will always want to come back, he underlined, even if they have moved to the city, or to foreign countries. Now that return is possible, they will also want to come back and 'start paddy cultivation at home. They will get a good yield. Sampur is a place of good health and wealth. The Kali temple is another reason people want to return. In Sampur nobody is born with disabilities. That is because our goddess is very powerful.' He told me in detail how the deity had survived the bombing. All of Sampur lay in ruins, but the goddess's statue at the heart of the temple had held out without a single crack.

With the return to Sampur, a clash over caste delineation (mixing different communities through relocation) was averted, but the contestation over *kudi* flared up instead. *Kudi*s are matriclans within a caste group which are associated with leadership roles, Hindu temple management and hierarchies of ritual honours (McGilvray 2008). Some castes, like the Kurukulak Karaiyar (or the 'casteless' Veddahs), do not have *kudi*s; others do (notably, the Vellala and the Thimilar). *Kudi* arrangements are broadly constitutive of social positions, but they become particularly acute and visible in the fierce and often contentious hierarchies of religious ritual. The composition of Hindu temple management boards is constituted on the basis of minute but tightly policed *kudi* differences. And they are highly present in the public displays of temple festivals, which are infused with the politics of honour, and smaller ritual occasions such as weddings or funerals (Klem and Maunaguru 2018; Maunaguru and Spencer 2013; McGilvray 2008; Whitaker 1997). While the hierarchies and the patterns of inclusion and exclusion tend to be quite persistent, they are almost invariably subject to contestation because different *kudi*s jostle, often endlessly, for their precise positions and privileges (see Chapter 3 for the standoff with the LTTE over the *kudi* dynamics of the temple festival). With the return to Sampur, Hindu temple boards jumped into action to generate funds for the reconstruction of their shrines and to organise the parades and ceremonies of seasonal temple festivals. As a result, *kudi* hierarchies moved back to the centre of attention.

In fact, Suriyamoorthy told me, the management of Sampur as a Hindu space was more important than ever after the war. People were deeply concerned about the activities of proselytising churches, which were very active in the aftermath of both the tsunami and the war. Now that the LTTE was no longer there to police this, there had been an upsurge of conversions. At the time, only few people in Sampur had been affected, but in the surrounding villages, Evangelical churches were rapidly gaining ground, first among followers of the mainstream churches (Catholic, Methodist) but then among Hindus as well (Spencer et al. 2015: 139–154).

Many new Christians were from destitute backgrounds – those outside Sampur were often Veddahs, and inside Sampur they often belonged to the poor strata of the Vellala fishermen. I interviewed some recent converts, and they associated conversion with better social practices and having their own pride of place. But for Suriyamoorthy, such conversions were a symptom of moral corruption and a threat to the social order. 'From birth they are all Hindu. Only because some benefits [do] they become Christian.' But 'mixing Hindus and Christians is seen as a problem', she said. 'People are not happy with that. They [Christians] have different manners.' Gnanasundaram concurred: 'Because of their poverty, they convert. They [Christian priests] are giving them money, that's why…. In Sampur, we are trying to block this.' Rules were being put in place to prohibit Christians from being buried in Sampur. When they died, they would have to be evicted from the area. Such strong leadership was required to preserve the Hindu constituency, according to Gnanasundaram. 'Sampur is a very rigid place,' he said, 'more than other places. [Unlike in Sampur] their leaders are not fit.'

People like Suriyamoorthy and Gnanasundaram – who were both in their thirties, occupied a position of social leadership and had a respectable family background – shared a disdain for mixture. This involved not only upholding ethnic boundaries and claiming ethnic space but also the preservation of supposed purities between castes and *kudi*s and associated delineations of religion, class, livelihood and gender. For the leaders of Sampur's prestigious Vellala *kudi*s, reconstituting pure Tamil space also meant assuring the Hindu character of the area (at the expense of Tamil Christians) and reinstating temple hierarchies (celebrating and honouring some *kudi*s while subverting or excluding others). And it comprised efforts to re-inscribe conservative norms of gendered conduct, particularly female chastity, as well as kinship structures and family life. This repertoire of identity politics, which predates ethno-nationalism, is mainly preoccupied with the preservation of cultural purities *within* the Tamil community rather than with the purity of the ethnic community as a whole.

Much in line with Thiranagama (2011), the effort of defining and delineating an ethnic community evokes struggles over caste, *kudi* and other forms of social differentiation, which then fracture that very ethnic community. And much in line with Spencer (2003), the preoccupation with purity, which centres on the need to mitigate mixture, is ultimately confronted with the problems of defining a national community in puritan terms. The accounts of Suriyamoorthy and Gnanasundaram show that the contradictions inherent to the spatial and cultural demarcations of the nation and its constituents came out in stark relief in the postwar context, when the landscape had been erased and the problematic foundations of puritan order were laid bare. Reconstituting Sampur as a pure Tamil space comprised the remaking of a cultural landscape that not only embodied ethnic territory but also religious space, caste positions and social practices.

An emancipatory Tamil nationalism

As the earlier discussion on reconstituting pure Tamil space in post-return Sampur shows, ethnic nationalism and cultural conservatism may converge. After all, Tamil nationalism is rooted in the idea of a Tamil genealogy, a Tamil homeland and the Tamil people as a demarcated community with a distinguished language and culture – cherishing cultural purities, traditional gender roles, spatial orders and caste hierarchies fits right in. The Tamil nationalist leadership has historically advocated broadly preservative positions on cultural issues, though reference to caste was generally shunned and religion de-emphasised. The gentlemen politicians of the Tamil nationalist movement espouse what we may call a conservative Tamil nationalism. Even if the leaders of the main post-independence Tamil party (Ilankai Tamil Arasu Kadchi, or ITAK) democratised Tamil nationalism and departed from the elitist approach of their predecessors (All Ceylon Tamil Congress, or ACTC), they sought to represent the masses with an all-Tamil agenda of collective grievances and aspirations, *not* a transformative agenda of mobilising the masses to address inequalities and injustices within the Tamil community (Sivarajah 2007; A. J. Wilson 2000).

As other scholars (De Alwis 2002; Hellmann-Rajayanakam 1994b; Sitralega Maunaguru 1995; S. Thiranagama 2011) have pointed out, however, there is a second strand of Tamil nationalism which marries ethnic liberation with a more encompassing programme of social justice. Many of the Tamil youth movements that sprouted up in the 1970s and 1980s had a leftist signature and revived the outlook of late colonial movements like the Jaffna Youth Congress in the 1920s and 1930s (Russel 1978). Nested within their separatist agenda was an emancipatory project aimed at abolishing caste and *kudi* hierarchies, overcoming class inequalities, redefining gender roles and age hierarchies, and embracing a secular worldview. For many of the youngsters, joining the militancy not only represented a nationalist duty but also an escape from the carefully surveilled confines of Tamil society (S. Thiranagama 2011: 183–227).

There has always been tension between the conservative and the emancipatory strand of Tamil nationalism, but persistent attempts at closing the ethnic ranks for a common cause have often kept these differences latent, simmering in the background, deferred to a later date. Significantly, the LTTE had an ambivalent position on these tensions. While notionally a secular leftist liberation movement that opposed the caste system and purported to redress class and gender inequality, it also cherished Tamil cultural traditions and eschewed outright confrontation over intra-Tamil issues of religion, caste and *kudi* (Hellmann-Rajanayagam 1994b). After the defeat of the LTTE in Mullivaikal, the lingering tension between conservative and emancipatory strands of Tamil nationalism came back out in the open.

Even in a rural backwater and a known 'high'-caste Hindu fortress like Sampur, this tension was evident. The person who first alerted me to this was a man I will call Nadarajah, whom I had come to know quite well over the years. He was a strong-minded activist. His achievements in education and business had enabled him to marry into a 'high'-caste family, and he had become a known political activist in and around Sampur. In the early days of the Tamil uprising, he joined the Eelam Revolutionary Organisation of Students (EROS), the Tamil nationalist youth movement that was most concerned with Marxist principles and social transformation. When the LTTE crushed the other Tamil militias in the mid-1980s, EROS cadres pre-emptively joined the LTTE. Nadarajah had also done things for the LTTE in the 1990s and 2000s. Fearing government reprisal, he was forced to spend some of the war years overseas. After the war, he became one of the organisers of the main Tamil party, ITAK, and its broader electoral vehicle, the TNA. He was one of the local assistants to party leader Sampanthan, whose home constituency is in Trincomalee. Nadarajah knew the ins and outs of Sampur society, the minute differences and their histories, the cultural boundaries within his electorate, the scuffles and sensitivities, and he was a man with a savvy political brain. He would generously educate me on the latest political rumours, problems and trickery, typically saving the more contentious issues for nighttime when we would bathe at the beach and chat away while watching the stars, floating in the lukewarm water of the Koddiyar Bay.

We usually talked about the larger political issues, ITAK/TNA positions and the struggle for return in Sampur, so it was only after several years that I came to know about his unease with internal Tamil divisions and the conservative strand of Tamil nationalism. That particular day, I had asked him to show me some of the Hindu temples around Sampur. As we walked past the impressive, newly furbished pillars and statues, he told me that his family's *kudi* was linked with this temple and that he himself had just contributed 70,000 rupees (some 450 US dollars, a significant amount of money) to the renovations. My interview habitus caused me to nod at him in admiration, but then he said: 'all wasted'. I couldn't resist a smile. He also laughed. 'My wife forced me to. I am not religious. I am a Marxist.' I was astonished by his forthright blasphemy in the middle of the temple.

From that day on, Nadarajah would regularly tell me about his frustrations with cultural conservatism and tussles over social positions. Two villages adjacent to Sampur, Chenaiyur and Kaddaiparichchan, were locked in battle over the naming and delineation of their respective territory, he complained. And in Hindu shrines in and around Sampur, there were regular conflicts over temple management and the associated *kudi* hierarchies. These fiercely contested politics of honour were a completely anachronistic waste of time, Nadarajah felt. 'The Sampur people have returned, but there are so many internal crises', he said and imitated the people involved: 'I am big! No, I am big! And so on. I am with this *kudi*! No, you are with that *kudi*!' These contentions had become more pronounced after the demise of LTTE's social policing, and Nadarajah found them particularly disturbing now that the Tamil plight was in such jeopardy. After the war, he felt, 'unity has collapsed. All people are leaders now. They don't follow anyone else.'

I had similar discussions with a handful of people in the area, but they were exceptional in Sampur in terms of their openly secular outlook and explicit rejection of caste and *kudi* traditions. The many other people I met in and around Sampur over the years did not adopt such an open ideological stance on intra-Tamil issues. At the same time, however, they were typically ambivalent and even apologetic about the thing that supposedly served as the backbone to whole cultural hierarchy: caste. Rigid caste hierarchies were seen to be a figment of the past. Even respondents from the most prestigious families, who were adamant about keeping out other ethnicities and religions, were embarrassed by caste issues. They readily conceded that strict caste segregation – for example, in marriage choices – was no longer defendable. The youth were more modern. The experiences of war had shifted, rearticulated or diffused social boundaries. People of all kinds had fought side by side, and they had suffered side by side in displacement camps. This mingling could not be undone. Cultural positions were adrift and attempts to reinstate a puritan order would face pushback. But what would come in its place? What would hold them together as a cultural community? This was the conundrum that the school principal referred to when he exasperated that the people had 'become singular'. They were puzzled about redefining a Tamil way of life now that traditions were eroding and postwar Tamil village society had to be built afresh (Photograph 4.2).

Photograph 4.2 Beachfront in Trincomalee

Source: Photograph by author.

Note: Families enjoy themselves in the evening on Trincomalee's beachfront in April 2010, a rare sight in the preceding war years.

Before their return to Sampur, tensions between conservative and emancipatory Tamil nationalism largely remained under the lid. It was not so difficult to keep the ranks closed when rallying against the dispossession of the government's special zone in Sampur, but subsequent attempts to reconstitute pure Tamil space exposed the underlying fissures. Scuffles over the hierarchies and performative honours of the main Kali temple came back out in the open, and this conjured up challenges for the coherence of Tamil nationalist politics. People like Nadarajah were dismayed by the fact that Tamil nationalist leaders seemed to be more worried about pleasing the 'high'-caste stratum and preserving temple prestige than about the everyday plight of the people. Nadarajah was active in the so-called Tamil People's Council (Tamil Makkal Peravai) and the Tamil Rise (Eluga Tamil) movement, popular initiatives with an uncompromising Tamil nationalist agenda that turned up the heat on the mainstream Tamil political parties and their leadership. Crafting an agenda to unite all Tamils in pursuit of shared aspiration was going to be more difficult for Sampanthan and his affiliates after the war.

Conclusion

Unlike many other civil wars, Sri Lanka's ethno-separatist war had a clear and definitive end point. It stopped on 18 May 2009, in Mullivaikal. After the comprehensive defeat of the LTTE, many things were fundamentally and irreversibly different. The insurgent sovereign experiment perished. The bounds of politics and legality were redefined, permanently redrawing the space for Tamil nationalist politics. The final military operations constituted a foundational sovereign violence that newly premised the fundamentals of the state, the law and democratic politics, much like the violence that had occasioned postcolonial states across South Asia six decades prior (Beverley 2020a; Chatterjee 1993; Mukherjee 2010; Purushotham 2021). The massacre that preceded the End weighed heavily on the Tamil political consciousness. Mullivaikal signified a watershed moment, but it was also clear that many things did not end at the End.

Postwar transition comprises a process of fundamental change that continues to grapple with what preceded it. In resonance with the term 'postcolonial', the prefix 'post' does not signify a definitive after but rather the continued struggle over the retrospective interpretation and the enduring legacies of what has happened (Klem 2018). Mullivaikal marks the beginning of Sri Lanka's postwar transition, but this transition is riven with contentions over Mullivaikal itself and over the framing of the ethno-political conflict more broadly. Mullivaikal harbours unresolved grievances and an enduring refusal to embrace the present predicament as the end stage of the Tamil nationalist struggle. As my discussion of postwar Sampur shows, Tamil grievances over militarisation, land appropriation, skewed development opportunities and the burden of what many Tamils consider genocidal violence are heavily present. In Sampur's case, these processes were initially manifest in a crudely physical form. The town's erasure was followed by the imposition of a special zone from which Tamils were barred entry.

Alongside these shared ethnic grievances, there was a whole raft of concerns with internal Tamil matters. The desire to preserve the cohesion of the Tamil collective and its cultural tradition was troubled by the resurfacing of intra-Tamil divisions. With the demise of the singular nationalism of the LTTE, the Tamil political arena opened up. In Sampur, this became manifest in attempts to reinstitute caste- and *kudi*-based hierarchies and claims to religious space. These attempts were driven by repertoires of purity aimed at mitigating unwanted mixture, both across the ethnic divide and within the Tamil community. Closely resonating with Spencer's (2003) work on nationalism and purification, the 'high' caste and 'high' *kudi* stratum was strongly preoccupied with reconstituting Sampur as a pure Tamil space, a notion that straddles the safeguarding of ethnic Tamil turf and the projection of a more particular cultural landscape with delineations of Hindu space and caste privileges.

Sampur can be seen as a crucible of Tamil society in Sri Lanka's northeast. Its recent history of conquest, displacement, sovereign erasure and troubled return resembles the plight of postwar Tamil society at large. It is indicative of the combined sense of freedom, subjugation, disorientation and loss in the void of the LTTE's de facto state, and the simultaneous opening up of a new political landscape with space for a plural kind of Tamil politics. It also underlines that these politics are not primarily about party politics but about a set of existential issues concerning land and social order, and about the anxiety of 'becoming singular' and losing the essence of what it means to be Tamil. Similar contentions over Tamil purity and delineations of caste, *kudi* and Hindu space have cropped up in other parts of Sri Lanka, probably most viciously in Jaffna, where a stiff tradition of caste discrimination has re-emerged after the war (Geetha 2020; Ratnajeevan Hoole 2013; Jeeweshwara Räsänen 2015; Silva 2020; Silva, Sivapragasam and Paramsothy 2009; Thanges 2014, 2015).

These tussles over *kudi*-based temple rites, caste-based land claims and the demarcation of Hindu space are not cultural phenomena detached from politics. They are pivotal to Tamil nationalist politics. They pertain to the political community – a Tamil *demos* – in whose name the claim to sovereignty is advanced. They concern the reflexive 'self' of self-determination. Struggles over the reconstitution of Tamil society after defeat expose a long-standing rift in Tamil nationalism, between a conservative strand of Tamil nationalism (which marries the agenda of national self-determination to a celebration of cultural tradition) and an emancipatory strand of Tamil nationalism (which extends the outlook of ethnic liberation to a more encompassing programme of social liberation thus taking issue with class, caste and gender-based inequalities within Tamil society). As became clear in my discussion of the wartime period (Chapter 3), the LTTE forced this variety of contentions into a singular nationalist outlook: a single cause and a single sovereign framework where authority was fused into one adulated body of *Führertum*, embodied by the *talaivar* Prabhakaran, with no space for dissent. The defeat of the movement and the death of Prabhakaran heralded a moment of decompression for Tamil politics. On the one hand, the space for Tamil nationalism at large became more confined now that it was condemned to the bounds stipulated by the Sri Lankan government. On the other hand, the political space for contestation within the Tamil nationalist arena radically opened up.

Notes

1   All India Anna Dravida Munnetra Kazhagam (AIADMK) is a 1972 breakaway of India's main Dravidian party Dravida Munnetra Kazhagam (DMK), in turn an heir of the Dravidian mother party: Dravidar Kazhagam. AIADMK was a significant pro-LTTE actor under M. G. Ramachandran in the 1970s and 1980s. Under Jayalalithaa, it resurfaced as a major political force in Tamil Nadu from the 1990s onwards.

2   For a detailed discussion, see Gaasbeek (2010: 90–95).

3   Panchamar castes, sometimes referred to as depressed castes or minority Tamils (Silva 2020), are considered the most underprivileged stratum. They have historically been conceptualised as servants, or even bonded labourers, to the land-owning castes, mainly the Vellala. While these groups are cognate to the Dalits in India and other countries, that term is rarely used in the Sri Lankan context, and the concurrent notion of untouchability no longer exists in the same strict terms.

4   On the densely populated Jaffna Peninsula, we have arguably seen a similar social mechanism that yielded an opposite outcome: some 'low'-caste communities remained stuck in camps (Silva 2020).

5 The Bureaucratic Evolution of Devolution

With the defeat of the Liberation Tigers of Tamil Eelam (LTTE), the experiment of establishing a de facto Tamil state had been violently erased. However, this was not the only institutional form created in pursuit of Tamil self-government. It had been dominant in the 1990s and 2000s, but there was a parallel institutional experiment, one that was premised on power-sharing within the framework of the Sri Lankan state: the North-Eastern Provincial Council (NEPC). The NEPC was created through the 1980s peace accord enforced by India, but it is part of a longer sequence of contested experiments with ethnic power-sharing in Sri Lanka, which dates to late colonial times and which continues to evolve. The central principle of these efforts is the devolution of government power from Colombo to sub-national levels. Ironically, the NEPC comprises an arrangement that none of the protagonists wanted, but which has nonetheless survived.

While the first part of this chapter takes stock of the NEPC's turbulent history, I will mainly focus on the postwar dynamics, when the council outlived the LTTE and emerged as the only remaining institutional legacy for some semblance of a Tamil government. My analysis zooms in on the day-to-day work of provincial bureaucrats. In a book about the grand historical themes of Tamil nationalism and Sri Lanka's civil war, it may seem unnecessary to become engrossed in bureaucratic processes, technical memos and departmental hierarchies. However, as I will elaborate in this chapter, the calm orderliness of the civil service and the turbulent conflict dynamics that engulfed provincial councils are not divorced realities. Civil servants enact the state, and the enactment of the state sits at the very heart of Sri Lanka's ethno-political conflict. The everyday work of neatly dressed bureaucrats with their paperwork, procedures and protocol, their tidy offices and stiff hierarchies (Photograph 5.1) is part of the same historical trajectory as the civil war and its aftermath.

Photograph 5.1 Provincial civil servant

Source: Photograph by author.

Note: Senior civil servant at his desk at the Northern Provincial Council in October 2018. The orderly appearances of bureaucratic attire and office environment contrasted with the turbulence of postwar transition and the acrimonious debates in Vigneswaran's council at the time (see Chapter 6).

There is valuable scholarship about what Sri Lanka's provincial councils *could* or *should* be doing, based on a diagnosis of the constitutional arrangements and governance structure (Coomaraswamy 2003; Rupesinghe 2006; Welikala 2012a). There is much less analysis of about what they *are* actually doing.[1] This chapter helps redress that dearth with an ethnographically founded analysis of the Eastern Provincial Council[2]. My approach follows suit with the growing ethnographic scholarship on bureaucratic realities (Amarasuriya 2010; Bear and Mathur 2015; Berenschot 2010; Gupta 2012; Hansen 2001; Hull 2012a, 2012b; Kelly 2006; Mathur 2015; Murray Li 2005). This scholarship debunks the conception of the state as a coherent set of institutions that operates according to legal mandate and rational procedure and instead focuses on the everyday negotiation of order, procedure, documentation and institutional performativity. The discourse of rational governance, coherent policy and institutional mandates – central to the self-legitimation of state actors – is often more reflective of the way state conduct is represented than of the workaday functionality of administrative processes.

This chapter describes how bureaucrats try to keep distance from politics by hedging their decisions and standing their ground with a discourse of 'rendering technical' (Murray Li [2005], drawing on Rose [1999]). Mitigating and regulating the forces of political interference is central to the bureaucratic endeavour. But for the provincial councils – which were created as an explicitly political platform to solve a fundamental political conflict over the nature of sovereignty with the devolution of political power to the peripheries – the preoccupation with keeping politics out is ironic. I will show that this tendency accounts for the tenacity of the provincial bureaucracy but simultaneously forces provincial councils to sacrifice the purpose they were meant to serve.

Performing a provincial Tamil government

The trajectory of the NEPC runs like a political artery throughout Sri Lanka's history of ethno-political conflict, but it is one of the island's least studied, and arguably least understood, institutions. After the 2009 end of the war, the NEPC resurfaced as a political body. In the absence of the LTTE's powerful experiment in staging Tamil self-determination, the provincial council was the only remaining institution that harboured a promise of Tamil self-government. The NEPC illustrates how an institution can assume a radically different political significance, depending on how it is enacted. The LTTE had violently opposed the NEPC after its creation in the late 1980s as a hostile Indian implant, but in the 1990s and 2000s, the movement adopted a more accommodative stance. I will briefly discuss the war-time evolution of the NEPC, before turning to its postwar struggles.

The NEPC was established through India's coercive imposition of a political compromise. The 1987 Indo-Lankan Accord enforced the thirteenth amendment to the Sri Lankan constitution, which devolved significant powers to the provinces. To assuage Tamil nationalist demands, the Northern and Eastern Provinces were provisionally merged to create an exceptionally large province that effectively matched the aspired territory of Tamil Eelam (see Map 2.1). This merger surrendered the Muslim community (a major group in the east, a small minority in the north) to a Tamil-dominated region. India implanted an institutional fix that met several important Tamil demands: the NEPC reversed the trend of watered-down compromises and broken pacts that had prevailed since the 1950s.[3] However, the thirteenth amendment inserted a layer of quasi-autonomous provincial governance into a centrist political system and precipitated severe competition between minimalist and maximalist interpretations of what had been agreed.[4] As a result, the NEPC was drawn into a dynamic of competing projects of statecraft between the Sri Lankan central government, the Indian federal government and the LTTE.

By bestowing or withholding the performative qualities and resources needed to enact political potency, an institution with a flimsy legal basis can assume a major role, while one that is well anchored in law can be made impotent (Gilmartin 2020; Hansen 2004; Ruud 2009). The Indian government spared no effort in enabling the NEPC to perform as a credible, legitimate and resilient institution (Abraham 2006; Dixit 2003: 239–254; Jayatilleka 2000). With the LTTE turning its back on the Indo-Lankan Accord and all other Tamil militant groups crushed in the onslaught leading up to the agreement, the Indian government thus threw its weight behind the Eelam People's Revolutionary Liberation Front (EPRLF). With its radical Marxist ideology, 'low' caste profile, no serious political track record and its recent decimation by the LTTE, the EPRLF was an unlikely ally, but the Indian government had no better alternatives.

Varatharajah Perumal, a leading EPRLF figure, was fielded as the preferred candidate for the key post of northeastern chief minister. Without Tamil rivals on the ballot, the EPRLF triumphed in this hampered performance of democracy, winning fifty-three of the seventy-one seats; with seventeen seats for the Sri Lanka Muslim Congress (SLMC), the Muslims became a marginal fraction in the merged northeast, as they had feared[5]. As the chief minister of the North-Eastern Province, Perumal headed the first-ever elected government of a territory resembling the Tamil homeland, but it was an institution that only existed on paper. When I interviewed him in 2018 to reflect on that period, he explained:

> There was nothing. Everything we had to [do ourselves]. Even the doormat ... we had to organise. Every secretary I had to search for. Whenever I got one ... the secretaries themselves started helping me to find other people.

The NEPC administration relied on the Indian military for its immediate survival, and it maintained close ties with Indian diplomats, most notably High Commissioner J. N. Dixit, who pressured, bullied and shamed the Sri Lankan government into taking action and resolving administrative blockages. Dixit's team devised workarounds to provide the council with resources that were not forthcoming from the central government: funding, training, vehicles (Dixit 2003: 268–285; Loganathan 2006: 84–100). These were needed not only to run an incipient administration but also to enact a new layer of government through idioms that people would recognise as such – four-wheel drive cars and prestigious office buildings are prerequisites for political potency in Sri Lanka. Much to the dismay of the central government, Perumal also insisted on referring to the whole of his institution as the provincial *government,* which then consisted of the elected legislature (the council) and the executive branch (the board of ministers), which commanded the provincial bureaucracy. This prompted President Premadasa to issue directives to newspapers to ban the term 'provincial government' in all advertisements and amend it to 'provincial council' (Loganathan 2006: 90).

The NEPC was not given much time to demonstrate its capacity to govern. Perumal was inaugurated in December 1988. President Premadasa assumed power in February 1989, and by April, his government denounced the Indo-Lankan Accord and reached out to the LTTE. In Delhi, the Singh government entered office and prepared to withdraw the Indian military. The LTTE was lining up to fill the void and unfold its own experiment of insurgent Tamil state-building.[6] Anticipating a violent confrontation with the LTTE, the EPRLF joined hands with other militant groups to erect a paramilitary force known as the Tamil National Army, with direct support from the Indian military and intelligence services. These troops were legitimised as a police force to come but effectively resembled a militia of forcibly conscripted youth, designed to rival the LTTE (Loganathan 2006: 93–97). The two competing forms of Tamil statecraft were starting to swap repertoire: the LTTE insurgency started to emulate a government, and the elected EPRLF administrators began adopting insurgency tactics.

These last-ditch efforts could not turn the tide, however. When the Indian military pulled out, the EPRLF politicians abandoned their posts. In their final administrative move, they pushed the NEPC experiment to, and arguably over, its limit, by converting the council into a constituent assembly tasked to draft the constitution of the Eelam Democratic Republic (Jayatilleka 2000: 126–127; Loganathan 2006: 98–100).[7] With this resolution, the EPRLF broke the bounds of devolution, and it discursively outmanoeuvred the LTTE, but it was a purely symbolic move that came at a high price, both for the EPRLF and for the provincial council. Days after its resolution, the EPRLF abandoned the offices of the NEPC and fled to India. Three months later, several EPRLF figureheads including party leader K. Pathmanabha were killed by the LTTE in Tamil Nadu. The institution of the provincial council lost out because the resolution prompted President Premadasa to amend the Provincial Council Act with a clause enabling the central government to dissolve a council that repudiated the constitution: yet another blow to the autonomy of provincial governance (Wickramaratne 2019: 19–20).

A devolution without politicians

The spectacular creation of the NEPC was followed by a dramatic collapse. With the departure of both the Indian military and Perumal's administration, the NEPC appeared moribund in 1990. After the councillors had left, it became a political void surrounded by enemies. Its buildings on Trincomalee's Inner Harbour Road were empty, and the administrative staff were awaiting the doom of an LTTE takeover. One of the senior bureaucrats, whom I will call Balasundaram, recalled that eerie period to me:

> Everyone was leaving. The councillors, the EPRLF, but also UNP and SLMC. And also all the staff. They were afraid. I was one of the few who stayed. I told the LTTE I am not an EPRLF man, I am a civil servant.

When the EPRLF abandoned its offices, the LTTE moved in to seize the instruments of government. The council's newly funded vehicles, furniture, files and other equipment were readily captured by the LTTE to be redeployed for their own governance experiment – institutional bricolage at its crudest. Balasundaram recalled, 'The LTTE came and they took everything. All the furniture, the fridges, everything.... I was only looking.' Even when everything else had become defunct, the central government bookkeepers went about their work: 'The audit for the council came and all had left, only I was there. The Public Services Commission investigated me.' They asked critical questions, but he was acquitted – what could they have expected him to do?

With the flight of the first elected council in 1990, the NEPC entered a protracted interim period. No new council was elected until 2008 (in the east) and 2013 (in the north). As a result, the provincial administration comprised a minimal bureaucratic structure under the governor (a presidential stalwart).[8] Tamil nationalists had agitated for a form of political self-rule, but what transpired during this period was a set of civil service departments that enacted the minimal administrative requirements of provincial governance – a devolution without politicians. Bureaucrats considered the absence of politicians interfering with procedure a mixed blessing, but they had other pressures to deal with instead. While the NEPC degenerated into an institutional apparatus without political leadership, the LTTE asserted itself as a de facto sovereign actor with gradually expanding institutions. As a result, space opened up for some degree of convergence between what had been competing modes of Tamil government.

Life goes on, even in times of civil war. Teachers need to be paid and hospitals maintained. Cooperative structures and basic administration of livelihoods continued in the northeast despite the unrest. Some of these structures were in territories controlled by the government military, but others were in the territories where the LTTE had gradually started to enact its own state structures. Even so, the NEPC needed to get on with its responsibilities, I was told in interviews with a wide range of civil servants. And when the NEPC tried to carry out its work, the LTTE started to bring parts of the provincial civil service into its orbit. I will reconstruct this phase of the evolving relationship between the NEPC and the LTTE by drawing on the accounts of three former provincial chief secretaries whom I will call Balasundaram, Sivankumaran and Rajasingham, all of whom were Tamil. I interviewed these top-level officers at various instances over the period 2010 to 2018. Balasundaram, whom I already cited earlier, worked with the council straight through the war:

> We had to deal with cleared [government-controlled] and uncleared [LTTE-controlled] areas. We provided for schools, hospitals, fishery, agriculture. Those kinds of things. But only the minimum. Just the basic salaries, no projects. The basic services. We had no money [to do more].

Rajasingham explained:

> The government was deeply suspicious of us. They thought we were with the LTTE. But still they were thankful we were working in those areas. A good number of my colleagues were killed. So the government was considerate. We had to manoeuvre between the LTTE and the government. They thought we were LTTE sympathisers, their henchmen. But that was also not fair. We were doing our job. Of course, we had sympathies for reasonable Tamil rights. We of course were also Tamil, but in the end, we are government servants.[9]

Provincial civil servants had a similarly convoluted relationship with the LTTE. Sivankumaran formulated it as follows:

> The LTTE did not support the council [NEPC] because they saw it as a half solution.... But [after IPKF] an understanding emerged. The LTTE was contempted for killing innocent people. And they seemed to have reached a level of confidence....

> With time, their stance changed because the council was a service delivery institution. Something the people needed. And they felt they should not cripple that any further. Also, they realised that when they would come to power, they needed some sort of mechanism. And they thought they could run a shadow administration. They took the council on remote control....

> The LTTE had their own administrative setup. So they communicated with government servants with letters, or just called them on the phone. Or they would send somebody. But they would only interfere with things that had an immediate impact on the ground. At local level. They had no interest in overall policies or our procedures or that kind of thing. They did not recognise those things in the first place....

Until the end they were very hard on government servants. The way they would speak to us. Not politely or with respect. They would maintain that authoritative voice. That superiority attitude....

The LTTE did not really trust civil servants, but it was a different kind of distrust than you would find from Colombo. Because they knew: these people will not betray us. They knew to which faction we belonged. But we were neutral, and that dissatisfied the LTTE. We resisted their ways and did not approve of them. We were not damaging them, but we did not support their ways.

As discussed in Chapter 3, the peace process of the 2000s offered a conducive context to push political boundaries and expand institutional experimentation. The existing practice of the LTTE surreptitiously co-opting the NEPC evolved into a practice of open mingling. Enabled by the more permissive government stance, foreign donors started resourcing interstitial institutions like the NEPC as a deliberate means of indirectly engaging with the LTTE. The trickle of public funding that had previously reached the council was augmented with large grants from the World Bank and the Asian Development Bank, and the German and Japanese governments started significant capacity building programmes with the council. After the 2004 tsunami, a new suite of multilateral projects followed, but the 2006 resumption of the war curbed these opportunities soon after they had started.

The resumption of political normalcy

The end of the war was a turbulent time for the provincial administration. In parallel to the government's military victory over the east in 2007, the North-Eastern Province was demerged when the Supreme Court – at long last – ruled the 1987 merger unconstitutional. Subsequent provincial elections in the east (2008) and north (2013) brought a normalcy of sorts to the two councils. The bureaucratic structures rapidly expanded, and reconstruction work was in full swing. At the same time, the politicians were back and so were the pressures of interference. The patronage machinery of the central government was working overtime, and the Rajapaksa administration was consolidating its control over the north and east with highly militarised means. Ethnic minorities were apprehensive about their postwar future.

When I interviewed senior Tamil bureaucrats in 2010, the fresh memory of the war and the tragic bloodshed in Mullivaikal overshadowed everything they had to say. Sivankumaran, one of the former provincial chief secretaries quoted earlier, had a habit of passionately gesticulating with his eyes twinkling when he elucidated the savvier insights of wartime bureaucratic survival, but his eyes turned hollow when he talked about the civilians who had been slaughtered in the final months of the military campaign. As a civil servant with good access to data, he knew that public estimates of death rates were far off the mark. The government claim that there had been no civilian casualties at all was clearly preposterous, but the United Nations figure (7,000 civilian fatalities at the time) was not much better. Basic math with the original population size, humanitarian assessments of displaced communities and how many people eventually came out in the days of LTTE defeat yielded a figure closer to 80,000, he implored with an insistent, whispering voice. It was as if he was burning inside, struggling to live with the knowledge of what had happened: a tragedy so grave that it stifled one's ability to act yet also foreclosed the thought of not doing anything.

The militarised nature of the immediate postwar years was reflected in the functioning of the eastern council. Its offices were hidden behind a fortified barrier with security guards patrolling the complex on Trincomalee's Inner-harbour Road. The newly demerged northern council was still in interim mode, as elections were yet to be held. Awaiting a more conducive environment in the north, it was temporarily housed in a large new complex on the outskirts of town, amidst the scrub that had once marked the beginnings of LTTE-controlled territory. Major buildings with several storeys had been constructed for the newly appointed northern governor and a minimal administrative staff, and it looked like a military complex. The surrounding walls and gates were at least 4 metres tall, and there was a major security presence. For all the defensive measures, little was going on inside. The newly demerged northern council was standing by for its new future.

I returned to the exact same complex eight years later, in 2018. The northern council had moved to Jaffna, and the premises now housed the departments of the Eastern Province, including the planning secretariat where I occupied a desk to conduct a bureaucratic ethnography. Though the buildings had not changed, it was a completely different place. Some of the tall ramparts were still there, but the metal gates were always open and had rusted in their hinges. The empty watchtowers had become like neoclassical decorations of the quadrangular walls (Photograph 5.2). In what had been a vacant swath of razed weeds reminiscent of military roadside clearing, the agriculture department had started a sample gardening plot. Entrance security was cordial. A friendly smile and handwave sufficed to get through. Every working day at about eight in the morning, a flurry of scooters and motorbikes along with office vehicles for the most senior staff made its way from Trincomalee's various neighbourhoods – women in colourful dresses and shawls, men in black pants and neatly ironed

Photograph 5.2 Walled provincial council

Source: Photograph by author.

Note: High security at the Northern Provincial Council complex in May 2010. The newly demerged northern council was still in 'interim mode' and provisionally housed at a walled compound outside Trincomalee.

white shirts, a tie or saree for heads of department and above. At the sun-sheltered bike stand, officers stored helmets, ruffled their hair, straightened jackets, checked cell phones and had a quick chat with colleagues before darting to their various departments to press their fingerprints onto the digital attendance clock.

While the political side of the council – the assembly hall, the assembly secretariat, the chief minister's office and associated entities – were in the old complex in town, the administrative leadership was housed in this new complex. The main building had an unspectacular central stairwell and a tiny lift, with the chief secretary's office right at the entrance. The provincial planning secretariat, my institutional home while I was there, was on the second floor and had the familiar lay out of a modern Sri Lankan office. Centrally located in the department was a separate office with a tinted glass door for the director of planning. Adjacent to it were slightly smaller offices, with shared air conditioning and a dividing wall that did not reach the ceiling for the four officers who were one or two rungs lower in the hierarchy. For all the others, there were open office spaces, with small desks of dark-brown veneer, a computer screen and a large office phone. All the staff in the offices were men; the vast majority of those at the desks were women, with notable exceptions like the IT technician and the caretaker. This gender division was typical but by no means absolute – some departments were headed by female officers. All planning staff except one were Tamils and Muslims. Most of them spoke good English.

It was normally quiet, though there was regular traffic across the office with staff whispering at each other's desks to consult, check a formulation or a figure, get a file signed – or gossip. Every now and then there would be a visiting delegation from Colombo to have a discussion. On most days, the office had an easy-going routine. For lunch, the senior cadre, who had an office vehicle at their disposal, would eat with their families in town, while the junior staff – that is, the women at the desks – gathered in the small kitchen to have their homemade rice and curry or a lighter meal. The caretaker brought around milk tea mid-morning and mid-afternoon while managing fans and air conditioning in his intermediary rounds. The bright daylight was dimmed by blinds with red, brown and yellow stripes (perhaps incidentally the colours of the Sri Lankan flag, though without green). The reception, run by a female intern, had a small bouquet of fake flowers and right across it, at the department entrance, was a small religious corner with icons of three prominent Hindu deities and a kit with the essentials for a *puja* (worship ritual). A distinctly secular ritual would start about 15 minutes after entering the office, at 8:45 a.m. Unprompted by prior warning, the intercom would air the national anthem. Without a word or hesitation, everyone would instantly stand up to silently pay respect, only to pick up whatever they were doing 3 minutes later.

The senior cadre was part of the Sri Lankan planning service and prided itself in an *esprit de corps* of dedication, integrity and efficiency. But even the development officers, who were not part of the public service corps (and thus had modest roles and career prospects), took their jobs very seriously. This was obvious from the way they engaged with me that they sought to emulate a modern kind of governance in service of the people. They were apologetic about delays in bureaucratic procedure and duplication between departments, and they did not want to be seen wasting time. They were keen to tell me about how they had improved transparency with a new website where all key documents were publicly available, and an internal database gave them a good overview of all the ongoing projects. Their institution was stiffly hierarchical, and they referred to their seniors with reverent respect, but they clearly respected some of their colleagues more than others. Some directors are 'completely flat', one member of the planning secretariat told me in private. He used his hands and face to underline his point. 'When they go to a meeting, all they worry about is the colour of their tie or saree. The public sector would be better off with half the people who earn double the salary and are recruited on merit. But that can't be changed.'

Other colleagues were admired, especially people of incorruptible character who stood up to anyone meddling with procedure, who had archival memories and therefore could never be cheated, who had the skill and perseverance to get things done and the experience and foresight to anticipate threats and problems early. Some of these people had been transferred precisely because of these abilities, for pushing back against the governor or politicians, but they were fondly remembered, and their former colleagues saw it as their task to continue the work in the same spirit. Senior and upcoming officers would not fail to mention their educational credentials. Many of them inquired about possibilities for further study. More than a few of their colleagues had left the service to become consultants. They had gained new skills and networks through the big World Bank and Asian Development Bank grants for the NEPC in the 2000s, and now they were advising their former colleagues and running workshops or evaluations – a life with less nuisance and the kind of salary needed to sustain a family in Colombo with children attending a moderately reputed school.

The orderly world of the provincial administration's offices contrasted with the society they were supposed to serve – the hot and often dusty towns and villages of the province, where people could only dream of working in a room with spotless tiles and the luxury of generator-powered air conditioning. Unlike frontline state entities, such as the divisional secretariats, the planning secretariat was not a place visited by civilians seeking redress for their problems, requesting registrations or filing complaints. It was a place of bureaucratic distance (Mathur 2015), a back office to the provincial administration, which was in charge of balancing funds and activities across all departments. Despite this distance, the harsh realities of the society around them, the suffering during times of war and anxieties of the postwar era, were very much present in the minds of these officers. They had all lived through the civil war for the biggest part of their lives – the younger ones had grown up in this context. They all remembered people who had been forcibly recruited, tortured or killed, and the 2004 tsunami had taken many more loved ones. Everyone knew colleagues, friends or relations who had gotten on an overloaded fishing boat after the war to escape their plight, sometimes to never give a sign of life again. Such tragedies and the plethora of smouldering conditions undergirding them were not abstract governance issues to provincial bureaucrats – these were life stories that were intertwined with their own.

One of the officers I came to know – I will call him Suren – had been stationed in Mullaitivu, the last major LTTE stronghold at the end of the war, to provide rudimentary government services for large groups of displaced people. Their means were very limited and there was a continuous threat of bombing. 'It was very difficult to work there. Very difficult', he told me and squinted his eyes to give expression to these arduous circumstances. 'But I was satisfied with my work. We were working for very poor people. And we were working at the ground level, directly with those people. Now I am sitting here, inside.' He pointed his arms at the calm office around us. Another phone call interrupted our chat. He made an apologetic gesture as he picked up the receiver with the typical, mutedly cautious 'hello'. 'These calls from other departments are a real challenge', he went on after hanging up. They were usually officers who were senior to him and there was always something else that needed doing. And then they had to reckon with the *kachcheri*, the district administration that was an extension of the central government apparatus. 'They are much more powerful than us.… They get four or five times the budget for one district that we have for a whole province. Their own funding plus the resources of line ministries who implement through the *kachcheri*.'

As he went on to talk about the stress and frustration of his job, Suren's voice started to break up. His eyes were watery. He took out his handkerchief and was struggling not to cry. A few years ago, he explained, a brain haemorrhage had put him in a coma. He pointed a finger to the temple of his head and groaned: 'when stress is coming now, it is intolerable'. His breakdown had occurred after several years of working around the clock in Mullaitivu. He was lucky to survive, but now he suffered from headaches and dizziness. He wanted to be strong and deliver good work, and he needed the salary to sustain his family and pay his mortgage, but it was difficult to sustain himself. All these calls from seniors and requests from juniors did not make it any easier.

Provincial finance: Enduring starvation and preserving insulation

To celebrate Navarathri, a ten-day Hindu festival in October dedicated to the universal mother figure, the meeting room in the rear section of the planning secretariat had been converted into a shrine of sorts. All tables and chairs had been removed. One of the staff members had spent hours pouring a large colourful mandala on the floor and there was a small make-do altar on a desk. It displayed a range of offerings including a small sample of bundled office files, which were to be consecrated as well. A Hindu priest had been invited to conduct the rituals. Having received his blessing, we sat back down on the floor along the walls with sacred white ash on our foreheads and a sequence of festive delicacies was passed around. I sat next to one of my close collaborators in the department, whom I will call Mansoor. He was Muslim but joined the festivities for collegial reasons. I had been away for a week and we were catching up on the latest news.

The calm devotion of the ceremony and the relaxed atmosphere of this get-together stood in stark contrast to the seasonal turmoil that had struck the council this week. October is the height of the eastern monsoon – just the day before, the downpour had been so heavy that flooding had brought Trincomalee to a standstill. There would be some clearing and reconstruction work to be done. More significantly in terms of governance, October marks a moment of truth for anyone concerned with public finance. The finance commission in Colombo had released the so-called impresst yesterday, Mansoor told me, as we were chewing on a gluey sweet with cardamom seeds. The impresst was a figure that informed them how much money the council would be given for the current year – this time about 70 per cent of what they had budgeted. They always anticipated such a cut, but one could never be sure of the exact amount, Mansoor explained. The planning machinery jolted into operation the moment the impresst was released, and the chief secretary immediately called a meeting with the planners and the key officers from all sectoral ministries and departments. This was always a tricky moment when the rivalry between provincial departments collided with the centre-periphery dynamic. It required a kind of bureaucratic finesse that not everyone could muster.

The catch in this whole dynamic hinged on a small piece of accountancy logic. Instead of simply transferring the whole sum, the finance commission would only cover the costs for 'bills in hand' – for activities that had been implemented, invoiced and paid by the provincial department. If a department spent money now without getting the invoices before the closure of the fiscal year, the costs would move to the following year and could create a liability for the next year's budget. If they expedited the work, finished it and had the 'bills in hand', it would be covered under this year's budget. But if all departments steamed ahead to generate such bills, they would risk exceeding the total impresst, and some of their spending would not be covered at all. Vice versa, if they all decided to cease expenditure, they would underspend and get less money, with possible negative knock-on effects for the future. And then of course, there were bookkeeping tricks: splitting activities in two and getting contractors to submit bills in hand for part of the work; or expediting procedures by getting on a motorcycle to physically collect bills from the ground level and personally run them by all the various desks where they would otherwise be at risk of getting stuck on a pile; or relabelling activities as recurrent expenditure, so they could be placed under a different funding channel. But this was all tinkering at the edges. The central challenge was to create an outcome where 70 per cent of this year's activities were completely finished and not a rupee was spent on the remaining 30 per cent. This required careful coordination and an accurate assessment and what really *needed* to be done and what *could* realistically be done.

Because of this, the day before had been packed with tense meetings. As Mansoor and I decided to give the next plate with snacks a miss, he told me today was a quiet day for the planners because the departments were consulting internally to strategise their actions. Next week, it would all have to be hammered out. He explained:

> The problem is, many officers don't really get the dynamic, so they start fighting for their budget, or they think: 'anyway I will get my salary, so I'll just the let activities run and take the receipt at the end and then we'll see'. So I have to tell them very clearly: 'if you do this or if this happens, you will not get the money. We'll have to take it off next year's budget, and there will be other consequences.' Even if I am junior to all of them, I have to mediate and tell them firmly what to do.

The underlying problem was that the impresst was only one of a sequence of steps in the funding cycle, and at each step provincial funds would lose out. Mansoor explained, 'It is very clear that the government wants to weaken the provincial council. They do this with constitutional means and with financial means. They are trying to starve the council.' The bulk of public funding was allocated to central ministries or the centralised institutional hierarchy that passed from Colombo to the *kachcheri* to the divisional secretaries, thus bypassing the province. To make matters worse, there was a long tradition of creating new authorities, which would then bypass not only the provinces but everyone else as well, to create a direct patronage channel between the grassroots and the very top of the political hierarchy.[10] This was driven by sinister motives, Mansoor explained. By starving the province while letting the work of central ministries flourish, the government created a situation where 'people themselves will ask for certain responsibilities to be moved to the centre'. Such requests from the public were not driven by ethnic chauvinism or political positioning for or against decentralisation. They just wanted the best facilities for their local school, market or clinic. Base hospitals, for example, could be under either the central ministry or the province, but the former group typically received more funding. 'Now there is a campaign in Kantale and Kinniya', Mansoor explained. Both these rural towns in Trincomalee District had a base hospital administered by the eastern council. 'They want the base hospital to be moved from provincial to central control because it would strengthen the way it is resourced. But with that logic, what is the point of having a provincial council?'

The eastern council (like the other provinces, except perhaps the Western Province) had become almost completely dependent on the impresst of the finance commission. Its own ability to collect revenue, which had been envisioned to be a significant part of Sri Lanka's tax base at the outset, had shrunk to negligible proportions.[11] During the peace process and the tsunami response, donor-funded projects had supplanted the provincial budget, but this was no longer possible now that donors had moved on to poorer countries. There had been various initiatives to reach out to the diaspora community to generate funding (though this was much more pronounced in the north than the east), for example by creating a chief minister's fund into which foreign parties could pledge, but such schemes had been obstructed by the centre.

As a result, the provincial council faced a permanent funding deficit, and it was poorly positioned to compete with national line ministries or the district administration in the *kachcheri*. This made it all the more important to plan and administer provincial funds meticulously and to prevent central and provincial initiatives from overlapping or working at cross-purposes. To do this, the provincial planners had come up with a suite of administrative creations, such as a meticulous database to scrutinise needs and a so-called provincial planning commission to push back against politicians interfering with procedure and prevent public resources from being hijacked by a patronage agenda that would invariably privilege one constituency, locality, ethnic group, or party block vote over another one.[12]

Remarkably, these mechanisms had no clear legal basis. As I discovered, they had not been formally created but rather been made into an established practice that instilled particular principles. They can be thought of as modest bureaucratic attempts at creating de facto institutions, which can be used to claim turf and push back against rivals. Through these de facto institutions, civil servants insulated public resources from political strongmen, as if to extend the blessings of a devolution without politicians that they had experienced during the interim period. Bureaucratic performativity was deployed as an antidote to patronage politics. The institutional repertoires of the civil service were far removed from the symbol-infused performances of the Tamil nationalist movement and the martial cult of the LTTE. To the extent that they engaged with ethnic identity, bureaucrats treated it as a distributional codifier. Ethnicity featured as a technical category to secure an equitable allocation of public resources, one that was *protected* from the sway of ethno-nationalism.

Provincial legislation: Stalled and diluted statutes

The provincial councils differ from line ministries, central authorities, district *kachcheris* and local government in the sense that they can legislate. Like parliament, they are empowered to write new law – a legislative entitlement originating from India's 1980s intervention in Sri Lanka's constitution. Provinces are thus licenced to acquire new kinds of executive authority and claw back terrain from the centre. More specifically, the thirteenth amendment mandates the councils to pass provincial laws, so-called statutes, about issues on either the provincial list or the concurrent list (shared competencies between province and centre). This includes sensitive matters like revenue collection, land control and law enforcement, but these powers are subject to a constitutional caveat that they do not infringe on the sovereignty of the Sri Lankan parliament. On an administrative level, this limitation was maintained by the governor, who assumed a gatekeeping role, and several adjudication mechanisms vis-à-vis the national legislature which work in parliament's favour.[13] Moreover, parliament had a significant head start in terms of claiming 'concurrent' turf, because the northeastern council was on hold for nearly two decades: without elected legislators, no statutes. Now that the eastern and northern council had regained their legislative capacity, they were trying to catch up.

The holy grail of statues in the north and east concerns the creation of a chief minister's fund, which would give the province a financial framework to bring in foreign funding from donors, diaspora or investors and reduce its dependence on the centre. This was the one significant statute that Perumal's northeastern council passed in the late 1980s, but the fund never materialised. The newly inaugurated eastern and northern councils initiated a similar statute, but the proposal got stuck in a constitutional loophole. If there were concerns about the constitutionality of a proposal, the governor could refer it to the president and the attorney general, who might then present it to the Supreme Court for a verdict, but there was a procedural catch: the laws did not specify a time limit for this, so the president or attorney general could also decide to *not* refer it to court, whereby the statute proposal ended up sitting on their desk indefinitely. Both the eastern and the northern statute for a chief minister's fund got stuck in such legal no man's land (Wickramaratne 2019: 47).[14] But several other statutes had been passed in the north and east, often replicating the statutes of the other seven provinces, which had started acting on these powers since the late 1980s.

To scrutinise the political and administrative dynamics around provincial statutes, I catalogued all the statutes initiated by the eastern council (including the ones that never made it through the legal process), and for a select sample I then adopted a method of 'following the statute' from its initial draft through the various revisions and blockages to the final text and the concrete results it yielded. I will focus here on the eastern tourism bureau statute, which attracted some attention for reasons explained below, but the basic dynamic and outcome were similar for other the statutes I studied.[15]

As with so many things in northeastern Sri Lanka, the tourism statute is not just about the whatever it says on the cover (a flourishing tourism industry) but also about sovereign claims to the territory on which it takes place (control over land) and about sovereign power (the authority to levy tax). As I have discussed in some detail elsewhere (Klem 2014), there was a scramble for land in the immediate aftermath of the 2009 LTTE defeat. Lots of people were on the move, returning to lost property or looking for new opportunities. Big swaths of land had been cordoned off by the military (as with Sampur's special zone, discussed in Chapter 4), and similar forms of enclosure were imposed in the name of development. In late 2009 and early 2010, the government initiated a tourism zone along the coastal strip of Kuchchaveli, north of Trincomalee town (see Map 2.1), a process spearheaded by three entities: the nation-building ministry (controlled by Basil Rajapaksa, brother of the president), the urban development authority (which had been moved to the defence ministry, controlled by another presidential family member, Gotabaya Rajapaksa), and the then government agent (head of district, in the *kachcheri*), retired army general T. T. Ranjith de Silva, who was known for his ruthless tirades against civil servants – or anyone else who dared to get in his way.

This tourism zone in Kuchchaveli would cover a large section of the shoreline, thus blocking entrance to the sea for coastal fishing communities and it stoked fears of ethnic colonisation and military occupation.[16] The zoning plans arranged for a whole suite of so-called five-star or boutique hotels in what had until then been a rural backwater.[17] A mammoth real estate scheme in a remote hinterland like Kuchchaveli clearly was not just about capitalising on regional tourism potential. It was pushed through the bureaucratic chain with coercive pace. The procedural correspondence, which officers working in the locality concerned leaked to me, churned out the key phrases about no objections being raised in the necessary consultations, the environmental impact assessment yielding no concerns and the necessary tender processes and land leases progressing smoothly. The dates on these letters revealed an unusual efficiency. Successive layers of government had provided accordance for a large and highly contentious scheme within a matter of weeks, sometimes days. I also met some of the people whose signatures adorned these letters – faced with full might of the Rajapaksa political machinery (including their boss De Silva, the militaristic head of district), they had seen no option but to underwrite these texts.

In constitutional terms, tourism is a concurrent subject upon which centre and province share power. Land appropriation is, technically, by and large a provincial subject (Amarasinghe and Selvakkumaran 2019b; Bastian 1996; Hasbullah and Geiser 2019). And the Kuchchaveli tourism zone was unfolding at the doorstep of the Eastern Provincial Council, which was in its first term under the leadership of a Tamil politician allied to the Rajapaksas: Chief Minister Sivanesathurai Chandrakanthan, alias Pillayan (whom we will encounter again in Chapter 6). Unsurprisingly, one of the first statutes initiated by the provincial administration was on tourism. The paper trail at the assembly secretariat, a messy bundle of folders which I consulted in 2018, dated back to mid-2010, when a first draft was sent to parliament for consultation. The draft statute evolved in parallel to a tug of war over the Kuchchaveli zone with gazettes, statements and threatening letters from Basil Rajapaksa's ministry and the national tourism authority. The provincial statute was delayed due to various procedural obstacles (such as the Tamil and Sinhala translations of the text) and vaguely worded objections.[18]

These procedural deadlocks were broken in 2015, when a new national government under President Sirisena came to power and the provincial council was reshuffled. A more accommodative governor (Austin Fernando) was appointed, and a team of constitutional experts from Colombo offered their services to the provincial legal officers to straighten out the finer juridical issues. Within half a year, by March 2016, the statute had cleared all the procedural steps – governor recommendation, the assembly passing it, governor assent and public announcement though a gazette. The Eastern Province Tourism Bureau had now come into legal assistance, but this breakthrough had less to do with provincial political prowess or constitutional erudition than with the enabling political environment of a collaborative central government and a conducive governor.

In order to pass the statute, however, its key components had been sacrificed. The initial draft of the statute of September 2010 endowed the proposed tourism bureau with two key powers, buried in quite a long list of more trivial matters: to 'take appropriate action' when land that had been alienated to a company for tourism purposes was not actually used for that purpose, and to generate revenue by mandating the bureau to 'levy fees or charges' from tourism accommodation, with the exception of hotels registered by the national tourism authority. Through the various drafts, both these powers were severely watered down. The power to act on land grabbing under the guise of tourism was diluted to a mandate to 'notify' the central ministry about such issues.

And the power to levy tax on hotels was curtailed to exclude accommodations that were under the local authority and pilgrim's rests under the religious ministry. Most significantly, the province's fiscal prerogatives excluded 'any premises which has [sic] more than five rooms'. If the plan of the province was to make money, this final proviso clearly nipped that in the bud.

When I interviewed a civil servant who had played a leading role in revising the statute, he readily agreed that final statute had been heavily diluted. 'Parliament wanted those limitations inserted. And we need their approval.... So we decided to accept that. That way, at least we have *something*. And perhaps it can then be amended later.'[19] Interestingly, the Kuchchaveli tourism zone, which had played a central role in triggering the tourism statute in 2010, had become moribund when the statute was finally passed. It only housed one major hotel, a luxury resort named Jungle Beach, while the rest of the zone's fences and signposts were rotting away (Photograph 5.3). The foundational structures that had been laid for two other hotels looked ever more like wartime ruins. This was entirely unrelated to the tourism statute or the provincial council: the business case for such a major development in a far-flung corner of the island had not been informed by a sound market assessment. Moreover, it was said that the Rajapaksa government had been intent on plenishing its coffers and had levied such high rates on the leases that investors had recoiled. The provincial tourism bureau was not empowered to resist the Kuchchaveli zone but realities on the ground had brought the megalomanic plan to a halt. The result, however, was precisely the scenario the province had meant to counter: land had been allocated, but it was lying idle. Bushes were growing but the plots could not be freed for more productive purposes. All that could be done was notify the central authorities about a situation they probably knew all too well and were unlikely to act on.

Even with the key teeth taken out, the statute empowered the Eastern Provincial Council to have a tourism bureau with its own staff and a legal mandate to engage in business ventures, promote the region as a tourist destination internationally, accept grants, purchase property, protect tourist attractions and promote employment opportunities. In practice, the tourism bureau was stillborn. Two years after the statute was passed, the bureau comprised a director who held the post alongside his regular role at the provincial health ministry and as director of the newly created housing authority. His supposed assistants had not been released from their home departments. The hard-fought tourism bureau had no actual office and no resources. The province's tiny projects aimed at the tourism sector matched this pitiful impression.[20] At the same time, grand new plans were being developed without any input from the province. Glossy reports commissioned to foreign consultants were circulating

Photograph 5.3 Overgrown tourism zone

Source: Photograph by author.

Note: Signpost demarcating the tourism zone on the coast of Kuchchaveli, north of Trincomalee. The zone blocked the local community from a large part of the coastline and was vehemently opposed. The eastern council tried to pass a law against the zone but failed. In the end, almost all land was lying fallow, because hoteliers did not see sufficient business prospect.

about the glamourous future of the so-called Trincomalee metropole as a hub of eco-tourism, modern industry and a top-grade harbour. The artist's impressions looked attractive, but they were completely out of touch with the Trincomalee region that I knew.[21]

On paper, provincial councils have the constitutional right to make law, an entitlement reflecting the ambitions of the Indo-Lankan Accord to appease Tamil separatists with a compromise premised on shared sovereignty in all but name. In practice, these legislative powers were crippled by parliament's prerogatives and administrative pushback. What thwarted the militarised land-grabbing of the Kuchchaveli tourism zone was not the law-making power of the Eastern Province but the botched business case of the Rajapaksa government and their eviction from power via national elections.

Conclusion

The turbulent history of the NEPC illustrates how a single institution can be enacted in dramatically different ways to serve diametrically opposed political interests. Its constitutional foundation, the thirteenth amendment, has not changed a word, but the political meaning, significance and utility of the council shifted significantly throughout the years of war, peace efforts and postwar transition. In its first stage, the NEPC was propped up by India to perform like a Tamil government of the northeast. With the military, diplomatic and budgetary back-up of a regional guardian (precisely what the LTTE had lacked during the 2000s peace process), Perumal's NEPC could make furore despite its minimal institutional and political clout, but when India pulled out, this bravado deflated like a balloon. In a second stage, the NEPC functioned in interim mode with a stripped core of administrative capacities. Its resources and institutions were redeployed as extensions of the LTTE's sovereign experiment. Furniture and fridges were carried over to LTTE offices, and the bureaucracy was brought under 'remote control'. These practices gained significance during the Norwegian-facilitated peace process, when foreign donors pumped resources and opportunities into the NEPC as way to indirectly engage with the LTTE. After the war, finally, a purported normalcy returned to the now de-merged northern and eastern councils. The politicians were back, and so were the hazards of a hostile central government. Administrative, budgetary and legal restraints reduced the performance of the councils to a politically impotent sideshow.

One of the startling things about the provincial councils is the very fact that they still exist. As a coercive implant of what was effectively an Indian military invasion, they were loathed and sabotaged by both the Sri Lankan government and the Tamil nationalists. They endured two decades of civil war and a powerful postwar Rajapaksa government that vehemently opposed devolution. The political environment for provincial governance was unconducive, even hostile, every step along the way, but the councils survived – partly because the little bit of pride that remained of India's involvement in the war was arguably invested in the provincial council system. The endurance of the councils is testament to the tenacity of bureaucratic institutions. Civil servants generate their own logics and precedents. Unmaking bureaucratic institutions leaves the kinds of loose ends that state entities are averse to. If the provincial councils were abolished, something would have to come in its place, which then would open up a whole new range of political conundrums – best not to pick at a wound.

Instead of abolishing the councils, they were curtailed. To endure the competing pressures, the NEPC constructed compromise on top of compromise and absorbed contestation in institutional forms and technical procedures. When a supposed political normalcy returned to the councils after the war, they continued to face competing pressures. The Sri Lankan government effectively starved the provincial councils. Provincial tax revenue had been stripped, and the disbursal of government funds favoured central ministries and authorities over the provinces. Planners and administrators scrambled to make the best of the trickle given to them with the tactics I have discussed (for example, by maximising the impresst by having 'bills in hand' for the right kinds of activities). Financial shortfall did not only impede the service delivery of the provinces; it also contributed to the continued erosion of a devolved system of government. When people want the administration of their base hospital, school or other public facilities to be taken from the province because anchoring it in a central line ministry makes for better resourcing, the provinces continue to lose ground.

The legislative power of the provinces was similarly compromised. In the conception of Sri Lanka's system of devolved governance, the ability of the councils to make law was a central part of the bargain. In practice, the provincial council system has fallen well short of any notion of shared sovereignty, as the tourism bureau statute illustrates. This proposed provincial law faced formidable opposition from both the governor and parliament. When it finally passed, this was not because of the devolved powers of the province but because of a political shift in Colombo. Moreover, the statute only materialised after it had been severely watered down: key provincial competencies over revenue and land were taken out. The tourism bureau convocated by the statute was a moot institution deprived of facilities, staff capacity and funding.

The tenacity of the council stems partly from the bureaucratic inclination to use technical procedures and institutional performances to mitigate political hazards. During the war, civil servants used bureaucratic rationales to legitimise and de-politicise their manoeuvring between government and LTTE. After the war, they tried to ward off attempts at political interference, from both central government institutions and their 'own' provincial politicians. The planning secretariat came up with databases, guidelines and a newly invented planning commission to safeguard an equal distribution of state resources insulated from the imperatives of patronage politics. The administrators I have described enact a performative repertoire that we may call a devolution without politics. This has yielded an apparatus that is not only institutionally resilient but also politically impotent. The hallmarks of a sovereign state – the ability to levy tax, regulate land, make and enforce law and control state officers – are scrupulously withheld from the provinces. The provincial bureaucracy has learned to circumvent these political challenges to sustain itself. What is left is the bureaucratic reproduction of the Indo-Lankan Accord's institutional legacy: an ironic outcome that none of the parties wanted and that serves no rational purpose but that nonetheless persists. Yet, as the NEPC's trajectory illustrates, institutional bricolage is never final. There is always some remaining potential for an institution to be resurrected when the political winds change.

Notes

1   For exceptions, though strongly focused on legal and constitutional dimensions, see Amarasinghe et al. (2019) and Welikala (2016). Thangarajah's (2012) chapter also touches on the real-life workings of the NEPC, but given the scope of his chapter, this discussion remains quite short.

2   This chapter draws on my engagement with bureaucrats in and around Trincomalee since the early 2000s. The main empirical foundation of this chapter comprises fieldwork visits in 2018 and 2019, when I was allowed to formally embed myself in the planning secretariat of the Eastern Provincial Council for several weeks at the time.

3   This 1957 Bandaranaike–Chelvanayakam Pact envisaged a pseudo-federal arrangement with regional councils that would have moderate powers, but it had no legal anchoring and was never implemented. Subsequent agreements offered more diluted versions of devolution: no constitutional underpinning, pitched at the micro level and ambiguous prerogatives. The 1965 Senanayake–Chelvanayakam Pact sufficed with vaguely defined local district councils, and the 1980 bargain on district development councils placed devolution firmly in the terrain of subsidiarity and decentralised development management (Edrisinha et al. 2008; Matthews 1982; A. J. Wilson 2000).

4   The provincial council system has been likened to a 'white elephant' – an impractical gift that one cannot get rid of (Amarasinghe et al. 2010). Despite its sobering results, the Indo-Lankan Accord fundamentally redefined Sri Lanka's devolution debate: since the late 1980s, the debate has arguably been more preoccupied with fixing the problems of the solution (the throes of the thirteenth amendment) rather than with finding new solutions to the original problem (Wickramaratne and Marasinghe 2010). More ambitious attempts to augment Sri Lanka's system of power-sharing, such as President Kumaratunga's 'devolution package' of the late 1990s (ICES 1996; Thiruchelvam 2000), have demised. As a result, the governance system that Sri Lanka has today is a direct legacy of Indian peace efforts in the 1980s.

5   The first NEPC elections (19 November 1988) were boycotted by the main opposition party (SLFP) and the Tamil political leadership (Ilankai Tamil Arasu Kadchi [ITAK]/Tamil United Liberation Front [TULF], as well as Tamil Eelam Liberation Organisation [TELO] and People's Liberation Organisation of Tamil

Eelam [PLOTE]), and the LTTE violently opposed them. In the northern districts of Vavuniya, Mullaitivu and Kilinochchi, EPRLF ran under the umbrella of the Eelam National Democratic Liberation Front (ENDLF) – once a joint platform of EPRLF, TELO and PLOTE, but with the latter two boycotting the polls, ENDLF effectively became a shell for EPRLF. The EPRLF proper gained forty-one seats and ENDLF twelve. The United National Party (UNP) gained one seat from Ampara, where the turnout in Sinhala divisions was very low; SLMC gained seventeen seats from Ampara, Batticaloa and Trincomalee.

6   While the NEPC was supported by the federal Indian government (a backing that was now waning), the LTTE enjoyed the support of Tamil Nadu's polity, most explicitly from Chief Minister Karunanidhi (from the Dravida Munnetra Kazhagam, or DMK).

7   In its last sitting on 1 March 1990, the NEPC formulated an ultimatum with nineteen demands to the central government. The resolution has entered the history books as a unilateral declaration of independence, though that wording was not explicitly used. When I asked Perumal, he admitted: '[the resolution] was a last-minute decision. Everybody had rejected our points. Everybody was telling us to dissolve the council. I said no. I won't dissolve. So last-minute, when we passed it, we had to put some emphasis.' One of Perumal's assistants phrased it more frankly: 'They did it as an affront to the LTTE. They had nothing to lose. Nobody was with them. Not that their statement was going to be effective. It was just not to be losers.'

8   This yielded one of the many ironies in the history of the provincial council system: the other seven provinces (which had never asked for autonomy) set out to institutionalise provincial devolution by exercising their powers and holding regular elections. But in the north and east (the region for which the whole setup had been created) the system was politically paralysed.

9   Despite these concerns, the central government did not want to completely cut these regions off. Such a move would imply that these were no longer Sri Lankan citizens, a tacit resignation to the LTTE's claim of sovereign rule. When I asked former president Chandrika Bandaranaike Kumaratunga about this, she explained the government did this, so that 'the Tamil youth began to see that a Sinhala government was doing things for them. And they started wondering, "Why should we kill ourselves for Prabhakaran?"' (Interview, London, 5 June 2011).

10   There are countless authorities of this kind. One of the oldest and most powerful ones is the Mahaweli authority. A salient intervention in the postwar Rajapaksa years was the attempted creation of a Divineguma authority, which would have created a patronage highway from the very top of the government to the grassroots, bypassing the provinces. It was defeated in the Supreme Court and then rolled out in more modest form.

11   Since the creation of the provincial council system in 1987, the central government introduced new taxes and marginalised or overhauled provincial taxes.

By 2017, the provincial share in Sri Lanka's overall fiscal revenue had shrunk to 4.4 per cent of national revenue; the revenue levied by the Northern and Eastern Province comprised meagre 0.33 per cent of national revenue (based on Gunawardena [2019: 237, 252]).

12 The provincial planning secretariat's database covered all constituent parts of the province: the three districts, the 45 divisions and the hundreds of village level units below them. It listed the basic characteristics of all these units – surface area, population, level of poverty – and quantified these with a set of coefficients to generate a baseline of neediness. It also factored in ethnic demography to prevent any group from losing out. This gave the planners procedural ammunition against the politicians seeking to divert benefits to their voters. A newly created provincial planning commission (consisting of the key planners, the chief secretary and other senior administrators) assessed the distribution of funds to assure adequate prioritising and balancing based on this database. Though created as an informal coordination mechanism – it had no official status – the commission had become an established forum and it sought concurrence for its decisions from the finance commission, the country's peak body overseeing public funding.

13 The schizophrenic nature of Sri Lanka's constitution and the thirteenth amendment becomes apparent here. While the amendment contains elements of provincial autonomy (which was the whole rationale of the Indo-Lankan Accord), they are embedded in a purportedly unitary constitution. Hence, the Supreme Court ruled that the provincial councils cannot perform 'sovereign legislative functions' and must be consistent with the constitution. As such, provincial statutes are considered subordinate law (Amarasinghe and Selvakkumaran 2019a: 191).

14 When I interviewed the eastern governor in 2010 about this statute (which had gotten stuck in 2009), he said he had to refer it to the president because the thirteenth amendment prohibits the council from getting foreign funds and because it excludes civil servants from the chief minister's decisions over funding allocation. This legal reasoning, which appears shaky at best, was not used to reject the statute, though; it was simply shelved.

15 The following statutes of the eastern council successfully gained governor assent: finance (2008), rules and procedures (2008), the road passenger transport board (2009, amended in 2014), the bureau of preschool education (2010), the emergency fund (2010), stamp duty (2010), court fines (2010), the housing authority (2014) and the tourism bureau (2016) (Overview drafted by the EPC legal unit). The northern council gained assent for the following statues: finance (2014), stamp duty (2014), health services (2015), education (2015), preschools (2015), child day care (2016), child development (2016), the road passenger transport authority (2017), the department of probation (2017), court fines (2017), mineral tax (2017), the tourism authority (2018), indigenous medicine (2018) and pawn brokers (2018). Two more were pending: the co-operative employee statute and the business name statute (Overview NPC Chief Secretary's Secretariat).

16 The extensions of the Mahaweli scheme (Weli Oya) were just interior from the tourism zone, and Mullaitivu District with all its military installations was just to the north.

17 At the time, there was only one tourism venue of significance: the Nilaveli Beach Hotel. It had been known for the coral around the neighbouring Pigeon Island (until the tsunami destroyed it), but during the war it was a run-down facility catering to humanitarian expats and an occasional backpacker for giveaway prices.

18 To illustrate this point, a parliamentary sub-committee sent the statute back after a 10-minute meeting in January 2011, saying that it 'has not been prepared as per standard procedure' without specifying the supposed irregularities. Three months later, the parliamentary legal draftsman's office summoned the province to 'send an officer conversant with the subject as there are certain issues that need clarifying'. The statute then got stuck in a procedural stalemate when the governor withheld his assent. The next provincial council tried to restart the process in 2013, but further disagreements over translation and procedural requirements prevented the statute from moving forward.

19 The key legal obstacle to the statute, he explained, was the parliamentary Tourism Development Act passed by the Wickremesinghe government in 2005: 'That expanded the powers of the Sri Lankan Tourism Authority. According to the thirteenth amendment, they need to consult with the provinces to do that, but in 2005 there was no council in the northeast.' A signature of the then-governor sufficed, and now it was difficult to redress the balance.

20 From 2013 to 2017, the budget for tourism activities was fixed at about 58 million rupees per year (roughly 300,000 US dollars). The 2015 creation of the tourism bureau had no effect on the expenditure. Moreover, many projects appeared to be driven by a general development impetus, rather than an attempt to nurture tourism-led growth and employment. Funds had been allocated to the improvement of pilgrim's rests in provincial outposts like Thennamaravadi and Dehiyathakandiya, and to lagoon shore beautification and peddle boats in Kinniya and Eravur – not exactly the sites that would boost the tourism industry.

21 To give one example, a new eco-tourism hub in Thopur had been slotted to generate 1,000 jobs – but the Thopur that actually existed was a small Muslim farmer's town with only a few rudimentary food stalls, where I had never seen a single tourist.

6 Tamil Nationalist Anti-politics in the Wake of Defeat

The old guard of Tamil nationalist politicians moved back to centre stage after the Liberation Tigers of Tamil Eelam's (LTTE) defeat. The gentlemen lawyers and parliamentarians of the main Tamil party, Ilankai Tamil Arasu Kadchi (ITAK), had made way for armed youth militants in the 1970s, when Tamil nationalism became Tamil national *liberation*. Pleas for federal power-sharing then escalated into uncompromising separatism, and constitutional bargaining yielded to guerrilla violence. In 2009, the pendulum swung back. The now-ageing ITAK leaders moved to the front seat again. But what could they bargain for without leverage? How could they claim heirship of the national cause when the new political reality forced them to shed the aspiration of an independent Eelam? ITAK was thus confronted with one of the central conundrums of this book: the schizophrenic plight of separatist political parties, which are forced to pursue their aspirations through the very democratic landscape that they reject on principle. To understand ITAK's postwar positioning, we also need to reengage with the provincial council system discussed in Chapter 5. The Tamil nationalist movement saw the provincial councils as treason to the Tamil cause. But after the defeat of the LTTE, they were the only remaining forum for a semblance of self-government in the north and east of Sri Lanka. If ITAK refused to govern the Northern and Eastern Province, rival Tamil parties would do it in their place.

A performative conception of politics sheds light on the way ITAK handled the schizophrenic condition of simultaneously opposing and participating in the prevalent political framework. By lifting our preoccupation with formal institutions and associated moral yardsticks of democratic behaviour, this conceptualisation directs our focus to the repertoires with which political aspirations are enacted, within or beyond official mandates and procedures.

More specifically, I will draw on the performative repertoire that Hansen (1999) has called 'anti-politics' in his work on Hindu nationalism. Anti-politics may be defined as a principled dissociation from the prevalent political arena. Evidently, the very attempt of extracting oneself from politics is itself a political act. Anti-politics should therefore *not* be understood as an apolitical phenomenon but rather as a performative attempt to construct a realm that is separate from (and typically elevated above) the established political arena. This anti-political realm is often legitimised in cultural or religious terms, and this then opens up space to construct 'the people' or 'the nation' as a cultural or religious, and therefore anti-political, category in the name of which transgressive practices are legitimised (Hansen 1999; see also Spencer 2008). South Asia has amassed an elaborate repertoire of anti-political performativity, with a plethora of pomp and ritual, ethnic or religious idioms, spectacle and enactments of potency, as well as a range of popular resistance tactics that include *satyagraha* (non-violent protests such as sit-in occupations), electoral boycotts, *hartals* (public shutdowns) and hunger strikes (Banerjee 2011; Harriss, Stokke and Törnquist 2004; Spencer 2007; Suykens and Islam 2013).

This chapter will distinguish three anti-political repertoires of the Tamil nationalist movement: oath-of-allegiance politics, politics of abstinence and the performance of institutional deficiency. I will argue that the 2009 defeat of the LTTE placed these anti-political repertoires under new strain. During the war, the Tamil nationalist movement could defer its paradoxical stance (in rejecting the framework of the Sri Lankan state but nonetheless participating in its institutions) by positioning itself as a moderate extension of the LTTE state experiment and a democratic placeholder for a new sovereign framework to come. With the defeat of the LTTE, such positioning no longer made sense: extension of what, placeholder until when? Moreover, the end of the war confronted the Tamil nationalist leadership with two practical challenges it was no longer familiar with: grappling with open disagreement in a multi-party Tamil arena and actually governing elected institutions, namely the provincial councils.

In shifting between local, provincial and national level politics, this chapter diverges from the tendency to discuss postwar Tamil politics on the basis of key national turning points (Höglund and Orjuela 2012; International Crisis Group 2017; Seoighe 2017; Stokke and Uyangoda 2011; Venugopal 2018; Wickramasinghe 2009). To help readers less familiar with Sri Lanka keep track of the different levels and their timelines, Table 6.1 provides a rudimentary chronology. As a brief crib sheet, the four key Tamil political figures that feature in this chapter among several other names are R. Sampanthan (leader of ITAK and the Tamil National Alliance [TNA]; member of parliament from Trincomalee), Mavai Senathirajah (ITAK/TNA deputy leader; member of parliament from Jaffna), C. V. Vigneswaran (chief minister of the first Northern

Table 6.1 Key political events at provincial and national levels, 2007–2018

	Eastern Provincial Council	Northern Provincial Council	National politics
2007	▪ De-merger of east and north comes into effect ▪ Defeat LTTE in east, continued warfare in north		
2008	♦ First elections Eastern Provincial Council (boycotted by TNA, Rajapaksa coalition wins, Pillayan chief minister).	In 'interim mode': no elected council	
2009			○ Defeat of LTTE
2010			○ Presidential elections: Mahinda Rajapaksa narrowly re-elected
2011	♦ Second elections Eastern Provincial Council (Rajapaksa coalition wins, Majeed CM, TNA in opposition)		○ Parliamentary elections: two-thirds majority for Mahinda Rajapaksa's coalition
2012			
2013		▫ First elections Northern Provincial Council (TNA landslide, Wigneswaran CM)	
2014			○ Presidential elections: Sirisena (common opposition) wins
2015	♦ Eastern Provincial Council reshuffled (Naseer becomes CM of TNA-SLMC coalition)		○ Parliamentary elections: Sirisena's "good governance" coalition wins
2016			
2017	♦ Council term expires (no election to date)	▫ Political crisis, Board of Ministers defunct ▫ Council term expires (no election to date)	
2018			○ Presidential coup and constitutional crisis

Source: Prepared by author.

Provincial Council; former Supreme Court judge from Colombo) and S. V. K. Sivagnanam (chairman of the first Northern Provincial Council, ITAK/TNA provincial councillor from Jaffna).

Historical antecedents of Tamil nationalist politics and anti-politics

As the political mainstay of Tamil nationalist politics, Ilankai Tamil Arasu Kadchi (ITAK) waxed and waned throughout Sri Lanka's turbulent conflict history. Literally translated, Ilankai Tamil Arasu Kadchi means Sri Lankan Tamil State Party, but in English it is known as the Federal Party. In 1949, the party broke away from G. G. Ponnambalam's All Ceylon Tamil Congress (ACTC) and became the primary platform of Tamil democratic agitation in the 1950s and 1960s. It was ITAK leader S. J. V. Chelvanayakam who negotiated pacts with the government in the 1950s and 1960s (Sivarajah 2007; A. J. Wilson 1994b, 2000). The party rejected the government's 'unilateral' drafting of the 1972 constitution and declared Chelvanayakam's 1975 by-election a constitutional referendum. ITAK carries the symbol of a house, an icon that resonates with protection and homeland. It also alludes to the party of 'father' Chelvanayakam offering an overall shelter for a wider gamut of Tamil groupings and formations. ITAK was the dominant player in the Tamil United Front (TUF), which later converted itself into the Tamil United Liberation Front (TULF) and took an explicitly separatist position with the 1976 Vaddukoddai resolution. This resolution marked a critical juncture in the history of the Tamil nationalist movement, by demanding the 'restoration and reconstitution of the Free, Sovereign, Secular, Socialist State of Tamil Eelam based on the right of self-determination', and calling 'upon the Tamil Nation in general and the Tamil youth in particular to come forward to throw themselves fully into the sacred fight for freedom and to flinch not till the goal of a sovereign state of Tamil Eelam is reached' (Edrisinha et al. 2008: 258).[1] The Vaddukoddai resolution also represented a moment of ambiguity. Despite the fierce calls to arms, the resolution signatories kept their seats in the Sri Lankan parliament (the TULF participated in the 1977 elections on the explicit premise of treating the polls as Tamil referendum on the separatist stance). Moreover, there was a discrepancy between the firm resolve of the resolution and the underlying difference and disagreements between the TULF's three constituents. Apart from ITAK, there was ACTC (both an ally and an electoral rival) and the Ceylon Workers' Congress (a party representing the *malaiyaha* Tamil constituency in the central highlands). The latter signatory unsettled the resolution's central point by adding a clause that registered the party's 'reservations in relation to its commitment to the setting up of a separate state of Tamil Eelam' (Edrisinha et al. 2008: 258).

With the rise of youth militias in the 1970s and the escalation of violence in the 1980s, ITAK/TULF lost its position as the orchestrator of the Tamil struggle to the LTTE. Several members, including its leader Amirthalingam, were assassinated by the movement. Under these circumstances, no new cohorts of political leadership emerged. The party assumed renewed significance in the run-up to the 2002 ceasefire, when the TNA was created (Whitaker 2007: 190–192) as a new joint platform of Tamil parties.[2] Officially, the TNA had no links with the LTTE. It was an elected party, composed of veteran politicians of the old days, largely drawn from the anglicised 'high' caste elite. The LTTE eschewed official support to the TNA, because it rejected the legitimacy of parliament. It had its own Political Wing and sought to establish its own sovereign state. But in practice, the TNA was a tactical LTTE mouthpiece in the heart of Colombo politics. If the movement considered itself the 'sole representative' of the Tamil people, the TNA became the 'sole representative of the sole representative'.[3] The TNA derived significance from this position.

Destined to eternally occupy a handful of opposition seats, the party was marginal to the horse-trading of party politics. But it gained prominence as a unified platform of the Tamil community, as an advance post of the LTTE's sovereign ambition and as the embodiment of a moderated and democratic Tamil nationalist force. Both domestically and internationally, TNA leader R. Sampanthan was perceived not just as the front man of a small political faction but as a spokesperson for the Tamil nation, a statesman-like figure. Both the institutional backbone and the leadership of the TNA had an ITAK signature. In everyday parlance, ITAK, TULF and TNA were in fact largely interchangeable[4]: different institutional outfits comprising the same people, networks and political repertoires.

After the war, ITAK (and the TNA) remerged as the primary Tamil formation, but it was confronted with a new set of challenges. The demise of its sovereign referent, the LTTE, newly exposed the party to the problems of democratically challenging the foundations of the democratic system. ITAK levelled fundamental critique against Sri Lanka's democratic system in rejecting the notion of a singular Sri Lankan nation, the validity of the constitution and the unitary nature of the state. But to act on that critique, it had to operate within the political architecture of one Sri Lankan nation, a unilaterally imposed constitution and a unitary state – the very system that had been upheld with the ruthless military violence in 2009, the same violence that had ultimately nullified Tamil Eelam. As a result, Tamil nationalists suffered from political schizophrenia: they could not simultaneously be good nationalists (by their own definition) and good democrats (by the prevalent legal and political norms). In what follows, I will argue that ITAK has navigated these challenges and paradoxes with three complimentary kinds of performance that combine elements of politics and anti-politics: oath-of-allegiance politics, the performance of political abstinence and the performance of institutional deficiency.

Oath-of-allegiance politics

The S. J. V. Chelvanayakam memorial in Jaffna commemorates the founder of ITAK and 'father of the Tamil nation', known by the short name *thanthai* Chelva (father Chelva). The grounds occupy a significant place in the symbol-infused urban landscape of the northern capital. At the edge of the old town, it lies adjacent to the Jaffna library, once a venerated repository of ancient Tamil sources, which was set ablaze in 1981 amidst escalating ethnic enmity and newly built after the war as a testament to the irreplaceable collection it once housed. The football stadium across the road carries the name of Alfred Duraiappah, the former mayor of Jaffna, now famous for being the first person to be killed by LTTE leader Prabhakaran. It is also the site of a mass grave. Beyond it lie the ramparts of the renowned Jaffna Fort, built as the heart of the local colonial administration and more recently home to government offices and the IPKF. Amidst those beacons of troubled Tamil history, the *thanthai* Chelva memorial comprises a slightly larger-than-life size golden statue of Chelvanayakam and a large tombstone with a tall white column towering over it. The ensemble is surrounded by a small but well-kept garden and a parapet wall.

My friend and mentor Shahul Hasbullah and I attended the annual Chelvanayakam memorial ceremony in April 2018. We were protected from the sun by a simple structure of wooden poles and tin sheets – perhaps fittingly, the party of the house (ITAK's electoral symbol) offered shelter that resembled refugee camp architecture. The audience trickled in to greet, chat and shake hands before finding a plastic chair. Many of the leading figures of the Tamil political community were present, including parliamentarians and provincial councillors, though the crowd was said to be smaller than usual. Several dignitaries were absent because they were attending the funeral of the wife of S. V. K. Sivagnanam – the chairman of the Northern Provincial Council was a respected face in ITAK circles. As would have been the case at that sad event, many of the attendants of the memorial lecture were dressed in solemn white. Almost all attendees were men well into retirement age. Most would have had their formative years in the 1950s and 1960s – a chapter of Tamil nationalism that was premised on parliamentary opposition and the Gandhian non-violent resistance of *satyagraha*. The memorial ground, similarly, was not only a homage to Chelvanayakam's persona, but it also harboured a nostalgia to his political era: a time before armed youth militias wrested command over the nationalist struggle, before the impressive but ruthless feats of the LTTE, and before the devastating end in Mullivaikal. A time when Tamil political leadership rested with a community of respected well-educated 'high' caste lawyers, legislators, and administrators in Jaffna and Colombo: civilised, learned and measured men, with impeccable manners and English rhetorical skills, a stratum once personified by Chelvanayakam, now a demographic cohort that earned ITAK the nickname 'pensioners' party'.

The master of ceremony was a priest from the Church of South India. Like many Tamil leaders of his time, Chelvanayakam was a Christian, though he claimed to be a 'Christian by religion and a Hindu by culture' (A. J. Wilson 1994b: 4). Following the main speech, the attendants flocked to the golden sculpture at the front of the grounds. An improvised platform with some scaffolded steps had been erected to enable the guests of honour to garland the statue. The priest, with his starkly purple cassock, ordained the sculpture with a first string of flowers (Photograph 6.1). A long sequence of dignitaries followed this act, including Mr. Chandrahasan, Chelvanayakam's now ageing son who had come from Chennai. The fusion of religious and political registers was remarkable – though not surprising for readers of Geertz (1980); Hansen (2004); Paley (2008); Siegel (1998); or Spencer (2007). Pomp and ritual curated by a priest mixed effortlessly with the political history of Tamil nationalism. The rickety stairs were a source of concern given the advanced age of gentlemen climbing it, but on a ceremonial day like this, it was not difficult to read symbolic meaning into their arduous yet steadfast journey to the top. These highly photogenic moments – and I was far from the only one taking pictures – were followed by the garlanding of the tombstone itself, an act in which the entire audience participated (Photograph 6.2). More greeting, chatting and handshaking followed, before the men dispersed with their motorbikes and cars, slightly more impressive vehicles for the dignitaries than the commoners.

Photograph 6.1 Celebrating Chelvanayakam

Source: Photograph by author.

Note: Priest garlanding the statue of 'father' Chelva at the annual commemoration event at the S. J. V. Chelvanayakam memorial ground in Jaffna, April 2018.

Photograph 6.2 Paying respect to Chelvanayakam

Source: Photograph by author.

Note: Commemorators decorating S. J. V. Chelvanayakam's tombstone at the memorial ground in Jaffna, April 2018. This photo is the original image that was used for the cover of this book.

This memorial event is a fitting representation of ITAK, not just because of the party's strong preoccupation with the past, its ageing political cadre and the adulation of past heroes and their offspring but also because the ritual illustrates what the party represents for the Tamil electorate. Voting for ITAK (or the TULF or the TNA) is to a large degree about nationalist articles of faith – an affirmation of the Tamil struggle, of the enduring plight of the Tamil people and of standing united in opposition to the Colombo government. Voting for 'the house' is only marginally political in the sense of steering the course of policy, endorsing the selection of party leaders or taking an ideological stance; it is primarily political in the sense of attesting to be part of a Tamil nation with unfulfilled aspirations. This ritual attestation of Tamil nationalism is congruent with Hansen's (1999) conceptualisation of the rise of Hindu nationalism in 1990s India and the use of anti-political repertoires to dissect nationalist ideology from small-fry politics, to project a mirage of Hindu puritanism that supersedes the politicking of democracy.[5]

Support to ITAK as a nationalist article of faith became all the more significant in the immediate postwar years, when ITAK/TNA presented itself as the only remaining bulwark against the government – within the country, that is, because the Tamil diaspora movement, with which the party had a complicated relationship, assumed a significant role in the oath-of-allegiance politics of Tamil nationalism. In December 2009, the immediate aftermath of the war, diaspora organisations initiated a referendum in several countries with a large Sri Lankan Tamil community in Europe, Canada and Australia. With a significant turnout (though no exact number can be given without an official voter registration system) and over 99 per cent majorities in each country, the Tamil diaspora endorsed the statement:

> I aspire for the formation of the independent and sovereign state of Tamil Eelam in the north and east territory of the island of Sri Lanka on the basis that the Tamils in the island of Sri Lanka make a distinct nation, have a traditional homeland and have the right to self-determination.[6]

If a codified oath of allegiance for Tamil nationalism ever existed, this is probably how it would read. While the referendum spawned some paradoxical questions,[7] it powerfully staged the large transnational support base of Sri Lankan Tamil nationalism. This added weight to ITAK's efforts, but it also complicated the challenge of keeping the ranks closed. Within Sri Lanka, ITAK firmly positioned itself as the heir of the LTTE's liberation struggle. The party was not able to stop the government's Sinhala nationalist and militarised interventions, but a vote for ITAK was one of the few remaining channels to voice dissent, if anything, to an international audience.

During the 2010 parliamentary elections, I was in Trincomalee, the home district of ITAK/TNA leader Sampanthan. His rallies were nothing like the government ones, which had a massive stage with large banners, a spectacular security arrangement, passionate shouting and an impressive congregation of acolytes. Government performances radiated political potency. Sampanthan's rallies were nothing of this kind. He would speak alone and on a tiny podium. People sat on the grass in an almost reverent quietness, while the 77-year-old ITAK leader placed the elections in their larger historical context with a soft-spoken but sonorous voice. If the government rally had felt like a rowdy, hot-tempered sport's match, the ITAK event seemed more like a tranquil meditative performance.

The government alliance boasted about its development plans and ability to deliver jobs and material progress. Roads were asphalted last-minute, new housing projects and industries foreshadowed, and small gifts distributed to secure votes (Photograph 6.3) (see Klem [2015] for a more detailed discussion). ITAK needed no such show of force to get the Tamil vote.[8] In the words of Nadarajah, the party organiser for Trincomalee District whom we encountered in the Chapter 4:

> We don't have to buy their votes. We have the weapon of being Tamil. That is a wrong thing, I know, but we are doing like that. We will say things like: so many people died, what did they die for? And so on. Without any expectation [of receiving material rewards] the people will come together.

Photograph 6.3 Election fever

Source: Photograph by author.

Note: Election posters for the 2010 parliamentary elections, displaying President Mahinda Rajapaksa with Susantha Punchinilame (*right*), the district strongman for the Rajapaksas in Trincomalee.

When I asked one of my other regular interlocutors, a Christian Tamil man from neighbouring Muttur, about the prevalent electoral sentiment among the Tamil community, he said, 'The LTTE was destroyed, but many people can't accept that. That's why most people will vote for ITAK.... Just to show their allegiance'.

Performing political abstinence

Political abstinence, the second repertoire I will discuss, was mainly present through electoral boycotts. The scholarly literature acknowledges this phenomenon as an occasional political tactic in South Asia.[9] I will approach electoral boycotts primarily as an anti-political performance: a call on the electorate (sometimes backed up by coercive force) to demonstratively sacrifice their voting rights and thus participate in a principled display of protest. In Sri Lanka, such boycotts date back to the emergence of proto-democratic institutions in the late British period: the Jaffna Youth Congress famously insisted on boycotting the island's first general elections for the State Council in 1931 (Russel 1978). In ITAK's history, such political abstinence played a significant, if inconsistent, role.[10] The party boycotted the presidential polls twice, in 1982 and 2005.[11] It never boycotted any parliamentary elections, though it did forfeit its seats twice: in protest against the 1972 constitution and when the government forced an anti-separatist oath on them in 1983. One of the most salient electoral boycotts was driven by a principled opposition to the forum on ballot (as well as by LTTE pressure): ITAK/TULF's opposition to the newly created provincial council, the NEPC, in 1988.

Boycotts can be powerful, but they are also perilous. After all, they carry the risk of demoting one's own relevance rather than that of the spurned institution, in which case political *abstinence* degenerates into political *absence* (as the first-ever Tamil boycott in 1931 had dramatically shown; Russel 1978). This risk became a major concern for the ITAK/TNA with the Eastern Provincial Council elections of 2008. These were arguably Sri Lanka's first postwar elections, even if there was still heavy fighting in the north, because the polls were prompted by the military's success in driving the LTTE out of the east in 2007. The 2008 elections were part of a government attempt to convert its military success into consolidated political control. ITAK/TNA continued to oppose the provincial council system (a stance underpinned by LTTE objection) and refused to participate in the polls. It was particularly resentful about the demerger of the northeast into an Eastern Province and a Northern Province (which dissected the claimed Tamil homeland into two administrative units and cut out the political heart of the 1987 Indo-Lankan Accord)[12] and the use of elections as a stabilisation tactic while fierce fighting continued in the north. The party had no way to enforce such a boycott among its constituency as the LTTE had done in the past, but the low turnout suggests that the party's moral authority did indeed convince a part of the Tamil electorate to refrain from exercising its franchise.[13]

This abstentionism was consistent with ITAK's boycott of the NEPC elections in 1988, but the context was different. The 2008 of the Eastern Provincial Council elections were a prelude to the Tamil political arena opening up to a plural kind of politics with competing claimants to Tamil leadership and open disagreement and political mobilisation on intra-Tamil issues. The ascendency of rival Tamil parties made the ITAK/TNA boycott of the 2008 elections in the Eastern Province a risky endeavour. President Rajapaksa was actively propping up the political platform of Karuna, the renegade eastern commander of the LTTE. The Karuna split of 2004 had exposed the latent but long-standing regional divide between the Tamil north and the east (Thangarajah 2012; A. J. Wilson 1994a). Karuna's newly created party, the Tamil Makkal Viduthalai Pulikal (TMVP, or Tamil People Liberation Tigers) offered obvious political utility to exploit that divide. Like all previous militant groups which had been driven into the hands of the government after falling out with the LTTE, the TMVP remained a fringe movement and it was subject to further splits. But the mobilisation of eastern Tamils, rather than the Tamil nation at large, with a narrative of redressing the dominance and arrogance of Jaffna Tamils and their stiff caste hierarchies, was a threat to the oath-of-allegiance politics of ITAK.

Only in the unique constellation of the first Eastern Provincial Council elections – the multi-ethnic east, President Rajapaksa desperate for a win, the void of the LTTE eviction, and ITAK/TNA stepping away from the vote – could a marginal movement like the TMVP claim electoral turf. And it was for that reason that the first chief minister of the Eastern Province, Sivanesathurai Chandrakanthan (commonly known by his fighter's name Pillayan), was a highly unlikely political figure. As a former LTTE child soldier from a modest social background and a school drop-out with no work experience (Sánchez Meertens 2013), Pillayan represented the opposite of ITAK's leaders. After breaking with TMVP leader Karuna, he headed the splinter of a splinter of the LTTE and had no party structure to fall back on, but he was to lead the newly created provincial administration with a coalition consisting of the Sinhala and Muslim constituents of Rajapaksa's electoral machine, both of which despised him.[14] Pillayan filled the vacuum created by ITAK/TNA's boycott, and for a brief period, he became a significant player as he set postwar precedents. He was governing a province in collaboration with Muslim and Sinhala parties, with the protection and backing of the formidable patronage networks of the Rajapaksa government. Offices started running, development projects were kickstarted, and Chief Minister Pillayan drove around with an impressive motorcade to attend public forums, cut ribbons and visit the halls of power in Colombo (see also Goodhand, Klem and Walton 2017).

Meanwhile, ITAK/TNA was absent from the scene. It steered clear of the Eastern Provincial Council and instead pleaded to an international audience with a discourse of Tamil rights and aspirations. On that front, however, it was not the most powerful voice either because diaspora networks assumed a prominent place. LTTE-associated outfits cried out about military violations during the final months of the war, particularly in Geneva, the seat of the United Nations Human Rights Council. The council continued to be a highly visible arena to perform competing political scripts after the war. While Western delegations and activists named and shamed the Sri Lankan government to push it towards accepting investigations and redressive measures, the Sri Lankan government used the same arena to perform its sovereign power and allude to Sinhala cultural idioms of preventing and deflecting shame.[15] Tamil diaspora, in turn, sought to connect war crime allegations to the broader discourse of Tamil human rights and the right to self-determination. This required significant adjustments to their routine script. The martial symbols and references of the Tamil struggle were inadequate for the legal idiom used in Geneva. Individual victim reports became the central performative tactic. Tamil aspirations, adulated leaders and the cult around martyrs dissipated from the plot, but this tactical severance from the LTTE created new tensions (Thurairajah 2020). The aforementioned diaspora referendums further boosted the transnational dimension of Tamil allegiance politics.

ITAK and the TNA had been conceived as the central platform in Tamil politics, but they were at risk of being outflanked from two sides: Pillayan was performing an executive kind of Tamil politics by catering to people's material needs, and diaspora players were performing oath-of-allegiance politics through their firm statements on the international stage. And this political rivalry was only the start. With the end of the war and the dissolution of the LTTE's coercive grip on society, the Tamil political arena opened up once more and a diversity of outfits proliferated. Militia movements like TELO, EPRLF, PLOTE (People's Liberation Organisation of Tamil Eelam) and EROS (Eelam Revolutionary Organisation of Students) re-emerged from hiding and hibernation to fashion themselves as democratic political platforms. ITAK's long-standing rival-cum-partner ACTC, now headed by GG Ponnambalam's grandson Gajen Ponnambalam, also joined the fray. Though there were differences, all of these parties professed some version of Tamil nationalist allegiance and drew on the same performative and discursive repertoires of Tamil politics.

This made it increasingly difficult for ITAK to paper over the divisions within Tamil society. The unifying narrative of Tamil nationalism edged on a preservationist stance on cultural traditions, but this outlook faced growing opposition. The postwar context offered fertile ground for mobilisation on intra-Tamil issues (as discussed in Chapter 4): turf battles between castes and *kudis*; youngsters and women seeking to release themselves from conservative trappings; Christians' anxiety about Hindu domination and Hindus' anxiety about Christian proselytisation; and the rural poor desiring economic development instead of nationalist rhetoric. With their emancipatory social outlook, some of the leftist Tamil movements found a receptive audience. The resurfacing of diverse versions of Tamil nationalism confronted ITAK with a dilemma: it was no longer able to perform the role of the statesmen-like advance guard of the LTTE's sovereign project, representing the Tamil people towards external foes and benefactors. Instead, it was faced with an internal Tamil political arena that encompassed this broad array of issues and parties. Given its association with the upper stratum of Tamil society and its leadership of well-educated 'high' caste men, ITAK was poorly positioned to launch an agenda of social transformation.

Running for the provincial council to perform its deficiency

Faced with these political hazards, ITAK did participate in the next eastern elections in 2012. Similarly, it decided *not* to boycott the first Northern Provincial Council elections. It was 2013. The war was well over and the Rajapaksa government was firmly in power. For the first time in ITAK's long and turbulent history, there was an opportunity to democratically govern the north. All the party's hesitations and frustrations with the provincial council system remained in place, and some civil society groups advocated another boycott of the polls to avoid a 'political Mullivaikal' (cited in Sathananthan 2013). But if ITAK (and its broader TNA alliance) recused itself from this arena, it would vacate a visible political stage for other Tamil groups – groups with a bigger clout and more authority than Pillayan had had in the east – and the party would risk losing relevance.

The northern election was a result of mounting international pressure against the Rajapaksa government (Photograph 6.4). Polls had been held twice in the east, but in the north they had been postponed indefinitely. The government's Machiavellian tactics in the multi-ethnic east would not work with the vast

Photograph 6.4 Northern Provincial Council complex

Source: Photograph by author.

Note: In 2013, the first-ever Northern Provincial Council was elected. It was accommodated in this complex in Kaithadi, outside Jaffna (photo taken in 2018). The entrance to the right comprised a large hall where people commonly queued up to present their problems to Chief Minister Vigneswaran, his cabinet and his officers.

Tamil majority in the Northern Province (see the ethnic geography depicted on Map 2.1), so the Rajapaksa government played for time. However, it was confronted with increasingly serious statements and resolutions in the United Nations Human Rights Council in Geneva. Aiming to alleviate pressure with gestures of goodwill without compromising on its key concerns, the Rajapaksa government conceded to schedule elections in the north.

The northern council elections brought fresh excitement to Jaffna: posters coloured the streets, party offices sprouted up, tuk-tuks with loudspeakers and rally speeches echoed through the neighbourhoods. The polls formed a major political juncture for the north and they were unfamiliar on three counts: all the key Tamil issues were openly on the agenda, people had a suite of parties to choose from and it was clear that Tamil parties would win and govern. A week before election day Hasbullah and I visited an ITAK campaign office to interview Mavai Senathirajah. As a long-time member of parliament and general secretary of the TNA, he yielded only to Sampanthan in the Tamil party hierarchy. ITAK had decided to run with the broader TNA umbrella (along with EPRLF, PLOTE, TELO and remnants of the TULF) to keep the ranks closed. But within the TNA campaign ITAK was clearly in the lead, and the speech Senathirajah gave us (and it was indeed more of a speech than an interview) was an ITAK speech. With his white robes, grey thinning hair and black moustache (a trademark of male Tamil potency), simple wire-framed specs (that is, not a 'modern' Colombo man), and his rhetorical ability to thread a whole range of historical events and legal notions into one flawless grammatical English sentence, he was easy to recognise as part of the old Tamil political cohort.

Senathirajah rehearsed the history of the Tamil struggle for us: the advocacy and civil disobedience, the pacts, the Indo-Lankan Accord, the limitations of the thirteenth amendment. But ITAK's stance had shifted now, he emphasised:

> We did not go back to the Vaddukoddai resolution [the separatist turn of 1976]. We accept a united Sri Lanka, but with devolution, so long as we clearly define what is central – defence, customs, monetary policy – and what is devolved – police, fiscal policy, land – and with no concurrent list.

The TNA election manifesto indeed walked a fine line. It rehearsed the foundational principles of the Tamil struggle: the Tamils as 'distinct People' and the northeast as the 'historical habitation' of the 'Tamil-Speaking People', a category subtly including the Muslims along with the Tamils. It underlined the 'right to self-determination' but avoided reference to homeland or a separate state and instead advocated a 'Federal structure' on the basis of 'shared sovereignty' with a merged north and east.[16] This was a narrative of Tamil nationalism with the separatist components redacted, a nationalism without liberation – or at least, without the explicit mention of thereof.

I asked Senathirajah about the Muslim community. After all, as the forthcoming government of the north, it was upon the Tamil leadership to act responsibly to its own minorities. He responded as if this was a routine matter: 'We are ready to accommodate the Muslim aspirations. The manifesto also says that.' Done and dusted. At that point, my companion Hasbullah, himself a northern Muslim and a victim of the LTTE Eviction of 1990, intervened. 'Is your party prepared to publicly acknowledge the fact that what happened to the Muslims was ethnic cleansing and that the Tamil leadership was responsible for that?' he asked with some vigour. The veteran ITAK leader was clearly not so used to being spoken to in such a confrontational way by a younger visitor, and he tried to shrug the question with some comments about how the party was ready to represent all Tamil-speaking people and how they were taking positive steps. Rhetorical fireworks ensued. Hasbullah, whom I knew to be an utterly mild-mannered man, fiercely rebuked this woolliness with a sternly raised finger and a seething voice. Senathirajah retorted that Muslim leaders were involved in political games and needed to be more accommodating. 'Then what about the Tamil leaders and the Jaffna bishop?' Hasbullah shot back, hinting at the overtly Tamil nationalist affiliation of the church leader. Having become a bystander to the debate, I waited for the tempers to calm down and politely wrapped up the interview. As so often, the most insightful words were spoken in the margin of this heated exchange. After we got back into our vehicle, the man who was facilitating our stay, himself a politically engaged Jaffna Tamil, said he was flabbergasted at Senathirajah's despotic rhetoric: 'It was like hearing the voice of [President] Rajapaksa!'

These concerns over the plight of minorities under a Tamil nationalist administration were not completely unfounded. In contrast to most other parts of Jaffna, the Muslim neighbourhood on the town's western fringe was still in ruins. Many of the Muslim victims of the 1990 Eviction had not returned, and those who had come back felt that the Tamil leadership gave them stepmotherly treatment, just as the LTTE had done. The position of the Muslims, a small proportion of Jaffna's electorate, was one of the several issues that had long been relegated to the background in Tamil nationalist politics. The end of the war brought the question with its rupturing potential back out in the open.

It was difficult enough for ITAK and the TNA to keep the Tamil ranks closed. They needed a leader who wasn't implicated by the violent and divisive past of Tamil nationalism, a unifying figure who could rise above the parties and proudly stand on par with the anglicised Colombo elite but also embody an innate Tamilness. In that perspective, the party's choice for C. V. Vigneswaran was a master stroke, or so it seemed at the time. A former judge of the Supreme Court, he was senior and articulate. He had unquestionable integrity and would command respect internationally. He was very much a Colombo Tamil, part of the ethnically intermarried elite of central Colombo with a life that was insulated from the war-torn north and east, but he was also an overtly devout Hindu and a quintessentially Tamil persona in terms of his demeanour, dress and diction – not one of the cosmopolitan urbanites despised by many northern Tamils. He had great rhetorical and poetic skills and had not been part of any previous fissures, mudslinging or worse because he was not a politician, let alone a militant. That lack of experience was also a potential problem, but for the time being it seemed an advantage. Vigneswaran in other words, resembled something of a stranger-king (Sahlins 2008; see also Gilmartin 2015) to the postwar Tamil political arena: a leader originating from beyond the bounds of society who nonetheless embodies that society; someone with reverential qualities of being a non-partisan exemplar who is simultaneously elevated above and embedded in a political community.

With the broad TNA alliance, a manifesto that was nationalist but not separatist, and a chief minister candidate with an almost regal aura who could rise above the parties, ITAK had smartly navigated some of the challenges and contradictions of postwar Tamil politics. Given all the historical baggage and the preoccupation with Tamil identity politics, the party did not say much about what it would actually do once in office: no grand development plans were launched in the campaign, no visions of material advancement projected. More than anything else, the impending task of governing the Northern Province was presented as a phase in a larger historical struggle, a phase that had been preceded by periods of both non-violent advocacy and armed liberation struggle and a phase that would not be the end game but a transient stage towards a more meaningful fulfilment of Tamil aspirations. And in view of that trajectory, the primary audience of the ITAK's performance arguably lay abroad. A TNA organiser from Vavuniya phrased it as follows:

> The elections are an important moment for the Tamil people, but they also realise that these elections will not solve the problem. We started as a political struggle, then it became an armed struggle. That is not possible now. So we continue the political struggle.... The government has the responsibility to respect the political choice of the people. If that fails, the international community has to take action. Both armed struggle and political struggle have then failed.

ITAK veteran Mavai Senathirajah alluded to such recourse in similar terms: 'The elections are very internationalised. We see that opportunity. There is no way to solve this internally.' Running for provincial office and governing the northern council was thus primarily a way to give expression to Tamil sentiments and display a constructive attitude to demonstrate that the present constitutional framework of stifled provincial councils was no adequate solution to 'the Tamil problem'. ITAK, in other words, had shifted from the performative anti-politics of a boycott to the performative politics of enacting provincial rule. But it did so *not* with the intention to legitimise the provincial councils (as the EPRLF the Indian federal government had tried so ardently in the 1980s) but to perform their insufficiency: to lay bare the inadequacy of the council.[17] Foreign powers, who were seen as capable of trumping the sovereignty of the Sri Lankan government, were the main target audience of this performance. Rather than an inward-oriented performance of provincial governance, ITAK's strategy was concerned with performing a residual aspiration of external sovereignty – a desperate clutch for the last straws of international recognition for the Tamil plight.

Tamil nationalists in office

The TNA won the northern elections with a landslide 78 per cent of the vote and thirty of the thirty-eight seats. ITAK came first among the TNA constituents with a safe fifteen seats. A quarter century after the Indo-Lankan Accord, the Tamil nationalist leadership thus set out to take hold of both the legislative and executive branch of government within Sri Lanka's arrangement of devolved governance. Vigneswaran was inaugurated as chief minister and set the tone in a public address at the first council meeting on 26 October 2013. The thirteenth amendment (the constitutional basis of the provincial council system), he argued, was 'like a vessel with a hole and seems good for nothing'.[19] He hoped to work with the centre to resolve the underlying issues, but the top priority was to de-militarise the north and release the occupied lands to the rightful owners. His speech gave voice to widely held feelings among the Tamil community, but it was entirely dedicated to issues that the council had negligible power over. The fields that Vigneswaran was empowered to act on – fully devolved subjects like health and education as well as poverty alleviation and agriculture – were hardly mentioned at all.

In subsequent months, the council caused controversy with staunchly Tamil nationalist resolutions on similar non-provincial issues. In January 2014, the TNA-dominated council passed a resolution calling for an international inquiry into 'ethnic cleansing' by government forces in the last stages of the war. After several rounds of debate, the term 'genocide' had been deleted from the resolution.[20] A year later, in February 2015, the council stepped up its efforts and passed a resolution that discussed in detail why government conduct during the war *did* qualify as 'genocide' and called for an 'international mechanism' to redress impunity and an 'international intervention … to ensure a sustainable future for self-determination, peace, and justice, in Sri Lanka and for the Tamil people'.[21]

Almost immediately after assuming office[18], however, questions arose about Vigneswaran's leadership. His conservative Hindu stance on cultural and religious issues instilled a fear that India's militant Hindu nationalism might lay down roots in Jaffna. In addition, there were doubts about Vigneswaran's administrative capacities.[22] His defiance towards the national government raised concern about his ability to broker the support that the north needed. Employment, infrastructure, service provision and economic opportunities were in a dilapidated state.

When I met Vigneswaran in 2019, a year after his term had ended, he agreed that his term in office had been a disappointment: 'I am not used to these things, because I have been in the judiciary. [Before becoming chief minister] I never knew anything about politics.' We were sitting in his residence in Nallur, northern Jaffna. He wore his signature dress, a collarless white robe, and his forehead was adorned with white stripes of sacred ash and a *pottu*. Much in line with his reputation, he was charmingly unpretentious and almost naively candid – if he had spin doctors, he clearly was not taking their cues. He knew that many people were disappointed with his accomplishments, he said, but they did not appreciate the limitations placed on the provincial council. He underlined the central government's long track record of constraining and starving the provincial councils. In their first operational budget, the northern council requested 12 billion rupees but received only 1.6 billion, 'not because the government does not have the money. That's not what happened. All that money was given to central ministers to do work in our province.' And even with the funds they had, the province's work was frustrated from Colombo.

The fall of the Rajapaksa government in 2015 offered Vigneswaran's northern council a much more conducive political environment.[23] The rainbow coalition of the Sirisena government came to power with ITAK backing and on an explicit agenda of addressing the ethno-political conflict. This transformation of the political landscape placed ITAK in a highly unusual position. It had been governing the north as a government adversary – it now became a government ally of sorts. In parliament, ITAK simultaneously positioned itself as a government partner *and* claimed the role of opposition leader.[24] Even if ITAK steered clear of an executive role in Colombo, its hands were closer to the levers of power than they had ever been. And this, combined with their ambitious campaign promises, stoked expectations. As illustrated in the final section, however, the Northern Provincial Council struggled to abandon its combative stance.

In the Eastern Provincial Council, meanwhile, the 2015 change of government prompted a major shift. In the immediate aftermath of Sirisena's presidential inauguration, the eastern board of ministers was reshuffled (see also Klem 2024).[25] The government adopted a supportive attitude to the province and vowed to resolve gridlocked issues, such as the resettlement of Sampur (discussed in Chapter 4). This success cast positive light on ITAK, which had regularly protested, either in situ or in speeches aimed at audiences abroad. The release of Sampur's land was ITAK's victory too. But once return had taken place, the party could no longer hold up Sampur as a scandal. It needed funding now to show that it could actually do something for the returning community. With great effort – and some luck – the responsible ITAK minister managed to mobilise resources,[26] but the loyalties of patronage require constant replenishing. If politicians disappear for too long or arrive empty-handed too frequently, they become the subject of criticism or mockery over their incompetence (cf. Ruud 2009).

This was precisely what happened to ITAK leaders in post-return Sampur, I was told by Nadarajah, a local ITAK organiser whom we encountered in Chapter 4 (where he commented money spent on the temple was 'all wasted') and earlier in this chapter (where he referred to the electoral 'weapon of being Tamil'). Nadarajah campaigned vigorously for ITAK leader Sampanthan, but in private he was critical of the party and its leadership. After 2015, the ITAK leadership was playing a macro-level game, forging a grand bargain with the government and mobilising international pressure in that pursuit. 'Sampanthan only comes to [his home district] Trincomalee for the elections and for the temple festival. People call him the "temple MP" [member of parliament]'. Given the fierce social conflicts over temple honours and *kudi* hierarchies within Sampur's Tamil community, such donations were not effective in nurturing a broad vote base. The 2015 change of government had a decompressing effect on ITAK, he observed. 'As Tamils, we were held together by the torture of the [Rajapaksa] government. That has stopped now, and Tamil politics will unfold.'[27]

Showdown of the Northern Provincial Council

ITAK/TNA leader Sampanthan had foreshadowed a grand constitutional bargain, when he called on Tamil voters to back President Sirisena's coalition in 2015, but negotiations on constitutional reform kept dragging on. Because of their partnership with the government, ITAK's statements became more moderate, much to the dislike of the party base. Meanwhile, the fruits of being in office – as the ruling party of the northern council (2013–2018) and a junior partner in the east (2015–2017) – had been meagre. Both in terms of nationalist aspiration and in terms delivering patronage, the party had disappointed. On the flank of nationalist politics, the Tamil opposition accused ITAK/TNA of squandering the LTTE legacy. Gajen Ponnambalan's ACTC was raking them over the coals for not speaking out to the central government. On the flank of development politics, there was disillusionment about the party's failure to use the northern council apparatus to improve everyday living conditions. The tactic of performing the deficiency of the provincial council system, as an intermediary step for mobilising international pressure, had not shown any returns either – if anything, foreign interest in Sri Lanka appeared to be waning.

Internally, the ITAK/TNA coalition governing the north had fractured. In fact, there had been a complete rupture between Chief Minister Vigneswaran and the rest of his party, and as a result, the council's board of ministers was no longer functional. The only meaningful political office that was still occupied when I visited the council in October 2018 was that of the chairman of the Northern Provincial Council (a role akin to the speaker in parliament).

I had awaited chairman Sivagnanam's return from the public accounts meeting, a large gathering that spans five long days to meticulously review all council expenditure. It was well after office hours when the chairman finally returned to his desk. Despite the preceding meeting, which must have been tedious and tiring, he appeared in no rush, and we talked until late in the evening. This was an ideal time to take stock of the Northern Provincial Council, as it would be dissolved upon completing its first five-year term in the following week. Sivagnanam's lone voice in the silent darkness of an otherwise abandoned provincial council complex matched his despondent account.

After some initial discussion, I wanted to ask about his opinion on the chief minister's credentials and started by saying that many praised Vigneswaran's honesty. Sivagnanam had been leaning back in his office chair, but he suddenly set up straight to interrupt me: 'Correct! He is honest. Financially, he is scrupulously honest. But that is not politics. Being honest is not enough in politics. You must also be a man of action.' Vigneswaran's key responsibility as the Tamil leader of the north was to 'keep his team intact. We have 30 seats of the 38. It should be easy to keep the team together. But he could not.' All of the above-discussed tensions within Tamil nationalist politics had become exposed in mid-2017, when a major schism had occurred, first in the council and then across the whole of ITAK and the TNA. This fissure had everything to do with the dynamics discussed in this chapter: the challenges of combining the repertoires of nationalist politics and patronage politics. Executive office requires political leaders to kickstart the state machinery and get the funds flowing by mobilising networks higher up in the patronage pyramid. This can be done in perfectly legal or not-so-legal ways, but it inevitably generates political adversaries and it makes leaders vulnerable to being tarnished as corrupt (Piliavsky 2014b; Price and Srinivas 2014).

In addition to the 'incorruptible' Chief Minister Vigneswaran, the Tamil executive of the north consisted of four TNA ministers: Ayngaranesan (EPRLF, agriculture), Deniswaran (TELO, fisheries), Kurukularajah (ITAK, education) and Sathiyalingham (ITAK, health). In 2016, Ayngaranesan was accused of administrative irregularities, possibly corruption, and the chief minister insisted on an independent inquiry. The tug of war over that inquiry revealed more irregularities, drawing fire to the other ministers, two of whom were ITAK men. Vigneswaran installed a board of inquiry for all four ministers, but the key witnesses for Ayngaranesan (EPRLF) and Deniswaran (TELO) did not turn up, so they were not found guilty, while Kurukularajah and Sathiyalingham (both ITAK) were. When Vigneswaran threatened to sack all four ministers in one grand clean-up, the party (both ITAK and the broader TNA alliance) pushed back and prepared a no-confidence motion against him.

Tamil politics was thus at risk of a complete, self-implicated breakdown at a key political juncture. At the national level, the Sirisena government had just entered office, and negotiations over a constitutional settlement had started, so there was an urgent need to at least try and stand united. At the level of the Northern Province, this should have been political harvesting time: the years of establishing the institution, having consultations for grand plans and mobilising funding had passed; now was the time to deliver and reap the fruits of all these efforts. ITAK/TNA leader Sampanthan and northern Chief Minister Vigneswaran managed to avert a complete escalation and agreed to a compromise in June 2017. The no-confidence motion was withdrawn and the board of ministers of the Northern Province was replaced. The newly inaugurated ministers were Kandiah Sarveswaran (PLOTE, agriculture), Ananthy Sasitharan (ITAK, women's affairs), Kandiah Sivanesan (EPRLF, education) and Gnanaseelan Gunaseelan (TELO, health). ITAK's new minister Ananthy was noteworthy appointment. She stood out as a rare female leader in an overwhelmingly male-dominated party landscape. Moreover, she was a formidable activist, who was widely known to the public for demanding accountability for her husband, LTTE leader Elilan, one of the many Tamil names on the list of people missing since the war. Her campaign as a widow calling for justice was powerful, and she secured an impressive 87,000 preferential votes, second only to Vigneswaran (Women's Action Network 2013), but commanding a ministry required a different kind of authority.

Soon after her appointment, she started to receive flak for her inability to deliver results. This reflected badly on her party: ITAK's role in the northern council had now been whittled down to one inconspicuous portfolio (women's affairs) held by a minister that lacked political experience.

With the Sampanathan–Vigneswaran deal, the crisis within ITAK and the northern council seemed to have been resolved, but there was a snag. Ironically, given the chief minister's profile as a Supreme Court lawyer, it was a legal one. Vigneswaran had removed Minister Deniswaran from office and told him the official notification would be sent by the governor, but that notice never came. The sacked minister appealed his dismissal, and after various legal procedures, he found the law on his side. In the absence of a formal dismissal letter, Vigneswaran was forced to reinstate Deniswaran in July 2018, but he refused to fire one of the four newly appointed ministers, which would have caused a new political crisis. The northern council was thus left with six ministers (the chief minister, the new four and a reappointed Deniswaran), but the constitution only provides for five. Unlike at the national level where bloated cabinets are the norm, one cannot add a portfolio to a provincial board of ministers. This left the northern council with the political version of the game of musical chairs. The only way forward, to stick with the metaphor, was to keep the music going to avoid having to sit down. The issue remained unresolved, and the next meeting of the board of ministers was deferred indefinitely, until their term ran out a few months later. The first elected Tamil government of the north had set out to demonstrate the deficiencies of the provincial council but ended its term with a defunct executive because of political infighting. As a result of the rivalry between Tamil factions and allegations of corruption, there were six people for five seats and therefore, it had become impossible – practically, politically and constitutionally – for the provincial executive to sit.

Conclusion

The tensions of separatist politics within a democratic arena came out in stark relief in postwar Sri Lanka. The difficulty of democratically contesting the foundational underpinnings of democracy confronted the Tamil nationalist movement with a fundamental problem. As the main Tamil nationalist party, ITAK/TNA could no longer position itself as parliamentary extension of the LTTE, a placeholder of a Tamil state to come. It was destined to participate in – and indeed govern – the democratic institutions that it had pitted itself against on principle grounds. After the annihilation of the LTTE in Mullivaikal, Tamil politics experienced a sense of decompression: all political registers were no longer forcibly aligned into a singular LTTE discourse. ITAK purported to represent the Tamil nation, but opening up the Tamil political arena forced the party to show its colours on issues that divided the Tamil collective.

This chapter placed postwar Tamil politics in the light of political performativity (Geertz 1980; Hansen 2004; Harriss, Stokke and Törnquist 2004; Paley 2008; Siegel 1998; Spencer 2007; Wedeen 2003), with particular attention to the repertoires of anti-politics (Hansen 1999; Spencer 2008). To navigate its postwar predicament, ITAK shifted between three different kinds of anti-political performance, though this evidently involved a very political kind of anti-politics. Each of these, this chapter has shown, came under heightened strain and then faltered, due to the forces of postwar transition.

ITAK's oath-of-allegiance politics, firstly, comprises a repertoire of rituals, historic narratives and nationalist articles of faith. It becomes visible at commemorative events, such as the one at the *thanthai* Chelva memorial, but it is also evident in electoral campaigns wielding, in the words of Nadarajah, 'the weapon of being Tamil' and the diaspora referendums on Tamil nationalist aspirations. It is anti-political in the sense that it is premised on the sphere of a people, their culture, language and history – a set of existential categories that is elevated above the mundane arena of party politics. It is a performance that depicts ITAK as a formation of statesman-like politicians. It steers clear of a left-right ideological divide, plans for running a government and intra-Tamil contentions over caste, clan and gender (which are shrugged under a carpet of broadly conservative cultural positions). Instead, it mobilises voters to testify that they belong to a Tamil nation with a long history of struggle over a well-known set of grievances and aspirations that remain unresolved. This approach continued to be highly effective when the wounds of war were still fresh, as is evident from ITAK/TNA's landslide victory in the 2010 parliamentary elections. But as the years passed, the repertoire of oath-of-allegiance politics started to unravel. ITAK could no longer position itself as the parliamentary avant-garde of the LTTE insurgency. Tamil electoral politics had become more competitive, and a variety of groups was elbowing to claim the political inheritance of liberation struggle.

ITAK's second set of anti-political performances comprises a repertoire of abstinence. Such performances were centrally important in the early decades of the nationalist movement. ITAK was known for its adaptation of Gandhian protest methods, such as *satyagraha* sit-ins – an approach the government struggled to respond to at the time (see the memoires of Jaffna's government agent of the 1960s, Jayaweera 2014: 105–128). The electoral boycott had become a common political instrument. ITAK was adamant about opposing the provincial council system as a hostile Indian implant that disabled a genuine solution to the Tamil problem. As substantiated in the previous chapter, these reservations were not completely unfounded – arguably, the provincial councils *were* politically impotent. ITAK therefore boycotted the 2008 Eastern Provincial Council elections, as it had done during the first original NEPC elections of 1988. Political abstinence carries the risk of turning into political absence, however. The 2008 boycott gave buoyancy to a rival form of Tamil executive politics: the outfit of Pillayan, propped up by the Rajapaksa government. After the LTTE defeat, boycotting the provincial council was no longer a tenable position for ITAK. It would be outflanked by more potent Tamil parties, and it risked being relegated to the annals of history. Despite its principled objections, ITAK therefore participated in the subsequent elections in the east (2012) and north (2013).

ITAK's participation in these elections then promulgated its third kind of anti-political performance: governing as a demonstration of institutional deficiency. Having assumed responsibility to govern the north with a landslide 78 per cent victory and a thirty (out of thirty-eight) seat majority for the TNA, ITAK needed to engage in real bargaining over coalitions, portfolios and all the manoeuvring, scheming and cunning that comes with executive politics. And it needed to take responsibility towards minorities within the northeast: most obviously the northern Muslim community but also marginalised communities of particular religions, castes, classes and regions within Tamil society. ITAK took on this challenge by assuming office on the explicit position that the provincial councils were a halfway house in the longer historical trajectory of pursuing Tamil aspirations. This yielded a peculiar form of political performance aimed at revealing the shortcomings of the system they governed, while simultaneously preserving the party's reputation as a capable and credible aspirant to state power. This produced myriad tensions, and the outcomes reflected badly on ITAK.

The entrenched political aspirations of Tamil nationalist parties do not easily combine with the pragmatic manoeuvring of patronage politics. In the east, party leader Sampanthan was lambasted for being a 'temple MP' who neglected his constituency, and ITAK struggled to carve out a role for itself in the reconstruction of Sampur. In the north, accomplishments were even more sobering. Even with a vast majority in the provincial council and in a firm position of power as kingmaker to Sirisena's national government, ITAK/TNA struggled to channel funding to the region they governed. To make matters worse, Vigneswaran's administration had fallen prey to allegations of corruption and political mudslinging, which eventually resulted in the self-implicated breakdown of the first ever elected Tamil government of the north. Rather than performing the deficiency of the provincial council system, ITAK/TNA had exhibited its own shortcomings. To stick with Vigneswaran's inaugural metaphor: the provincial ship of state went down, not because it was leaky but because it was wrecked by a poorly executed mutiny against a swaying captain.

Notes

1 This text is widely available in English translation. See, for example, https://www.sangam.org/FB_HIST_DOCS/vaddukod.htm (accessed 15 November 2023).

2 The TNA was created on 22 October 2001, by four parties: the TULF, the ACTC (previously part of the TULF), the Tamil Eelam Liberation Organisation (TELO) and the Eelam People's Revolutionary Liberation Front (EPRLF).

3 This phrase has been attributed to Ketesh Loganathan.

4 The position of the TULF in this process adds yet another layer of complexity. TULF leader V. Anandasangaree, a staunch LTTE opponent, resisted the creation of the TNA (after he was himself kept out by the LTTE). While almost the entire party joined the TNA, he persisted in his opposition, forcing the other TULF members to revive ITAK (the main TULF constituent) as their political vehicle. As a result, the TNA ran under the icon of ITAK's house, rather than the TULF's sun.

5 In contrast to India's Bharatiya Janata Party, Tamil nationalists resorted to anti-politics from the arguably rather more suppressed position of an ethnic minority.

6 This text is widely available on the internet. See, for example, Canadian Broadcasting Cooperation, https://www.cbc.ca/news/canada/toronto/tamil-canadians-vote-for-independent-state-in-sri-lanka-1.810846 (accessed 15 November 2023).

7 These referendums were puzzling on several fronts. What to make of a plebiscite on an article of faith? With what legitimacy could those who had left Sri Lanka decide over the plight of those who had not? And how to deal with the profound contradictions of a transnational community vying for a nationalist cause, a sovereign claim by people who had become foreign citizens and the validation of an ethno-territorial (and potentially xenophobic) discourse by a de-territorialised electorate domiciled in dispersed multi-cultural societies? The referendums remained inconsequential (when considered in the formal legal and political terms through which referendum outcomes are normally effected). But as a political performance, they were a significant articulation of citational practice – what had started with ITAK leader opting out of Sri Lanka's sovereign constitutional arrangement in the 1970s (and had been reiterated at key junctures like the 1985 Thimpu talks, Perumal's 1990 unilateral declaration of independence and the 2003 ISGA proposal) now continued on a transnational level.

8 Sampanthan swept the Tamil vote in Trincomalee in 2010 and easily secured his parliamentary seat, as did the vast majority of his party men across the north and east, with the exception of the Jaffna islands (a known stronghold of the Eelam People's Democratic Party) and some electorates along the east coast where Karuna's electoral outfit and the Muslim vote challenged ITAK in some seats.

9 See, for example, Banerjee on 'vote bahiskar' (Banerjee 2014: 155–158).

10 On several key junctures, ITAK decided not to abstain from political participation. Most saliently, ITAK briefly joined Senanayake's 'national government' in 1965 and M. Thiruchelvam, a leading ITAK member, became the cabinet minister for local government. A more recent example was the first postwar presidential election in 2010, when voters could choose between Mahinda Rajapaksa (who had presided over LTTE defeat and the brutal military campaign leading up to it) and Sarath Fonseka (the most senior army general in charge of that very campaign) – if there ever was a race without a remotely reasonable choice for Tamils, this was it. But ITAK did not boycott these elections and advised its supporters to vote for who it thought would be the lesser evil: Fonseka.

11 In both cases, the boycotts tipped the election to favour a belligerent Sinhala nationalist candidate. In 1982 (the first presidential race), the boycott enabled Jayawardena to gain an absolute majority; in 2005, the boycott (which was clearly driven by LTTE instructions) helped paved the way for Mahinda Rajapaksa's victory.

12 In 2006, the Supreme Court had declared the merging of the North-Eastern Province unconstitutional. The resulting demerger came into effect in January 2007 and cleared the way for elections in the east, while the war continued in the north.

13 The turnout was 66 per cent in a province where Tamils comprise 40 per cent of the electorate. According to Department of Census and Statistics (2012) data, the Eastern Province was home to 39.79 per cent Tamils, 36.72 per cent Muslims and 23.14 per cent Sinhalese. In the 1971 census, this was 43.89 per cent (Tamils), 34.86 per cent (Muslims) and 20.69 per cent (Sinhalese). While the overall turnout was similar in the next elections of the Eastern Provincial Council (66 per cent), the turnout in the Tamil dominated districts Batticaloa and Trincomalee was several per cent point lower in 2008 (61 and 62 per cent respectively) than in 2012 (64 and 67 per cent).

14 The mainstream Sinhala-dominated SLFP and two Muslim parties organised around strongmen: the All Ceylon Muslim Congress (ACMC, led by Rishad Badiutheen) and National Congress (NC, led by A. L. M. Athaulla). Both constituents had expected the president to give their candidate the chief minister post, rather than inexperienced Pillayan, who was considered by many as a former terrorist.

15 My thinking on this issue has been informed by Chulani Kodikara who kindly shared with me her work-in-progress article (under review with the *Journal of the Royal Anthropological Institute*) on the dynamics of cultural pride and shame in relation to the UNHRC.

16 https://www.colombotelegraph.com/index.php/full-text-tnas-northern-provincial-council-election-manifesto-2013/ (accessed 22 May 2021).

17 A similar, though arguably more dramatic, performative effort of incriminating one's own institution may be found at the end of Hansen's *Wages of Violence*

(2001: 227), where he describes Shiv Sena leader Ramesh Vaiti, who – as the elected mayor of Thane – participates in a Shiv Sena riot that ransacks his own office.

18 The caption of this section (Tamil nationalists in office) resonates with Nicole Watt's book *Activists in Office* (2010) on the manoeuvring of Kurdish nationalists in Turkey who are elected at a provincial level.

19 https://www.thehindu.com/news/international/south-asia/sri-lanka-northern-council-holds-historic-first-session/article5273775.ece (accessed 22 May 2021).

20 http://dbsjeyaraj.com/dbsj/archives/27637 (accessed 22 May 2021).

21 https://www.tamilguardian.com/content/npc-passes-resolution-asking-un-investigate-genocide-tamils-sri-lanka-state?articleid=13726 (accessed 22 May 2021).

22 Some of the problems of Vigneswaran's provincial administration were self-inflicted. In the first weeks of his tenure, a dispute with his chief secretary (the most senior civil servant of the council), Mrs Vijiyalakshmi, escalated to damaging proportions. Since such senior staff are part of the national civil service, not the provincial one, there were fears that the loyalties of Vijiyalakshmi (who is Sinhalese) would lie with President Rajapaksa. To pre-emptively rein Vijiyalakshmi in, instructions were issued to prevent her from leaving the province or communicating with the central government without Vigneswaran's permission. This attempt to display overlordship backfired. 'She took me to the Supreme Court, and I was about to lose the case', Vigneswaran admitted. He had to withdraw his decision to avoid an affront at the bar. This defeat reflected badly on him. Much of his authority derived from having been a Supreme Court judge himself. As a result, one of my informants commented: 'the secretaries [senior bureaucrats] felt the chief minister could not be relied on. If he can't even confront his own chief secretary.... So they wanted to play safe from then on.'

23 In the run-up to the 2015 presidential elections, scheduled by Rajapaksa himself to get a fresh mandate at a time of his choosing, a remarkable rainbow coalition of hitherto archenemies emerged behind one of his renegade ministers, Maithripala Sirisena, who became the joint opposition candidate. Vital support to Sirisena's victory came from ITAK/TNA. The party successfully called on its voters to support Sirisena, foreshadowing that the Tamil problem would be resolved, no less, under the next administration. Upon their victory, the Sirisena government established a whole suite of *yahapalana* (good governance) measures and initiated negotiations with the Tamil leadership on constitutional reform and ethnic power-sharing. However, soon after, these initiatives balked and the coalition started showing the first signs of disintegration.

24 The 'leader of the opposition' is an official title in Sri Lanka, which comes with certain privileges and resources. In political terms, it was obvious that Mahinda Rajapaksa (the defeated former president) led the opposition: he commanded

many more members of parliament and, unlike Sampanthan's TNA, he avidly opposed the Sirisena government. However, given that Rajapaksa was technically a member of the SLFP, the same party as his rival presidential candidate Sirisena, the post of opposition leader went to the TNA.

25 No new elections were held, but the main Muslim party – the Sri Lanka Muslim Congress (SLMC) – changed alliance and joined hands with the Tamil ITAK/TNA. Two ITAK ministers were newly inaugurated: opposition leader S. Thandayuthapani (from Trincomalee) became the education minister; K. Thurairajasingham (from Batticaloa) was put in charge of agriculture. The fifth minister (Ariyawathi Galappaththi, SLFP) was appointed minister for road development. In addition, and arguably more significantly, the governor of the Eastern Province, retired Admiral Mohan Wijewickrama, was replaced by a veteran civil servant, Austin Fernando.

26 India, one of the few donors still active in Sri Lanka, supported a housing reconstruction project in Sampur, but ITAK was not involved in the delivery of such assistance. The provincial minister of education (Thandayuthapani, who also had personal links to Sampur) was also responsible for resettlement, but this portfolio came with a mere 17 million rupees (roughly 95,000 US dollars), as he told me. Almost all resettlement work was administered by the central line ministry. Coincidentally, one of the big World Bank projects from the 2000s (the North-East Local Service Improvement Project, NELSIP) had a final line of funding left. It was not designed for what Thandayuthapani wanted to do, but with a slight creative adjustment, unspent funds could be deployed for reconstruction in Sampur. What comprised leftovers for the World Bank represented a patronage goldmine for ITAK minister Thandayuthapani. 297 million rupees (about 1.6 million US dollars) could be disbursed under his tutelage for roads, schools and health centres.

27 When I met Nadarajah in 2018, he had left ITAK and returned to his first love in Tamil politics, EROS, which was gradually coming back to life as a political party. His political enthusiasm was back. When I met him again in 2019, EROS had also disappointed him. He had started a restaurant and was no longer active in politics.

7 Conclusion

Big questions sometimes present themselves in small form. The grand themes of Sri Lanka's contemporary history – its quagmire of nationalist politics, the hampered solution of provincial devolution and the incessant friction between constitutional, administrative and political realities – became manifest in the minutiae of a marginal bureaucratic problem when I was in Colombo in October 2019. For just a moment, all the central concerns of this book were folded into a discussion between a civil servant and a constitutional lawyer about a topic that would never have occurred to me as one of my research interests: the appointment of schoolteachers.

I was attending a seminar titled 'Thirty Years of Devolution' at the Galadari Hotel in the historical heart of the capital. Constitutional experts were launching a book (Amarasinghe et al. 2019) to an audience of civil servants: chief secretaries and legal officers from various provinces. The debate centred on the unresolved problems of the provincial council system three decades after its creation. Any talk of fixing devolution felt like a rear-guard battle, though. We all knew that the world outside our elegant conference room had moved on. Whatever had been left of the consultative process on constitutional reform, which had started with much excitement under the Sirisena–Wickremesinghe government in 2015, had been thrown off the rails by the constitutional crisis of 2018 (Welikala 2020). The governing coalition had become defunct. The country was now holding its breath for the presidential elections, which would be in two weeks. Until the race between Sajith Premadasa (United National Party, or UNP) and Gotabaya Rajapaksa (Sri Lanka Podujana Peramuna, or SLPP[1]) was adjudicated, all other political matters were on hold. Quite literally so at the provincial level: by now, all councils had been dissolved. Their term had expired, but new elections had been postponed time and again due to a stalemate over electoral system reform. In effect, we had entered a new 'interim period' where the provinces were ruled by presidential appointees (the governors) rather than elected politicians (the provincial council and the board of ministers), not just in the north and east this time but in all nine provinces.

The intricacies of schoolteacher appointments arose when the keynote speaker wrapped up his talk on the constitutional challenges of provincial devolution and one of the participants raised his hand. The teacher nominations that his province was grappling with were explicitly mentioned on the 'devolved list' of the thirteenth amendment: the constitutional turf of the province. But without elected councillors, who could act on this prerogative? Would it be constitutional for the governor to appoint these teachers? After all, as a presidential appointee, he did not have a mandate from the provincial electorate. The central education ministry had gone ahead and appointed teachers at provincial schools and was now asking the province for consent, but who was there to give or withhold it? Several participants started leafing through their booklet copy of the constitution and the provincial council act. The initial spell of frowning and consternation soon gave way to agitated debate and snigging in small groups around the room. The trouble was that the constitution framed these prerogatives as a governor's decision based on the 'advice' of the chief minister (and the provincial board of ministers). But what did advice mean? The prevalent interpretation among constitutional experts was that this was a grandiloquent phrase for what in fact amounted to an order, but what if the governor interpreted this advice as just another opinion that he might heed or not?

'Even if the statute empowers the minister', one of the provincial officers interjected, 'we often see the governor taking decisions'. Her tone and gestures suggested that she thought that this was just how it was – why make a big fuss over it? 'But', the keynote speaker riposted, 'the drafters of the constitution never anticipated a situation where the councils are dissolved for such a long time'. One of the chief secretaries (the top provincial administrator) scratched his chin and suggested that the council's chairperson (an elected councillor with a role akin to speaker of the house) could be a possible way out: 'The chairman stays when the council is dissolved …' The keynote speaker paused to appraise this suggestion and then responded: 'But there may be cases where the chairman dies or faces disciplinary action. Then the chief secretary does not have the power to appoint teachers on behalf of the council, so who is there?' Chuckled laughter across the room. 'What does the constitution expect us to do if nobody is empowered to take disciplinary action against a teacher who engaged in misconduct?' More laughter. 'Why on earth does the thirteenth amendment specifically mention schoolteachers but not other officers?' asked one of the participants. 'I don't know,' the constitutional expert replied with a smile, 'I did not write it'. Another civil servant sat up and asked with a slightly worried voice: 'Does this also apply to sport teachers?' A new spate of questions and concerns ensued.

My empirical account started with the institutional jungle across the frontline in Sampur, an east coast backwater, a decade before the end of the war. It ends with a debate between lawyers and civil servants in a boutique hotel in Colombo a decade after the war. Very different times, very different places, but many parallels. When we start dissecting the multitude of institutions that we call the Sri Lankan state, what emerges is a Gordian knot of constitutional principles, administrative structures, political interference and violent impositions. We encounter a lived reality that is shaped by all the official rules and stipulations but which at the same time diverges radically from the original institutional design. Deliberation on the adequate constitutional form for sharing the sovereignty of a diverse nation eventually results in bureaucratic tribulations over schoolteacher appointments. And vice versa, the workaday improvisation of marginal administrators complicates and compromises the manifestation of the state's constitutional composition.

This book has untangled some of these complicated institutional realities. I have taken a performative perspective on political contestation to show that the lived reality of political order is produced in friction with the legal and political architecture of the state. An analysis of separatist conflict should not be held hostage to these formal categories, neither should it simply surrender to militant claims. In navigating this epistemic battlefield, this book has shown that the Tamil nationalist movement encompasses several competing political repertoires. Among these, the Liberation Tigers of Tamil Eelam's (LTTE) sovereign experiment (Chapter 3) was dominant for two decades, but this effort interacted with other performative experimentation, particularly those emerging from within the Tamil-dominated bureaucracy (Chapter 5) and the democratic arena of Tamil nationalist parties (Chapter 6). Each of these parallel trajectories of political performativity had a probationary character. They advanced through improvised citational practice, bending state rationalities and gaining implied acceptance, and as such the status and significance of these performative experiments were always contingent and precarious. Junctures that opened new space for manoeuvre were followed by moments of rupture, curtailment or complete erasure. With the faltering of one experiment, others regained potency, causing the political centre of gravity of the Tamil nationalist movement to shift, thus yielding new constellations and performative adaptation.

These observations resonate beyond the new-built houses of Sampur, the government offices in Trincomalee and the rally grounds in Jaffna. This final chapter brings the different analytical threads of my analysis back together and discusses their broader merits and ramifications. The first two sections take stock of my findings to, first, revisit the theoretical problems of sovereignty and, second, review the merits of a performative perspective in addressing these problems. The third section appraises broader implications of my analysis for the scholarship on insurgent governance, on violent democratic politics and on the lived realities of war. I will close with a section to discuss whether devolution, as a constitutional antidote to conflict, has a future in Sri Lanka.

Revisiting sovereignty

Sovereignty is the ultimate mark of state power, and as such it is the notion through which states and national citizenship are legitimised, but it has no referent that lends itself to adjudication. International law (as codified in the 1933 Montevideo convention) premises the right to sovereign self-determination on the existence of a defined territory, a permanent population, a government and a capacity to enter into relations with other states, but these benchmarks offer little solace to sovereign aspirants. After all, such sovereign characteristics are typically a historical consequence, rather than a prerequisite, of state-building (Anderson 2006 [1983]; Anghie 1999; Benton 2009; Chatterjee 1993; Mukherjee 2010; Hansen and Stepputat 2005; Pahuja 2011; Purushotham 2021). The question of self-determination is not a matter of ground realities meeting the criteria; it is drenched in violent political struggles over making and interpreting ground realities.

Sovereign power is capricious. It does not merely harbour disciplinary force but also (*pace* Foucault 1997) excessive violence. It is encoded in the law but produced through violence, and (*pace* Schmitt 2005 [1922]) it ultimately centres on the sovereign exception of suspending the law. It is typically legitimised in a political idiom of state benevolence but (*pace* Kantorowicz 1997 [1957]) needs recourse to the transcendental to make sense. The central quality of sovereignty, as Gilmartin (2015, 2020) points out, is that its contradictions are inherently irresolvable. Sovereignty is intractable because it simultaneously constitutes the moral framework that legitimises the power, legal authority and violent capacities of the state *and* the ability to supersede this framework – to change the rules, to invent exceptions, to unleash violence. Rather than seeking to resolve or circumvent these tensions, this book has placed the unsettled nature of sovereignty at centre stage, thus making the book *about* the intractability of sovereignty, which then forces us to critically reflect on the way we understand and diagnose conflict.

Sri Lanka's postcolonial constitutional settlement and subsequent debates on the devolution of state power grappled with the notion of shared sovereignty, but these efforts crumbled in face of the contradictions inherent to that term: how to draft rules for sharing a kind of power that encompasses the ability to break the rules? Rather than serving as a framework of redress (mitigating ethno-nationalist conflict with an inclusive constitutional arrangement), Sri Lanka's constitution became a primary corrosive. The government's 'unilateral' constitution of the early 1970s definitively estranged the Tamil leadership, who demonstratively stepped away from this new legal framework and declared it invalid to the Tamil nation. With the escalation of political hoodwinking and violent confrontation in the 1970s and 1980s, contestation over sovereignty changed vessel, and the LTTE violently advanced the aspiration of Tamil separatism by gradually establishing 'de facto sovereign' structures.

In the 1990s, the LTTE established an elaborate institutional framework – grafted onto its violent control over Tamil society – to enact Tamil Eelam as an independent state in the making and then tried to sediment this disciplinary regime with self-authored legal underpinnings. This sovereign experiment was rife with tensions. The movement crafted new institutions by mimicking state departments but also co-opted existing state institutions. It emulated a procedural form of order with courts and departments but simultaneously remained unruly: recourse to ruthless violence was always a possibility, and the movement's *talaivar* (leader) Prabhakaran remained an ungraspable figure. While these tensions arguably apply to recognised states as well, they are especially stark with an insurgent movement like the LTTE. To bolster the territorial establishment of a de facto Tamil Eelam, the LTTE tried to appropriate external sovereignty by taking its sovereign performance to the international level during the peace process of the 2000s. The preparedness of the Norwegian mediators to treat the LTTE like a state – an entity on par with the Sri Lankan government – offered the LTTE an entry point into the circular logics of sovereign recognition. However, the apparent symmetry of the Norwegian peace effort was situated in a regional and global environment that considered the LTTE in staunchly asymmetrical terms. The peace process gave the LTTE an unusually conducive platform to vie for external sovereignty, but when that scaffolding collapsed, the downfall came with heavy repercussions: the sovereign erasure of 2009. The de facto LTTE state was wiped out, and its leader Prabhakaran, the ultimate referent of LTTE sovereign power, was killed. Acts committed in his name lost their validation. Any claim to insurgent legality became null and void. The government military victory reaffirmed Sri Lanka's unchallenged sovereignty and marked the triumph of an all-Sri Lankan nation concept over rival renditions of nationalism.

The notion of shared sovereignty suffered a slow death after the war – though one can never rule out a reincarnation. The regional autonomy arrangement of the provincial councils had once alluded to a compromised form of self-government, but the abilities of the councils crumbled precisely because they lacked the necessary sovereign underpinnings: control over land, bureaucracy, law-making, tax collection. As a result, provincial governance was legally truncated and starved of resources. In institutional terms, the councils were remarkably resilient throughout the years of war and the subsequent decade of highly centralised government. But in order to function, ironically, they needed to surrender the ambition they were created for: a form (however minimal) of self-government. The eastern council, in particular, eschewed playing an openly political role and thus degenerated into a regional welfare distribution scheme.

The end of the war brought the plight of Tamil nationalism full circle to the legal-political tensions around sovereignty of the 1970s, if in even starker form. The LTTE defeat left the Tamil nationalist movement in a precarious position. From the early 2000s Ilankai Tamil Arasu Kadchi (ITAK) (and its wider political platform, the Tamil National Alliance [TNA]) had positioned itself as a democratic extension of the LTTE struggle, a political placeholder for a Tamil state to come. After the LTTE defeat, this no longer made sense. ITAK had no recourse to the de facto sovereignty of the LTTE, and it struggled to project a credible pathway to a future sovereign Tamil state. It had difficulty presenting itself as a state-like representative of the Tamil nation because Tamil politics had once more become a diverse arena. To retain political relevance, ITAK was forced to engage in intra-Tamil party politics and run for office. In that context, it could no longer defer the fundamental contradiction between the Tamil nationalism it propagated (which rejected the sovereign underpinnings of the Sri Lankan nation and state) and the Sri Lankan democratic framework through which it tried to do so (which embroiled ITAK in the sovereign constellation it opposed).

The literature on Sri Lanka's ethno-political conflict attends to these issues (Edrisinha et al. 2008; Ludsin 2012; Saunders and Dziedzic 2012; Spencer 2007; Welikala 2012a; A. J. Wilson 2000), but the question of sovereignty is rarely confronted head on. My account underlines the need to explicate the intractability of sovereignty. Skimming over this yields a whole range of imbalances and omissions. For example, the question of sovereignty underlines that government recourse to the law (branding the LTTE as illegal, rejecting proposals as unconstitutional) is self-referential. Conversely, the Tamil nationalist claim to self-determination follows a systematic but similarly circular reasoning. Ultimately, it pivots on a question that is impossible to adjudicate, for both lawyers and social scientists: Do the Tamils constitute a nation, and is the northeast of Sri Lanka their homeland? The de facto state institutions created by the LTTE projected their own self-referential logic of national demarcation, law, institutions and violence. It was de facto sovereign in its capacity to autonomously exercise discipline, but the qualification de jure sovereignty spawns more questions: What basis do we have to judge the legal, political and moral underpinnings of a sovereign Tamil state? Both international law and democratic theory are implicated by the circular logics between the definition of a national community, moral claims to self-determination, the legal and political codifications of sovereign statehood and the political dynamics of international recognition.

The absence of a firm normative or analytical framework to resolve these questions deserves reiteration because this fundamental problem is often clouded in the discursive projections of democracy, the rule of law and institutional legitimacy. This became especially obvious after the war. To understand the reservations of Tamil nationalists about postwar power-sharing, autonomy, minority protection and development, we must confront the fact that such proposals are contingent on the bootstrapping logics of the Sri Lankan constitution, and these derive from the sovereign power of the Sri Lankan state. And as such, these purported compromises are ultimately steeped in the violent assertion of sovereignty on the battlefields of the Vanni, where the massacres of the war's final offensives took place. To recognise the self-referential nature of sovereignty is to face the analytical swamp beneath our feet: our inability to adjudicate the fundamental questions underpinning the demarcation of sovereign states, the justification of democratic consent and the foundation of law. It cautions us to be more transparent about how the intractability of sovereignty raises questions that we tend to avoid, and how the analytical choices we make tend to stabilise the order and knowledge systems of recognised sovereign powers at the cost of sovereign aspirants that seek to challenge them.

Insurgent performativity

The empirical shape that government institutions and interventions take in practice may radically diverge from the way they are supposed to look from an official standpoint. Some institutions assume a role that differs from their legal mandate: some have a powerful mandate but become irrelevant; others do not have an official mandate but play a big role. The practices and performances of an institution are thus no derivative of its legal authorisation; rather, they are in constant interaction with this authorisation. This is an important analytical premise because a large body of scholarship has been dedicated to identifying suitable constitutional designs and institutional architectures for conflict-ridden societies. Constitutional reform with a new institutional architecture for power-sharing may be a prerequisite for an inclusive settlement of some sort (Bastian and Luckham 2003; Choudry 2008; Reynolds 2002; Rothchild and Roeder 2005; Stern and Druckman 2000), but however brilliant a constitutional design the negotiators come up with, its actual shape and functionality will likely change beyond recognition when exposed to the forces of politics. A steadfast focus on defining institutional mandates sits uneasily with the widespread realisation that politicians routinely break the rules. Many South Asians would consider such transgressive practices normal politics (Klem and Suykens 2018; Michelutti et al. 2018; Mines 1994; Piliavsky 2014a; Price and Ruud 2014; Ruud 2009; Spencer 2007; Witsoe 2013). Setting norms is not the exclusive domain of those who write the lawbook or bargain over a new constitutional settlement. It is also shaped by the way conflict belligerents enact the political landscape in everyday reality.

I have therefore turned to the rich literature in political anthropology (Bertrand, Briquet and Pels 2007; Hansen 2001; Michelutti et al. 2018; Paley 2008; Siegel 1998; Spencer 2007; Wedeen 2003) and related fields (Gregson and Rose 2000; Haraway 1997; Harriss, Stokke and Törnquist 2004; McConnell 2016; Leigh and Weber 2018). This scholarship places official mandates aside and instead explores institutions through their everyday enactment (Geertz 1980; Goffman 1959; Hansen 2009; Rutherford 2012). It is often through symbolic performativity and spectacle that political institutions assume meaning in society. Such performance is not a mere façade to an otherwise rational order of the state – this staging of power and authority, so the argument goes, is what the state *is* (Abrams 1988 [1977]; Geertz 1980; Gilmartin 2012; Hansen 2001; Mitchell 1991). Many political entities are in fact 'twilight institutions' (Lund 2006); they may be subject to 'institutional bricolage' (Douglas 1970), and they are often replicated through 'citational practice' (Weber 1995) or 'mimicry' (Bhabha 1994).

This perspective opens the door for sovereign aspirants, of which the LTTE was but one example, to stage their authority in forms that people recognise as state-like – and lay the legal foundations afterwards (Klem and Maunaguru 2017; McConnell 2016; Watts 2010; Alice Wilson 2016). They are 'rehearsing the state', to use McConnell's (2016) phrase, in aspiration of a future status. They engage in 'make-believe' politics (Navaro-Yashin 2012) and a subversive variant of 'as-if' politics (Watts 2010) to instil probationary subjectivities and project political imaginaries. The implied logic of the institutional design literature suggests that legal foundations define what is normal, and institutions are shaped on that basis. Insurgencies and unrecognised states remind us that this logic may be reversed: institutions are performed to make them look normal, which then enables them to grow legal roots.

Yet, when sovereign aspirants unfold their own institutional landscape, the performative effort of depicting this apparatus as real and authentic embodies its own denial. It is simultaneously factual and factitious (Bryant and Hatay 2020: 20–21, 269–271). The state-like institutions of an insurgency derive significance from their transgressive character – the very fact that they exist is a source of amazement. And because of their aspirational outlook and their backdrop of unresolved grievances, these institutions inevitably exhibit their own incompletion and ambivalence. They must be provisional to be credible. Sovereign experimentation, as I have argued in this book, comprises contingent and precarious institutional performance, which is invariably conjugated with the institutional frameworks that it seeks to quash, supplant, subjugate or co-opt.

Examples of creative institutional performance – with varying degrees of transgression – abounded throughout this book. The 1970s Bandaranaike government transformed parliament (a body *conferred by* the constitution) into a constituent assembly (a body *conferring* a new constitution). Provincial Chief Minister Perumal in 1990 replicated this legal gambit – though with much less impact – when he declared the provincial council authorised to draft the constitution of an independent Tamil state. Tamil nationalists engaged in demonstrative walkouts, marches and sit-ins, each part of a transgressive repertoire that uses public state arenas to contrarian ends. As an extension of this repertoire, they shifted the political significance of elections by discursively turning them into constitutional plebiscites or by boycotting them to voice political dissent. Understanding the significance of these institutions – and the manoeuvring around them – is clearly not just a matter of consulting the lawbook to verify their official status.

During the war, performative innovation went well beyond legal finesse and institutional tweaking. LTTE performativity set out to rewrite the political landscape altogether. To enact a de facto state, the movement founded departments without a legal basis (or rather, it founded the legal basis along with the departments), and it co-opted elements of state bureaucracy to work towards its separatist aim. Institutional mimicry and encroachment were central to this performative practice. The LTTE enacted state institutions in ways that its subject population could easily recognise as such: they closely resembled the institutions of the Sri Lankan state, which they were supposed to supplant. At the same, the awe and excitement about the LTTE's conduct underlined that its normalising performance was not in fact so normal at all. After all, the movement's institutional framework was underpinned by a martial cult of devotion, sacrifice and martyrdom, and it established a cadre of boys and girls that lopsided many of the traditional norms and hierarchies of Tamil society. And when it managed to sustain itself, despite government attacks, 'the boys' (the masculine vernacular euphemism for the LTTE) put on suits and travelled to distant countries to be received by foreign dignitaries. During the ceasefire period in the 2000s, the LTTE boosted its state performance in the Vanni and expanded its performative repertoire to international diplomatic circles, giving rise to a radical experiment in political theatre. The movement dispatched diplomatic teams to other continents, started formalising its borders with customs officers and hosted foreign delegations with measured diplomatic pomp to showcase its emerging state.

Boundaries were tested and pushed from all sides. The LTTE's theatrical experiment raised excitement precisely because it was precarious: it was not so clear what the LTTE would get away with and for how long. The moment of truth could not be averted indefinitely. The peace process collapsed and, in the resulting showdown, the LTTE was rapidly pushed on the defensive. Its performative action on the international stage lost its validating stage and audience and was at risk of impressing as farcical. Its elaborate institutional architecture in the Vanni crumbled. When the movement finally perished, the government put Prabhakaran's corps on photographic display and built ostentatious victory monuments to lay claim to the land.

In parallel to the rise and fall of the de facto LTTE state, the everyday institutional practices of state departments continued. In contrast to the spectacular performativity of the insurgency, these bureaucratic efforts were a story of procedural hedging, compromise and institutional tenacity. The civil service adapted to the shifting tectonic plates of the war. Government bureaucrats continued to work in LTTE-held territory, and the LTTE started percolating into the purportedly adversarial institutions of the government. This was particularly poignant in the provincial council. The North-Eastern Provincial Council (NEPC) has received little serious public or scholarly attention but embodies a unique crumble zone between competing assertions of sovereignty. It was used by Indian peacemakers to enact a moderated version of Tamil self-government in the 1980s and was then subjected to the institutional encroachment of the LTTE in the 1990s. During the peace process of the 2000s, the NEPC emerged as a nucleus for experimenting with informal shared governance between the LTTE and the government, bankrolled by development donors. After the war, the LTTE's remote control over provincial bureaucratic apparatus was replaced by a different kind of interference: the tricks and trades of democratic patronage politics. To shield themselves from these pressures, bureaucrats reverted to a similar strategy of keeping politics out by technical and procedural means. To expose attempts to appropriate resources for narrow political ends, civil servants invented new databases, paper trails and unofficial oversight bodies. State institutions were remarkably resilient because of their pliability. Frontlines came and went, a de facto sovereign LTTE state was established and then erased, peace processes took off and then collapsed, and bureaucratic institutions persisted throughout, including highly contentious ones like the NEPC.

Political performance often takes place in pursuit of normalisation – even if this normalcy is premised on its own denial, as discussed earlier – but the reverse may also occur. Aspirational performativity may explicitly exhibit a state of incompletion, of being stuck, of insufficiency, or even absurdity. The anti-political performance of Tamil nationalist parties comprised an effort of counter-normalisation. Expanding on its opposition to the prevalent democratic system in Sri Lanka in the 1970s (with self-declared referenda and electoral mandates for secession), Tamil nationalist parties continued to unsettle the purported normalcy of government institutions after the war. ITAK, the main Tamil party, engaged in oath-of-allegiance politics, providing its constituents with symbolic articles of faith to attest being part of a Tamil nation with unfulfilled aspirations. It also engaged in political abstinence through electoral boycotts to discredit the institution on the ballot during the Eastern Provincial Council elections in 2008. And when it could no longer afford to do that (that is, when it ran for the northern council in 2013), ITAK engaged in the performance of institutional deficiency, governing the northern council so as to demonstrate that the 'leaky boat' of provincial devolution fell short of a solution for the Tamil problem. These three repertoires debunked the legitimacy of Sri Lanka's democratic arena (and the provincial councils in particular) and they imbued ITAK (and their broader TNA alliance) with a heightened level of political significance and authority. However, the line between looking authoritative and losing face can be quite thin. ITAK's anti-political repertoires came under increasing strain after the war, partly because of the increased competition from other Tamil parties. This became most visible with the implosion of the Northern Provincial Council in the period 2016–2018. The crisis within ITAK and other constituent parties of the TNA culminated in a humiliating affront. The council could literally not sit because it had six people for five seats as a result of the schisms between Tamil political factions: a political version of the game of musical chairs. Rather than exhibiting the deficiency of provincial devolution in Sri Lanka, what was on display was the inability of the Tamil leadership to govern.

Broader implications

Some of the political skulduggery and transgression that I describe are routinely mentioned in historical accounts (Edrisinha et al. 2008; Spencer 2007; A. Wilson 2000), and the de facto LTTE state has received academic attention (Hellmann-Rajanayagam 1994b; Korf et al. 2010; Mampilly 2011; Provost 2021; Stokke 2006; Terpstra and Frerks 2018; Trawick 2007). My analysis deepens these insights by highlighting the historical chains of citation and mimicry and the ramifications of such transgressive institutional bricolage. These observations resonate with broader scholarly debates across several fields and disciplines. I will review some pertinent implications and merits by discussing the three fields of study that I started out with in the introductory chapter, respectively: on rebel governance, on violent democratic politics and on the everyday realities of war.

My analyses, especially the observations in Chapter 3, corroborate the broad strokes of the rebel governance literature (Arjona 2016; Arjona, Kasfir and Mampilly 2015; Mampilly 2011; Mampilly and Stewart 2021; Staniland 2014; Provost 2021; Stokke 2006; Terpstra and Frerks 2018). The sophisticated institutional array erected by the LTTE matches the central contention of this literature that insurgent movements are capable of establishing meaningful bureaucratic and judicial institutions. This body of work describes insurgent forms of governance, sometimes in meticulous empirical detail, to refute the narrative of war as anarchy, the reductionism of the terrorism paradigm and the concurrent juridical orthodoxy that no legal thing can emerge from an illegal entity. While my account readily endorses this line of argument, it also points to limitations in the rebel governance literature and offers complementary insight.

Let me illustrate this with reference to the two academic pieces that analyse the LTTE in greatest detail, Mampilly's (2011) account of the LTTE administrative system and Provost's (2021) discussion of the LTTE judiciary. Both are comparative books with a lengthy chapter on Sri Lanka that offers a more detailed overview of LTTE institutions than I have given: the different administrative levels and divisions are listed, the array of departments reviewed, and the framework of laws and courts unravelled. To aid the reader's comprehension of these fine-grained structure, both authors include organograms that depict institutions in different shades and connect them with solid or dotted lines (Mampilly 2011: 117; Provost 2021: 223, 225). Provost even adds table with the complete three-year curriculum of the LTTE law college (Provost 2021: 240), and Mampilly reviews the effectiveness of LTTE governance with indices such as the proportion of underweight babies, the number of completed court cases and school drop-out rates (Mampilly 2011: 110,

118, 123). These analyses, based on interviews and online documents, offer a rich empirical discussion, and they convincingly argue that an insurgent movement can establish effective administrative order (Mampilly 2011) and that it is imperative to countenance rebel jurisdiction in the margins of international law (Provost 2021).

These merits notwithstanding, there is something uneasy about the overriding tidiness of these accounts.[2] The rundown of institutions and the graphs depicting mandates and hierarchies instil a narrative that this is simply how it was: these were the laws, these were the courts, these were the duties of the education council, this is where they were in the hierarchy and these were their accomplishments. But in each of these assertions, the affirmative verb 'were' stands in the interpretative place of a Shakespearian question: 'To be or not not to be?' An overly formalistic rendition of LTTE institutions shrouds the central socio-political dynamic around this institutional framework (not least among the supposed Tamil subjects), which was one of awe and excitement, anticipation and suspense, perturbation and dismay. The LTTE's boldness in presenting its institutional architecture as normal derived political energy and significance from the fact that it was in fact not so normal at all. In short, the rebel governance literature is at risk of offering an academic replication of the LTTE's institutional framework, thus presenting the neat landscape of courts and departments as a discrete phenomenon that is severed from the capricious character of the movement.[3] We know that a rational, instrumental conception of the political arena misses crucial dimensions of politics in well-established democracies like the United States or India (Banerjee 2008, 2014; Spencer 2007) or authoritarian regimes like Syria or Yemen (Wedeen 1999, 2003). It suffers from similar limitations in the context of a separatist insurgency. Projections of legitimate government must be understood as contingent, especially in the context of coercion and violent conflict.

The performative perspective adopted in this book thus complements the rebel governance literature by situating the institutional framework of insurgent rule within a broader arena of contingent performative practices around competing claims to sovereignty. Insurgent experimentation with governing institutions must be considered in conjunction with the inherent uncertainty and unruliness stemming from the transgressive and capricious nature of sovereign performativity. Institutional logics matter, but rather than adopting them as our analytical categories to describe what an institution 'was', they must be understood as part of a performative script. LTTE courts and departments were subject to the probationary character, the dubious status and the uncertain permanence of the movement's sovereign experiment. Institutions could mingle with and encroach on other institutions, or create new offspring;

they could emerge in one era or arena and end up in another. Tamil nationalist parties like ITAK preceded the militancy, were subverted by the LTTE in the 1980s and 1990s, then became its parliamentary mouthpiece in the 2000s and struggled to claim its political inheritance in the 2010s. The NEPC was violently subdued, then co-opted as an interstitial institution and then outlived the LTTE as a resilient but politically moot power-sharing apparatus. What an institution 'was' thus remained uncertain: it could change, sometimes rapidly, and it could assume new meaning and potency, or lose it. As I have shown, the experimentation with institutional bricolage, twisting political entities and self-appropriated legal mandates did not start with the LTTE. These transgressions have a long history – one that escalated with the legal and political hoodwinking of the 1970s and militarised with the pogroms, violent skirmishes and India's military intervention of the 1980s. Similarly, the significance of the LTTE's sovereign experiment did not perish with their 2009 defeat in Mullivaikal. The symbolic repertoires, the institutional precedents *and* their subsequent violent erasure continue to shape the Tamil political consciousness and lend themselves to new forms of citational practice.

Second, the literature on violent democratic politics (Arias and Goldstein 2010; Hagmann and Péclard 2010; Hansen 1999; Hansen and Steppuat 2001, 2005; Michelutti et al. 2018; Peabody 2009; Piliavsky 2014a; A. Sen 2007; Spencer 2007; Witsoe 2013) resonates closely with the malleable institutions, the fluid boundaries and the political trickery that I have described in this book. The pre-war staging of Tamil dissent, the wartime courts and cults of the LTTE and the postwar projection of subversive aspirations all have cognates elsewhere. The most obvious South Asian parallels may be drawn to the political strongmen, revolutionaries and thugs of what Michelutti et al. (2018) describe as 'Mafia Raj'. While many of these figures operate in the democratic arena and the state bureaucracy, they also muster the 'de facto sovereign' (Hansen and Steppuat 2006) capacity to instil their own variant of public discipline: they impose rules, extract resources, adjudicate disputes, mete out penalties, wield armed violence and propagate leadership cults (Hansen and Steppuat 2005; Malik 2018; A. Sen 2007; Spencer 2007; Witsoe 2013).

However, the aspiration of nationalist self-determination distinguishes the LTTE's sovereign experiment (and the Tamil nationalist movement more widely) from the political strongmen that prevail in South Asia's democratic landscape. This bold ideological outlook complicates the relationship with state institutions, and it heightens the significance of international audiences. It necessitates the performance of parity vis-à-vis the state and thus deepens the schizophrenia of operating in a democratic landscape that one rejects on principle grounds. Broadly in the spirit of Hansen and Steppuat's attempt to place diverse manifestations of political authority and de facto sovereignty into one conceptual frame (Hansen and Stepputat 2001, 2005, 2006), the preceding chapters have straddled the spheres of violent insurgency, democratic politics, constitutional law and bureaucratic administration. The NEPC trajectory illustrates this well: it was framed and constrained by Sri Lanka's constitution and administrative structure, but it was deployed to project rival interpretations of sovereignty by the Indian government (in the late 1980s), the LTTE (in the 1990s and 2000s) and the TNA (in the 2010s).

By placing specific episodes of strong-arm politics, insurgent governance and political protest on the broader trajectory of Sri Lanka's ethnopolitical conflict, the tremors of routine political contestation – a fight won, an election lost, patronage wrested or ceded – become connected to the much larger ruptures of the state's tectonic plates that occur when a violent insurgency escalates, transforms and ends. Consider ITAK's postwar repertoires of performative anti-politics. The party engaged in transgression, but as a political outfit, it comprised the inverse of 'Mafia Raj', the rule of the strongmen described in the literature in violent politics in India (Berenschot 2011; Michelutti et al. 2018; Piliavsky 2014a; Witsoe 2013). These strongmen may have great political potency and an ability to project force, but they do not typically have aspirations of establishing a new state. ITAK made every effort to retain that aspiration but lacked political muscle. India's political bosses have a sovereign capacity but no ambition of formal sovereign status; ITAK has the ambition but not the capacity. As a result, ITAK's political performativity did not project the agentive ability and intractable power that political strongmen (and the LTTE) are known for, but rather enacted repertoires of dissent, subversive allegiance, suffering and victimhood. These performative efforts embed ITAK's present political weakness in the *longue durée* of the Tamil struggle, thus drawing potency from a past of thwarted rebellion (with references to the 'genocidal' end of the war, the military feats of the LTTE and the legitimating narratives of the pre-war Tamil nationalist movement) and a future of aspiration (parrying awkward questions about the internal fissures, the ageing leadership and the lack of results with promises of a state to come). Seen in this light, parallels emerge between ITAK's postwar politics and the broader South Asian repertoires of commemorating collective hardship, adulating slain leaders, glorifying sacrifice, staging victimhood and prophecies of new kingdoms to come (Das and Poole 2004; A. Sen 2007; Shah 2019; Singh 2012; Spencer 2007).

Third, my analysis resonates closely with the scholarship on everyday realities of societies at war (Kelly 2008; Lubkemann 2008; Pettygrew 2013; Richards 2004; Spencer 2007; S. Thiranagama 2011). These ethnographic accounts unsettle established master narratives of conflict (its assumed causes, dynamics, parties, and phases) and instead adopt the vantage point that lived realities are self-reflexive: the material realities of a society at war shape their interpretation, and vice versa. Violent conflict has epistemic effects. The boundaries of gendered conduct are redrawn, subjectivities are rearticulated, the abnormal becomes the norm, the normal becomes exceptional. And as a result, what the conflict is about is itself subject to transformation. Tamil nationalism is a central component of Sri Lanka's ethno-political conflict, but what it means to be Tamil has changed through the experience of escalating conflict and civil war. The resultant reworking of boundaries, repertoires and political positioning affected the whole range of subjectivities – ethnicity, gender, age, religion, region, class, caste, *kudi* (Sitralega Maunaguru 1995; S. Thiranagama 2011; Winslow and Woost 2004).

As shown in Chapter 4, this process did not stop with the end of the war. Postwar Sampur was rife with confusion and struggle over the cultural fibre of Tamil society. Attempts to reconstitute a 'pure Tamil space' after the war conjured up anxiety and discord. Any attempt to define or demarcate the Tamil community after three decades of suffering, displacement and mixture conjured up new problems and divisions. With the dissipating clasp of wartime dispositions, Tamil boundaries, virtues and hierarchies were all in flux, and as a result, it appeared as if the very essence of being Tamil was slipping away, leaving people to feel disoriented and 'singular'. Efforts to reinstate traditional caste and *kudi* hierarchies, affirm Hindu space and police cultural practices were met with opposition and rival interpretations of postwar Tamil identity (similar observations were made in Jaffna; Geetha 2020; Silva 2020). These fissures and scuffles transposed to the political arena, where the culturally conservative leadership of the TNA was confronted with the renewed buoyancy of intra-Tamil struggles over social emancipation and the concurrent re-emergence of rival political parties. My analysis does not fundamentally challenge Thiranagama's (2010, 2011) work or related scholarship (McGilvray 2008; Walker 2013; Whitaker 1997). Rather, it complements this literature with observations on more recent postwar dynamics and by extending the perspective of everyday social realities to the spheres of the Tamil bureaucracy (Chapter 5) and Tamil nationalist politics (Chapter 6).

This extension of temporal scope brings questions about the postwar condition into the purview of this scholarship. The 2009 LTTE defeat marked a watershed moment that heralded a process of fundamental change, but the resultant shifts and struggles are completely embroiled with the conflictual past. This ambiguity is embodied in the ambivalence of the prefix 'post'. The 'post' in postwar transition does not mark a 'definitive after' but a 'continued struggle against legacies of'. It denotes a societal process that is shaped by attempts to diverge from the recent past while being in a state that continues to be marked by it. Postwar transition does not denote a fresh start. It comprises a transition away from what was – war – but this involves a continued struggle against and over the enduring implications of that past. The ethnography of war literature retains its relevance after war ends. Many cultural repertoires, forms of authority, the crafting of social spaces beyond conflict and norms of gendered conduct remerge in the postwar era – if often in rearticulated form. As I have argued elsewhere (Klem 2018), parallels could be drawn here between the postwar condition and the postcolonial condition. In both contexts, the impact and legacy of the recent past leaves an imprint in the categories of knowledge, which in turn shape identities and subjectivities. And the foundational violence that preceded the new sovereign order curtails the bandwidth of legitimate politics. Not dissimilar to newly declared post-colonies, Sri Lanka's violent apotheosis of 2009 precipitated the postwar political order. The experience of the preceding years heavily shaped the militaristic inclinations, the closure of political space, the unbounded potency of the ruling family and the imposition of a 'peace without ethnicities' wherein President Rajapaksa's Sinhala nationalist outlook declared ethnic identity irrelevant.

Whither shared sovereignty?

Is there hope for Sri Lanka's provincial council system? Can anything be done to fix its faults? Can it serve as a compromise to assuage ethno-nationalist conflict? To end this book with firm projections or prescriptions would go against its foundational analytical premises. My chapters have shown that breezy attempts to predict the trajectory of Sri Lankan politics invariably capsize, and recommendations for an institutional fix yield unforeseen outcomes. It is possible, though, to take stock of how the provincial council system has evolved and to identify what space it leaves for meaningful regional autonomy and power-sharing.

The provincial council system has failed to deliver on the rationale of resolving or even palliating Tamil nationalist aspirations and the grievances of Sri Lanka's ethnic minorities more widely. It was stifled, sabotaged and starved from the outset and remained a marginal layer of government after the war. To retain the little capacity that they have, provincial councils compromised their autonomy by finding allies in Colombo and by steering clear of controversial political issues. Effectively, they have become a framework for distributing a trickle of welfare services across the island's diverse regions, but that is not what the provincial councils were created for, and one does not need provincial councils to secure balanced regional development.

At the same time, the councils have proven remarkably tenacious. They were created amidst an escalating war, and they were fiercely opposed from all sides. Yet their institutions held out. The postwar political climate was marked by unprecedented centralisation of power and minimal political space for dissent or minority protection. The constellation could hardly have been less conducive for devolved governance, but the provincial councils survived the postwar Rajapaksa years. The victory of the Sirisena–Wickremesinghe 'good governance' government in 2015 raised new hopes, but these were short-lived. Within two years, the coalition crumbled. In 2018, President Sirisena tried to replace his prime minister (Wickremesinghe) with former president Mahinda Rajapaksa but was forced to reverse his decision. This aborted 'self-coup' prompted a constitutional crisis that made the skulduggery of the 1970s look tame: unprecedented transgressions followed in rapid sequence.

The November 2019 elections broke the resulting political paralysis. Mahinda's younger brother Gotabaya Rajapaksa (SLPP), former defence secretary and self-claimed architect of the military victory over the LTTE, became president. Ethnic minorities braced themselves for newly unleashed bouts of Sinhala-Buddhist nationalism, authoritarian measures and military-style governance. It was in the eerie calm before this storm that I found myself at the Galadari Hotel attending the seminar on devolution described in the first paragraphs of this chapter. The position of the yet-to-be elected provincial councils (polls continue to be deferred) was more constrained than ever. It was too early to conduct a post-mortem on the provincial council system, but it certainly impressed as terminal. And yet, the tenacity of the provincial apparatus suggests that it will salvage a residual spirit of autonomy in delivering public services and resources. In terms of *realpolitik*, this is what maximal devolution entails in the present constellation.

In *constitutional* terms, maximal devolution would honour a veritable sense of shared sovereignty and thus ease the excessive legal, financial and administrative constraints on provincial councils. As many studies, reports and public consultation mechanisms have argued before me (Amarasinghe et al. 2019; Bastian 1994; Coomaraswamy 2003; Edrisinha et al. 2008; Thiruchelvam 2000; Welikala 2012a, 2016; Wickramaratne 2014), it would involve rationalisation of devolved subjects, with clearly delineated central and provincial roles and no concurrent list (currently a smorgasbord of shared central and provincial prerogatives). It would safeguard Sri Lanka's national interest by giving the centre authority over security, foreign affairs, major natural resources and strategic maritime matters but make the province responsible for police, land, taxation and the ability to attract investment. It would also empower provinces to release themselves from the clutches of the constitutional clause that national policy prevails on all subjects, and it would bolster provincial autonomy in terms of staffing and resources. Provincial prerogatives would have to be constitutionally protected and a balanced mechanism for legal redress would need to be in place to adjudicate disputes between centre and province. It would require a conception of citizenship that reflects the diversity of Sri Lankan society, for example by framing popular sovereignty in plurinational terms. This would yield a democratic constellation of complementary *demoi* that transcend provincial boundaries and a bill of rights (Samararatne 2019) to protect all individuals and minorities from state misconduct at both central and devolved level. Finally, to comprise a geography that makes political sense (that is, one that comprises regions with a reasonable coherence and a distinct historical, cultural and socio-economic signature), the geographical conception of the provinces would need to be redefined to create a smaller number of entities that are larger in size: for example, some version of the (Tamil- and Muslim-dominated) northeast, some version of the ('Rajarata') northern flatlands, some version of the ('Kandyan') upcountry, some version of the south ('Ruhuna') and some arrangement around the national capital.[4]

All of this would elicit major political, legal, ethical and, frankly, sovereign problems. It would require a new constitution, probably a constitution with unamendable foundational clauses. It raises questions – some would say forgone conclusions – about political viability. It raises issues of legitimacy, and it conjures up the fundamental problems I started out with. What political community/communities, demarcated on what basis, would be entitled to decide on this? How to regulate sovereign power if that power is premised on the ability to supersede regulation? How to prevent a framework to assuage ethno-nationalism from inadvertently fuelling it? How to endow ethnic minority regions with autonomy without giving them the autonomy to impose majoritarian rule over their own regional minorities? In other words, a framework of maximal devolution would not resolve the central theoretical problems of this book; they would come up in different, possibly starker, forms.

Yet, given the perseverance of Tamil nationalism over the past century and the resilience of devolution (in terms of both discourse and institutions), we should not write off the possibility of a new settlement of some sort to emerge in ten or twenty-five years. Institutional performance never reaches a static end stage, and thus there always remains a potential for subtle or radical shifts in the political landscape due to new repertoires – or old repertoires that assume different meanings in a new context. If a new settlement materialises, it is unlikely to be completely new. Hardly anything ever is. All the bargains and debacles, alliances and fissures, escalations and de-escalations that we have seen over the past decades have rearticulated existing components into new configurations. They reassembled legacies rather than shedding them. Any future bargain would likely be shaped by the institutions and idioms of provincial devolution. And as such, any future settlement would be indebted to the struggles, the tenacity and the innovations of many of the people I have described in this book.

Notes

1   The SLPP, or the Sri Lanka People's Front, was the newly created political vehicle of the Rajapaksa family after they failed to wrest their original political home base (the Sri Lanka Freedom Party, or SLFP) back from President Sirisena. The SLPP was created in 2016 as a reassembly of an earlier Sinhala-Buddhist nationalist outfit: Ape Sri Lanka Nidahas Peramuna (Our Sri Lanka Freedom Front), which was in turn a reincarnation of the Sri Lanka Jathika Peramuna (Sri Lanka National Front).

2   Both authors, though mainly Provost, acknowledge some rough edges around this tidy organisational structure. For example, in Provost's (2021: 243) discussion of the LTTE's 2006 Child Protection Act, which prohibited child recruitment, he highlights that there was an element of window-dressing to the international community and that LTTE military practice did not yet match this commitment in practice (Provost 2021: 243).

3   As mentioned in Chapter 3, this issue fuelled fierce academic debate. When Stokke (2006) discussed the sprawling of LTTE institutions after the 2002 ceasefire, Sarvananthan (2007) accused him of taking LTTE propaganda at face value and thus lending it academic credibility, a claim that Stokke (2007) firmly rejected.

4   While this is extremely controversial, it has been suggested that a division along these lines would match historical precedents of Sinhala kingdoms and the graduated impact of colonial rule (Perera 1997). The devolution package of the 1990s proposed a similar model of a union of regions (Thiruchelvam 2000).

Epilogue

I wrote the initial drafts of this book over the period November 2018 to April 2020. Every time I had finished a draft chapter, Sri Lanka's appetite for power-sharing seemed to have crumbled further. The scene at the Galadari Hotel and the dim prospects of devolution in the concluding chapter are reflective of this. With Gotabaya Rajapaksa's election to president in late 2019 a new era appeared to start, and I decided to draw a line under my analysis. Academic books cannot continue to keep up with events, and it would be foolhardy to try.

Or so I told myself. Until an economic maelstrom of debt and shortages precipitated a popular uprising that ousted the Rajapaksa government, leaving Sri Lanka's entire political landscape in disarray. With the resulting whirlwind of ideas, hopes, puzzles and disillusions – as present in many readers' minds as in mine, I presume – an epilogue is warranted to grapple with the afterthoughts to this book. As my manuscript wormed its way through the academic machinery of reviews and revisions, radio stations called me to comment on a country that appeared to have changed beyond recognition. Everything that had seemed unchangeable – the very genetic coding of Sri Lanka's political system and culture – got in flux. Through the *aragalaya* (struggle), as the uprising came to be known, the edifice of the state and its foundation of a sovereign people made a volte-face in the first half of 2022 – only to land roughly where they had always been, though maybe not quite, in the second half of that year. Many of the characteristics of this revolt connect to the central concerns of this book.

In late 2021 and early 2022, Sri Lanka spiralled into a foreign debt trap. The seeds for this had been sown in the immediate aftermath of the civil war, when the Rajapaksa government initiated a lending spree to bankroll a trajectory of postwar development that combined sensible infrastructural upgrades with misguided megalomanic prestige projects, as well as soaring corruption (Ruwanpura 2016). The impressive growth figures of the immediate postwar years and visions of becoming a new Malaysia or Singapore muted concerns over the debt burden from multilateral, Chinese and other loans. When growth flattened off in the mid-2010s, these concerns became more acute (Klem 2020). Due to the combined impact of the COVID-19 pandemic (Peiris 2021) and government mismanagement, the economy took a nosedive. When the island's primary sources of foreign currency (tourism, remittances, along with the export of apparel, tea and other commodities) dried up, Sri Lanka became unable to service its debts and pay for essential import (De Mel, de Mel and Kapilan 2021; DeVotta 2022). Endless queues at the fuel station and enduring power cuts became the norm. Vital commodities like medicine became scarce. Soaring inflation pushed large parts of the population into poverty. Unlike war-time destitution, which had disproportionately affected the northeast, this crisis affected everyone, including the urban middle class, which had long considered itself safe from such shocks. University lectures were scrambling for cooking gas canisters, senior bureaucrats struggled to feed their families and established businessmen went bust.

The general state of anger and anxiety was aggravated by haphazard government policies and the continued repression of dissent. Even in 2021, before the economic crisis hit with full vigour, the farmer's movement was on the streets to protest the government's sudden ban on important agrochemicals (prompted by the need to save dollars but legitimised as a strategy to mitigate the kidney disease that plagued rural areas). Supporters of the Catholic Church protested to demand investigations into government maleficence around the 2019 Easter bombings. The teacher's union was on strike over salary arrears. University teachers fulminated against the militarisation of higher education (Gamage 2022; Klem and Samararatne 2022). These diverse nodes of protest gradually converged around their opposition to Gotabaya Rajapaksa's government, and in early 2022 they eventually fused into one focal point of popular uproar: the Galle Face Green. Hitherto disparate voices joined the protest chorus of the *aragalaya* movement: rural and urban, men and women, cis-gender and queer, Sinhala-Buddhist nationalist and liberal cosmopolitan, leftist and conservative, the peasant movement and the bar association, office clerks and youth activists. And the Galle Face Green – Colombo's premier parading ground, a waterfront surrounded by government buildings, prestigious hotels and the most visible of flopped megalomanias (the interrupted Port City project) – became the stage where the nation demanded Gotabaya Rajapaksa's eviction from the presidential palace across the road. The protest assumed a permanent character when an improvised settlement emerged on the green. What started as rudimentary lodging for the protesters grew into a theme park of political imagination with a people's library, a people's university, an art gallery, arenas for debate and consultations, and venues for press statements. The central slogan of the protesters – 'Gota go' – earned the settlement its name: Gota go *gama* (the Gota go village in Sinhala). Hash-tagged slogans, pamphlets, videos, artwork, caricatures and gaffes went viral on social media. Far from a rowdy street protest butting heads with the police, Gota go *gama* became an attraction for the general public, both online and on-site. Families started making outings to show their children the spectacle.

This book grappled with a set of fundamental normative and conceptual problems around sovereignty, including the self-referential character of key sovereign notions, like the legitimacy of the state, the foundation of law and the demarcation of the people or *demos*. All of these were out on display in Gota go *gama*, but in ways that differ from the Tamil nationalist tribulations with sovereignty that I have described in the preceding chapters. With its persistent emphasis on 'the people', it was easy to read the *aragalaya* as an invocation of popular sovereignty, a movement by the people, for the people that set out to redress the unwarranted appropriation of Sri Lankan sovereignty by a corrupt political family and the dynastic political cartel more widely. Though the Rajapaksas had been democratically elected several times, their democratic legitimacy was voided – so the protestors argued – when they crippled the rule of law and sacrificed the welfare of the entire nation for their personal spoils. This warranted 're-activation of the sovereign people's extra-legal constituent power' (Wijayalath 2022) – words that seem to echo the Ilankai Tamil Arasu Kadchi's (ITAK) rejection of the 1972 constitution, or the 1976 Vaddukoddai resolution, or the 2003 Liberation Tigers of Tamil Eelam's interim self-government proposal.

Gota go *gama* created a well-televised stage to give performative shape to a notion that often remains vague, if not vacuous: the people. It remained deliberately leaderless (though there were some charismatic spokespersons), and it successfully projected unity in diversity – no small feat considering Sri Lanka's history of political splintering. Most significant of all, it maintained its peaceful character, even in the face of violent provocation by government thugs and security forces (DeVotta 2022), until 9 July 2022 – the moment of dramatic climax – when the crowd crossed the road, broke through the barricades and poured into the halls of the presidential office. The performative stage of the street absorbed the stage of the palace, leaving spectators – in Colombo, around the island and across the globe – in amazement and shock. President Rajapaksa fled in haste and left the country. When he conceded his resignation, the revolution of the people appeared to have triumphed.

OK, a people's revolution, a re-assertion of democracy, a performance of popular sovereignty. But what *kind* of 'people'? What kind of *demos*, defined and demarcated how? The community enacting 'the people' on the Galle Face Green notably included Tamil, Muslim and Christian leaders and supporters, as well as many other minorities (Gamage 2022; Imtiyaz 2023), and Sinhala activists made a deliberate effort to highlight minority grievances and amplify minority voices, but the *aragalaya* emerged from a groundswell disgruntlement from the majority community. It advocated a broad and encompassing agenda of system change and re-democratisation, but its unifying demands concerned economic hardship, outrage over the Rajapaksa political family and objection to the extreme concentration of power in the executive presidency – not ethnic power-sharing, justice for wartime violence, postwar land-grabbing or ethnic minority rights (Samararatne 2022; Uyangoda 2022). When Tamil and Muslim protesters were out on the streets in the years prior to the 2022 uprising, demanding justice for war crimes and disappearances, demilitarisation and self-determination, their demands were routinely cold-shouldered. The *aragalaya* uprising derived the power to occupy Colombo's public space and overrun the president's office from being a movement representing virtually every layer of *Sinhala* society. Everyone could see that these were not the sinister elements that Gotabaya had promised to protect his voters from; these *were* his voters. Had Tamil or Muslim activists initiated a Gota go *kiramam*, they would have been driven away at the very least. Had they tried to storm the presidential office, they would have been shot or incarcerated. In fact, long before this uprising, one of the first major Tamil nationalist protests had started on the exact same Galle Face Green. In 1956, ITAK leaders opposed the 'Sinhala only' language bill with a *satyagraha*, a peaceful sit-in protest in the scorching heat of the green, then the square across from parliament. They were attacked and evicted by thugs with government officers standing by. A wave of anti-Tamil violence followed.

The 2022 *aragalaya* was a genuine and broad-based movement for civic democracy (Uyangoda 2022, 2023), but it stood apart from the protracted opposition by Tamil (and Muslim) rights advocates that long preceded it (Satkunanathan 2022). The protest movement afforded unprecedented space for minority concerns, but to be a part of the struggle, Tamil concerns would need to fit in with this civic democracy agenda. And as such, *aragalaya* as an arena of people's democracy confronted Tamil nationalist leaders with the same conundrums as Sri Lanka's formal democratic institutions. To participate in a democratic arena, one must shed fundamental political convictions that clash with the foundations of that arena. The agenda of re-democratisation afforded no space for a different *demos*, for a Tamil claim to self-determination (Samararatna 2022; Uyangoda 2023). Moreover, it required alignment with a broad range of parties and constituencies, many of which had been instrumental in bringing the Rajapaksa government to power (and in solidifying the violent, anti-minority character of the state in the preceding decades). Where were 'the people' before milk and fuel became so expensive, critical minority voices wondered: when Muslims were attacked in Aluthgama, when Tamils were detained and tortured under draconian anti-terrorism law or (long before the Rajapaksas came to power) when Tamil houses were burned in Black July, when the 1956 satyagraha on Galle Face Green was violently dispersed?

Notwithstanding these uneasy questions, the *aragalaya* offered an unusually permissive scope to proclaim grievances and aspirations. Rather than performing strained anti-political repertoires, as Tamil nationalists had done after the war (see Chapter 6), Gota go *gama* offered a comprehensively anti-political arena, a permanent stage elevated above small-fry politics, wholly dedicated to the castigation and mockery of the island's political elite. The agenda of re-democratisation (Uyangoda 2023) – aimed at a constitutional reset with a fundamental re-conception of electoral democracy and the institutional design of the state – afforded potentially fruitful space to rearticulate Tamil aspirations in civic terms. Power-sharing, greater transparency, stronger anchoring of fundamental rights and more robust measures against political manipulation would be welcome, even if these measures were taken in the name of good governance rather than the redress of Tamil grievances. Joining the bandwagon would require silence on Tamil nationalist articles of faith, but it would arguably increase the chances of success.

Soon after the apparent triumph of Rajapaksa's resignation, however, it became clear that the fruits of the *aragalaya* revolt were no less bitter for its Sinhalese proponents than they were for minority rights activists. Both the prime minister and the president had been driven away, but parliament – with its majority of Rajapaksa backbenchers – remained intact (DeVotta 2022). Ranil Wickremesinghe, a veteran politician representing the quintessence of the arrogant established elite of dynastic families, rose from the ashes when a parliamentary vote mandated him as the new president. After he assumed office, President Wickremesinghe cracked down on the protestors, clearing the Galle Face Green (Keenan 2022). Austerity reforms – the seal of Wickremesinghe's politics throughout his long career – were initiated to court the International Monetary Fund. A first instalment of emergency credit was finally agreed in early 2023 (after China conceded to restructure some of its loans, a condition from multilateral donors). Long before that, the Rajapaksas returned to Sri Lanka and patched up with Wickremesinghe. The majority of ministers in the post-*aragalaya* cabinet belong to the Rajapaksa party (SLPP).

After the dramatic staging of Sri Lanka's 'Bastille Day' (Wijayalath 2022), the curtain was drawn. The political stage has been reset, and it looks remarkably like what it used to. But there is no doubt that the events of 2022 have enriched Sri Lanka's political imaginary. The *aragalaya* showed that a powerful but peaceful campaign for civic democracy is possible. It demonstrated that no government, even the despotic apparatus of the Rajapaksas, is impervious to opposition. It left a trail of images, ideas, hashtags, jokes – a new idiom of popular democracy – that remains inscribed in Sri Lanka's collective political consciousness. And it harnessed the realisation that many across Sri Lanka's fractured society share a commitment to democratic values and constitutional rights, even if they disagree on the sovereign constellation that underpins them.

Glossary

aragalaya	struggle (Sinhala), denoting the popular uprising against the Rajapaksa government in 2022
arasu	state, government or, much less commonly, king (Tamil)
gama	village (Sinhala)
grama niladari	village- or ward-level officer (Sinhala, also used in English and Tamil)
kachcheri	district administration, headed by the government agent (used in Sinhala, Tamil and English)
kadchi	political party (Tamil)
kudi	clan (Tamil)
malaiyaha Tamil	upcountry Tamil, referring to Tamils of recent (colonial era) Indian origin who have historically resided in Sri Lanka's central highland region
pottu	a coloured dot adorning the forehead (Tamil)
satyagraha	non-violent protest (Sinhala; Tamil cognates)
talaivar	leader (Tamil)
thanthai	father (Tamil)

References

Abeles, Marc. 1988. 'Modern Political Ritual: Ethnography of an Inauguration and a Pilgrimage by President Mitterrand'. *Current Anthropology* 29(3): 391–404.

Abraham, Thomas. 2006. 'The Emergence of the LTTE and the Indo-Sri Lanka Agreement of 1987'. In *Negotiating Peace in Sri Lanka: Efforts, Failures and Lessons*, edited by Kumar Rupesinghe, 1:9–23. Colombo: Foundation for Coexistence.

Abrams, Philip. 1988 (1977). 'Notes on the Difficulty of Studying the State'. *Journal of Historical Sociology* 1(1): 58–89.

Achniotis, Panos. 2021. 'Sovereign Days: Imagining and Making the Catalan Republic from Below'. In *The Everyday Lives of Sovereignty: Political Imagination beyond the State*, edited by Madeleine Reeves and Rebecca Bryant, 175–196. Ithaka, NY: Cornell University Press.

Agamben, Giorgio. 2005. *The State of Exception*. Translated by Kevin Attell. Chicago, IL: Chicago University Press.

Akhter, Majed. 2019. 'The Proliferation of Peripheries: Militarized Drones and the Reconfiguration of Global Space'. *Progress in Human Geography* 43(1): 64–80.

Alison, Mirinda. 2003. 'Cogs in the Wheel? Women in the Liberation Tigers of Tamil Eelam'. *Civil War* 6(1): 37–54.

Amarasingam, Amarnath. 2015. *Pain, Pride and Politics: Social Movement Activism and the Sri Lankan Tamil Diaspora in Canada*. Athens, GA: University of Georgia Press.

Amarasinghe, Ranjith, Asoka Gunawardena, Jayampathi Wickramaratne, A. Navaratna-Bandara and N. Selvakkumaran, eds. 2010. *Twenty Two Years of*

Devolution: An Evaluation of the Workings of Provincial Councils in Sri Lanka. Colombo: Institute for Constitutional Studies.

———. 2019. *Thirty Years of Devolution: An Evaluation of the Workings of Provincial Councils in Sri Lanka.* Colombo: Institute for Constitutional Studies.

Amarasinghe, Ranjith and N. Selvakkumaran. 2019a. 'Legislative Functions of Provincial Councils'. In *Thirty Years of Devolution: An Evaluation of the Workings of Provincial Councils in Sri Lanka*, edited by Ranjith Amarasinghe, Asoka Gunawardena, Jayampathi Wickramaratne, A. Navaratna-Bandara and N. Selvakkumaran, 191–218. Colombo: Institute for Constitutional Studies.

———. 2019b. 'The Workings of Provincial Councils: Centre-Province Relations'. In *Thirty Years of Devolution: An Evaluation of the Workings of Provincial Councils in Sri Lanka*, edited by Ranjith Amarasinghe, Asoka Gunawardena, Jayampathi Wickramaratne, A. Navaratna-Bandara and N. Selvakkumaran, 277–308. Colombo: Institute for Constitutional Studies.

Amarasuriya, Harini. 2010. 'Guardians of Childhood: State, Class and Morality in a Sri Lankan Bureaucracy'. PhD diss., Edinburgh University and Queen Margaret University.

Amirthalingam, Kopalapillai and Rajith Lakshman. 2009. 'Displaced Livelihoods in Sri Lanka: An Economic Analysis'. *Journal of Refugee Studies* 22(4): 502–524.

———. 2014. 'Impact of Internal Displacement on Agricultural Livelihoods: Evidence from Sampur, Sri Lanka'. *Migration and Development* 4(1): 143–162.

Ameerdeen, Vellaithamby. 2006. *Ethnic Politics of Muslims in Sri Lanka.* Kandy: International Centre for Ethnic Studies.

Anderson, Benedikt. 2006 (1983). *Imagined Communities: Reflections on the Origins of Nationalism.* London: Verso.

Anghie, Anthony. 1999. 'Finding the Peripheries: Sovereignty and Colonialism in Nineteenth Century International Law'. *Harvard International Law Journal* 40(1): 3–71.

Ann, Adele. 1993. *Women Fighters of Liberation Tigers.* Jaffna: LTTE Publication Section.

Arasaratnam, Sinnappah. 1994. 'Sri Lanka's Tamils: Under Colonial Rule'. In *The Sri Lankan Tamils: Ethnicity and Identity*, edited by Chelvadurai Manogaran and Bryan Pfaffenberger, 30–53. Boulder, CO: Westview Press.

Aretxaga, Begoña. 1997. *Shattering Silence: Women, Nationalism, and Political Subjectivity in Northern Ireland.* Princeton, NJ: Princeton University Press.

Arias, Enrique Desmond and Daniel Goldstein, eds. 2010. *Violent Democracies in Latin America.* Durham, NC: Duke University Press.

Arjona, Ana. 2016. *Rebelocracy: Social Order in the Colombian Civil War.* Cambridge: Cambridge University Press.

Arjona, Ana, Nelson Kasfir and Zachariah Mampilly, eds. 2015. *Rebel Governance in Civil War.* Cambridge: Cambridge University Press.

Arrhenius, Gustaf. 2005. 'The Boundary Problem in Democratic Theory'. In *Democracy Unbound: Basic Explorations I,* edited by Folke Tersman, 14–19. Stockholm: Filosofiska Institutionen, Stockholms Universitet.

Balasingham, Anton. 2004. *War and Peace: Armed Struggle and Peace Efforts of Liberation Tigers.* London: Fairmax Publishing.

Banerjee, Mukulika. 2008. 'Democracy, Sacred and Everyday: An Ethnographic Case from India'. In *Democracy: Anthropological Perspectives,* edited by Julia Paley, 63–96. Santa Fe, NM: School of Advanced Research Press.

———. 2011. 'Elections as Communitas'. *Social Research* 78(1): 75–98.

———. 2014. *Why India Votes?* London: Routledge.

Bárcena, Miguel de. 2020. 'The Persistence of the Catalan Sovereignty Process before the Spanish Constitucional Court'. *Revista Española de Derecho Constitucional* 120 (September–December): 199–230.

Barker, Joanne. 2006. 'Gender, Sovereignty, and the Discourse of Rights in Native Women's Activism'. *Meridians: Feminism, Race, Transnationalism* 19(S1): 219–254.

Barnett, Randy. 2004. *Restoring the Lost Constitution: The Presumption of Liberty.* Princeton, NJ: Princeton University Press.

Bartelson, Jens. 1995. *A Genealogy of Sovereignty.* Cambridge: Cambridge University Press.

Baruah, Sanjib. 2007. *Durable Disorder: Understanding the Politics of Northeast India.* New Delhi: Oxford University Press.

Bastian, Sunil. 1994. *Devolution and Development in Sri Lanka.* Colombo: International Centre for Ethnic Studies (with Konark Publishers).

———. 1996. 'Control of State Land: The Devolution Debate'. In *Sri Lanka: The Devolution Debate,* edited by ICES, 61–86. Colombo: International Centre for Ethnic Studies.

Bastian, Sunil and Robin Luckham. 2003. *Can Democracy Be Designed? The Politics of Institutional Choice in Conflict-Torn Societies.* Chicago, IL: Chicago University Press.

Bear, Laura and Nayanika Mathur. 2015. 'Introduction: Remaking the Public Good; A New Anthropology of Bureaucracy'. *Cambridge Journal of Anthropology* 33(1): 18–34.

Benton, Lauren. 1999. 'Colonial Law and Cultural Difference: Jurisdictional Politics and the Formation of the Colonial State'. *Comparative Studies in Society and History* 41(3): 563–588.

———. 2002. *Law and Colonial Cultures: Legal Regimes in World History, 1400–1900*. Cambridge: Cambridge University Press.

———. 2009. *A Search for Sovereignty: Law and Geography in European Empires, 1400–1900*. Cambridge: Cambridge University Press.

Berenschot, Ward. 2010. 'Everyday Mediation: The Politics of Public Service Delivery in Gujarat, India'. *Development and Change* 41(5): 883–905.

———. 2011. *Riot Politics: Hindu–Muslim Violence and the India State*. New York, NY: Columbia University Press.

Bertrand, Romain, Jean-Louis Briquet and Peter Pels, eds. 2007. *Cultures of Voting: The Hidden History of the Secret Ballot*. London: Hurst.

Beverley, Eric. 2013. 'Frontier as Resource: Law, Crime, and Sovereignty on the Margins of Empire'. *Comparative Studies in Society and History* 55(2): 241–272.

———. 2020a. 'Rethinking Sovereignty, Colonial Empires, and Nation-States in South Asia and Beyond'. *Comparative Studies of South Asia, Africa and the Middle East* 40(3): 407–420.

———. 2020b. 'Old Borderlands: Sovereignty and Autonomy in the Hyderabad Deccan, ca. 1800–2014'. *Comparative Studies of South Asia, Africa and the Middle East* 40(3): 454–467.

Bhabha, Homi. 1994. *The Location of Culture*. London: Routledge.

Bhungalia, Lisa. 2020. 'Laughing at Power: Humor, Transgression, and the Politics of Refusal in Palestine'. *Environment and Planning C: Politics and Space* 38 (May): 387–404.

Bilgiç, Ali. 2018. 'Migrant Encounters with Neo-Colonial Masculinity: Producing European Sovereignty through Emotions'. *International Feminist Journal of Politics* 20(4): 542–562.

Blight, James and Janet Lang. 2005. *The Fog of War: Lessons from the Life of Robert S. McNamara*. London: Rowman and Littlefield.

Bloemraad, Irene. 2018. 'Theorising the Power of Citizenship as Claims-Making'. *Journal of Ethnic and Migration Studies* 44(1): 4–26.

Bobick, Michael. 2017. 'Sovereignty and the Vicissitudes of Recognition: Peoplehood and Performance in De Facto State'. *PoLAR: The Political and Legal Anthropology Review* 40(1): 158–170.

Boege, Volker, Anne Brown, Kevin Clements and Anna Nolan. 2009. 'Building Peace and Political Community in Hybrid Political Orders'. *International Peacekeeping* 16(5): 599–615.

Bose, Sumantra. 1994. *States, Nations, Sovereignty: Sri Lanka, India and the Tamil Eelam Movement*. Thousand Oaks, CA: Sage.

———. 2002. 'Flawed Mediation, Chaotic Implementation: The 1987 Indo-Sri Lanka Peace Agreement'. In *Ending Civil Wars: The Implementation of Peace Agreements*, edited by Stephen Stedman, Donald Rothchild and Elizabeth Cousens, 631–659. London: Lynne Rienner.

Bosia, Michael. 2018. 'Do Queer Visions Trouble Human Security'. In *Routledge Handbook of Gender and Security*. https://www.taylorfrancis.com/chapters/edit/10.4324/9781315525099-8/queer-visions-trouble-human-security-michael-bosia. Accessed 29 June 2023.

Bratton, Michael and Nicolas van de Walle. 1994. 'Neopatrimonial Regimes and Political Transitions in Africa'. *World Politics* 46(4): 453–489.

Breman, Jan. 1974. *Patronage and Exploitation: Changing Agrarian Relations in Southern Gujarat*. Berkeley, CA: University of California Press.

Bremner, Francesca. 2013. 'Recasting Caste: War, Displacement and Transformations'. *International Journal of Ethnic and Social Studies* 1(2): 31–56.

Brenner, David. 2017. 'Authority in Rebel Groups: Identity, Recognition and the Struggle over Legitimacy'. *Contemporary Politics* 23(4): 408–426.

Brilmayer, Lea. 1989. 'Consent, Contract, and Territory'. *Minnesota Law Review* 74(1): 1–35.

Brow, James. 1996. *Demons and Development: The Struggle for Community in a Sri Lankan Village*. Tucson, AZ: University of Arizona Press.

Brubaker, Rogers. 2004. *Ethnicity without Groups*. Cambridge, MA: Harvard University Press.

Brun, Cathrine. 2008. 'Birds of Freedom'. *Critical Asian Studies* 40(3): 399–422.

Bryant, Rebecca and Mete Hatay. 2020. *Sovereignty Suspended: Building the So-Called State*. Philadelphia, PA: University of Pennsylvania Press.

Butler, Judith. 1990. *Gender Trouble*. New York, NY: Routledge.

Buur, Lars. 2005. 'The Sovereign Outsourced: Local Justice and Violence in Port Elizabeth'. In *States of Imagination: Ethnographic Explorations of the Postcolonial State*, edited by Thomas Blom Hansen and Finn Stepputat, 192–217. Durham, NC: Duke University Press.

Byrne, Sarah and Bart Klem. 2015. 'Constructing Legitimacy in Post-War Transition: The Return of "Normal" Politics in Nepal and Sri Lanka?' *Geoforum* 66: 224–233.

Caspersen, Nina. 2012. *Unrecognized States: The Struggle for Sovereignty in the Modern International System*. Cambridge: Polity Press.

Chandler, David. 2000. *Bosnia: Faking Democracy after Dayton*. London: Pluto Press.

Chandra, Kanchan. 2004. *Why Ethnic Parties Succeed: Patronage and Ethnic Head Counts in India*. Cambridge: Cambridge University Press.

Chatterjee, Partha. 1986. *Nationalist Thought and the Colonial World: A Derivative Discourse*. London: Zed Books.

———. 1993. *The Nation and Its Fragments*. Princeton, NJ: Princeton University Press.

———. 2004. *The Politics of the Governed: Reflections on Popular Politics in Most of the World*. New York, NY: Columbia University Press.

———. 2005. 'Sovereign Violence and the Domain of the Political'. In *States of Imagination: Ethnographic Explorations of the Postcolonial State*, edited by Thomas Blom Hansen and Finn Stepputat, 82–100. Durham, NC: Duke University Press.

Cheran, Rainford, ed. 2009. *Pathways of Dissent: Tamil Nationalism in Sri Lanka*. Thousand Oaks, CA: Sage.

Choudry, Sujit. 2008. *Constitutional Design for Divided Societies: Integration or Accommodation?* New York, NY: Oxford University Press.

Chowdhury, Mahfuzul. 2003. 'Violence, Politics and the State in Bangladesh'. *Conflict, Security and Development* 3(2): 265–276.

Clausewitz, Carl von. 1976 (1834) *Vom Kriege*. Cologne: Anaconda.

Cleaver, Frances. 2012. *Development through Bricolage: Rethinking Institutions for Natural Resource Management*. London: Earthscan.

Cockburn, Cynthia and Susan Ormrod, eds. 1993. *Gender and Technology in the Making*. London: Sage.

Cockburn, Cynthia and Dubravka *Zarkov*. 2002. *The Postwar Moment: Militaries, Masculinities, and International Peacekeeping*. London: Lawrence and Wishart.

Coomaraswamy, Radhika. 1994. 'Devolution, the Law, and Judicial Construction'. In *Devolution and Development in Sri Lanka*, edited by Sunil Bastian, 121–142. Colombo: International Centre for Ethnic Studies (with Konark Publishers).

———. 1996. 'Tiger Women and the Question of Women's Emancipation'. *Pravada* 4(9): 8–10.

———. 2003. 'The Politics of Institutional Design: An Overview of the Case of Sri Lanka'. In *Can Democracy Be Designed? The Politics of Institutional Choice in Conflict-Torn Societies*, edited by Sunil Bastian and Robin Luckham, 145–169. London: Zed Books.

———. 2012. 'The 1972 Republican Constitution in the Postcolonial Constitutional Evolution of Sri Lanka'. In *The Sri Lankan Republic at 40: Reflections on Constitutional History, Theory and Practice*, edited by Asanga Welikala, 125–144. Colombo: Centre for Policy Alternatives.

Coomaraswamy, Radhika and Nimanthi Perera-Rajasingham. 2009. 'Being Tamil in a Different Way: A Feminist Critique of the Tamil Nation'. In *Pathways of Dissent: Tamil Nationalism in Sri Lanka*, edited by Rainford Cheran, 107–138. New Delhi: Sage.

Cooper, Frederick. 2002. 'Decolonizing Situations: The Rise, Fall, and Rise of Colonial Studies, 1951–2001'. *French Politics, Culture and Society* 20(2): 47–76.

———. 2014. *Citizenship between Empire and Nation: Remaking France and French Africa, 1945–1960*. Princeton, NJ: Princeton University Press.

Corcuff, Stéphane. 2012. 'The Liminality of Taiwan: A Case-Study in Geopolitics'. *Taiwan in Comparative Perspective* 4 (December): 34–64.

Daniel, Valentine. 1996. *Charred Lullabies: Chapters in an Anthropography of Violence*. Princeton, NJ: Princeton University Press.

Das, Veena and Deborah Poole, eds. 2004. *Anthropology in the Margins of the State*. New Delhi: Oxford University Press.

De Alwis, Malithi. 2002. 'The Changing Role of Women in Sri Lankan Society'. *Social Research* 69(3): 675–691.

Degregori, Carlos. 2012. *How Difficult It Is to Be God: Shining Path's Politics of War in Peru, 1980–1999*. Madison, WI: University of Wisconsin Press.

De Mel, Neloufer. 2001. *Women and the Nation's Narrative: Gender and Nationalism in Twentieth Century Sri Lanka*. Washington, DC: Rowman & Littlefield Publishers.

———. 2004. 'Body Politics: (Re)Cognising the Female Suicide Bomber in Sri Lanka'. *Indian Journal of Gender Studies* 11(1): 75–93.

———. 2007. *Militarizing Sri Lanka: Popular Culture, Memory and Narrative in the Armed Conflict*. London: Sage.

De Mel, Nishan, Deshal de Mel and Anushan Kapilan. 2021. 'Charting a Path for Debt Sustainability in Sri Lanka'. Verité Research, Working Paper, 1 October 2021. https://www.veriteresearch.org/publication/charting-a-path-for-debt-sustainability-in-sri-lanka/. Accessed 29 June 2023.

Demmers, Jolle, Lauren Gould and David Snetselaar. 2020. 'Perfect War and Its Contestations'. In *Spaces of War, War of Spaces*, edited by Sarah Maltby, Ben O'Loughlin, Katy Parry and Laura Roselle, 231–246. New York, NY: Bloomsbury.

DeMunck, Victor. 1998. 'Sufi and Reformist Designs: Muslim Identity in Sri Lanka'. In Buddhist Fundamentalism and Minority Identities in Sri Lanka, edited by Tessa Bartholomeusz and Chandra De Silva, 110–132. New York, NY: State University of New York Press.

De Silva, Kingsley. 2005. *A History of Sri Lanka*. Colombo: Vijitha Yapa Publications.

De Silva-Ranasinghe, Sergei. 2010. 'Strategic Analysis of Sri Lankan Military's Counter-Insurgency Operations'. Strategic Analysis Paper, Future Directions International, West Perth.

DeVotta, Neil. 2004. Blowback: Linguistic Nationalism, Institutional Decay, and Ethnic Conflict in Sri Lanka. Stanford, CA: Stanford University Press.

———. 2022. 'Sri Lanka's Agony'. *Journal of Democracy* 33(3): 92–99.

De Waal, Alex. 2009. 'Mission without End? Peacekeeping in the African Political Marketplace'. *International Affairs* 85(1): 99–113.

Dimova, Rozita and Ludmila Cojocaru. 2013. 'Contested Nation-Building within the International "Order of Things": Performance, Festivals and Legitimization in South-Eastern Europe'. *History and Anthropology* 24(1): 1–12.

Dixit, Jyotindra. 2003. *Assignment Colombo*. Colombo: Vijitha Yapa Publications.

Dixon, Paul. 2019. *Performing the Northern Ireland Peace Process: In Defence of Politics*. London: Palgrave.

Douglas, Mary. 1970. *Natural Symbols: Explorations in Cosmology*. New York, NY: Pantheon Books.

———. 1987. *How Institutions Think*. London: Routledge.

Duschinski, Haley, Mona Blan, Ather Zia and Cynthia Mahmood, eds. 2018. *Resisting Occupation in Kashmir*. Philadelphia, PA: University of Pennsylvania Press.

Edrisinha, Rohan, Mario Gomez, V. T. Thamilmaran and Asanga Welikala, eds. 2008. *Power-Sharing in Sri Lanka: Constitutional and Political Documents 1926–2008*. Colombo; Berlin: Centre for Policy Alternatives and Berghof Foundation for Peace Support.

Edrisinha, Rohan and Asanga Welikala. 2008. 'The LTTE's ISGA Proposal (2003)'. In *Power-Sharing in Sri Lanka: Constitutional and Political Documents 1926–2008*, edited by Rohan Edrisinha, Mario Gomez, V. T. Thamilmaran and Asanga Welikala, 662–667. Colombo; Berlin: Centre for Policy Alternatives and Berghof Foundation for Peace Support.

Enguix Grau, Begonya. 2021. 'Rebel Bodies: Feminism as Resistance in the Catalan Pro-Independence Left'. *European Journal of English Studies* 25(2): 225–248.

Egnell, Robert and Peter Haldén, eds. 2013. *New Agendas in Statebuilding: Hybridity, Contingency and History*. London: Routledge.

Featherstone, David. 2008. *Resistance, Space and Political Identities: The Making of Counter-Global Networks*. Chichester: Wiley-Blackwell.

Feldman, Ilana. 2008. *Governing Gaza: Bureaucracy, Authority, and the Work of Rule (1917–1967)*. Durham, NC: Duke University Press.

Fernando, Austin. 2008. *My Belly Is White*. Colombo: Vijitha Yapa Publications.

Fluri, Jennifer. 2019. 'What's So Funny in Afghanistan? Jocular Geopolitics and the Everyday Use of Humor in Spaces of Protracted Precarity'. *Political Geography* 68 (January): 125–130.

Fonseka, Bhavani and Mirak Raheem. 2009. 'Trincomalee High Security Zone and Special Economic Zone'. CPA Report. Colombo: CPA.

———. 2010. 'Land in the Eastern Province: Politics, Policy and Conflict'. CPA Report. Colombo: CPA.

Foucault, Michel. 1997. *'Society Must Be Defended': Lectures at the Collège de France, 1975–76*. Edited by Mauro Bertani and Alessandro Fontana. New York, NY: Picador.

Friedman, Sara. 2021. 'Aspirational Sovereignty and Human Rights Advocacy: Audience, Recognition, and the Reach of the Taiwan State'. In *The Everyday Lives of Sovereignty: Political Imagination beyond the State*, edited by Madeleine Reeves and Rebecca Bryant, 89–113. Ithaka NY: Cornell University Press.

Fuglerud, Øivind. 1991. *Life on the Outside: The Tamil Diaspora and Long-Distance Nationalism*. London: Pluto.

———. 2009. 'Fractured Sovereignty: The LTTE's State-Building in an Inter-Connected World'. In *Spatialising Politics: Culture and Geography in Post-Colonial Sri Lanka*, edited by Cathrine Brun and Tarik Jazeel, 194–215. New Delhi: Sage.

Fuller, Chris and Véronique Bénéï, eds. 2009. *The Everyday State and Society in Modern India*. New Delhi: Social Science Press.

Gaasbeek, Timmo. 2010. 'Bridging Troubled Waters? Everyday Inter-ethnic Interaction in a Context of Violent Conflict in Kottiyar Pattu, Trincomalee, Sri Lanka'. PhD diss., Wageningen University.

Gamage, Gayathri. 2022. 'Aragalaya: A New Page of People's Resistance in Sri Lanka'. *Protest* 2 (January): 269–277.

Gangwala, Glen. 2015. 'The Creation of Governments-in-Waiting: The Arab Uprisings and Legitimacy in the International System'. *Geoforum* 66: 215–223.

Gardezi, Hassan and Jamil Rashid, eds. 1983. *Pakistan, the Roots of Dictatorship: The Political Economy of a Praetorian State*. Oxford: Oxford University Press.

Gayer, Laurent and Christophe Jaffrelot, eds. 2009. *Armed Militias of South Asia: Fundamentalists, Maoists, and Separatists*. New York, NY: Columbia University Press.

Geertz, Clifford. 1980. *Negara: The Theatre State in Nineteenth Century Bali*. Princeton, NJ: Princeton University Press.

Geetha, Krishnamurthy Alamelu. 2020. 'Housing the Unhomely: A Study of Srilankan Panchamar Fiction'. *Interventions* 22(7): 951–965.

Gellner, David, ed. 2007. *Resistance and the State: Nepalese Experiences*. New York, NY; Oxford: Berghahn Books.

Gilmartin, David. 2012. 'Towards a Global History of Voting: Sovereignty, the Diffusion of Ideas, and the Enchanted Individual'. *Religions* 3(2): 407–423.

———. 2015. 'Rethinking the Public through the Lens of Sovereignty'. *South Asia: Journal of South Asian Studies* 38(3): 371–386.

———. 2020. 'Introduction: South Asian Sovereignty: The Conundrum of Worldly Power'. In *South Asian Sovereignty: The Conundrum of Worldly Power*, edited by David Gilmartin, Pamela Price and Arild Engelsen Ruud, 1–34. London: Routledge.

Gilmartin, David, Pamela Price and Arild Engelsen Ruud, eds. 2020. *South Asian Sovereignty: The Conundrum of Worldly Power*. London: Routledge.

Goffman, Erving. 1959. *The Presentation of Self in Everyday Life*. New York, NY: Doubleday Anchor.

Goodhand, Jonathan. 2010. 'Stabilising a Victor's Peace? Humanitarian Action and Reconstruction in Eastern Sri Lanka'. *Disasters* 34(S3): S342–S367.

———. 2012. 'Sri Lanka in 2011: Consolidation and Militarization of the Post-War Regime'. *Asian Survey* 52(1): 130–137.

Goodhand, Jonathan, Bart Klem and Gunnar Sørbø. 2011. 'Pawns of Peace: Evaluation of Norwegian Peace Efforts in Sri Lanka, 1997–2009'. Norad report, May 2011.

Goodhand, Jonathan, Bart Klem and Oliver Walton. 2017. 'Mediating the Margins: The Role of Brokers and the Eastern Provincial Council in Sri Lanka's Post-war Transition'. *Third World Thematics* 1(6): 817–836.

Goodhand, Jonathan, Benedikt Korf and Jonathan Spencer, eds. 2011. *Conflict and Peacebuilding in Sri Lanka: Caught in the Peace Trap?* London; New York, NY: Routledge.

Gooneratne, John. 2007. *Negotiating with the Tigers (LTTE) (2002–2005): A View from the Second Row*. Pannipitiya, Sri Lanka: Stamford Lake.

Government of Sri Lanka. 2009. 'Sri Lanka: The Largest Hostage Rescue Mission in the World Launched'. Press release, Government of Sri Lanka,

10 April 2009. http://www.reliefweb.int/rw/rwb.nsf/db900SID/SNAA-7QYDAB?OpenDocument. Accessed 30 June 2023.

Gowrinathan, Nimmi. 2017. 'The Committed Female Fighter: The Political Identities of Tamil Women in the Liberation Tigers of Tamil Eelam'. *International Feminist Journal of Politics* 19(3): 327–341.

Gregson, Nicky and Gillian Rose. 2000. 'Taking Butler Elsewhere: Performativities, Spatialities and Subjectivities'. *Environment and Planning D: Society and Space* 18 (4): 433–452.

Gunaratna, Rohan. 2003. 'Sri Lanka: Feeding the Tamil Tigers'. In *The Political Economy of Armed Conflict: Beyond Greed and Grievance*, edited by Karen Ballentine and Jake Sherman, 197–223. Boulder, CO: International Peace Academy/Lynne Rienner.

Gunasingam, Murugar. 2016. *Tamils in Sri Lanka: A Comprehensive History*. Sydney: MV Publication, South Asian Studies Centre.

Gunawardena, Asoka. 2019. 'Fiscal Devolution: Challenges in Realizing Governance and Development Objectives'. In *Thirty Years of Devolution: An Evaluation of the Workings of Provincial Councils in Sri Lanka*, edited by Ranjith Amarasinghe, Asoka Gunawardena, Jayampathi Wickramaratne, A. Navaratna-Bandara and N. Selvakkumaran, 219–276. Colombo: Institute for Constitutional Studies.

Gunes, Cengiz. 2012. *The Kurdish National Movement in Turkey: From Protest to Resistance*. New York, NY: Routledge.

Gupta, Akhil. 1995. 'Blurred Boundaries: The Discourse of Corruption, the Culture of Politics, and the Imagined State'. *American Ethnologist* 22(2): 375–402.

———. 2012. *Red Tape: Bureaucracy, Structural Violence, and Poverty in India*. Durham, NC: Duke University Press.

Guruparan, Kumaravadivel. 2016. 'Customary Law of Stateless Nations: Some Observations on the Question of Who Can Reform the Thesawalamai, the Customary Laws of the Tamils in Sri Lanka'. *Jindal Global Law Review* 7(1): 49–59.

Hagmann, Tobias and Didier Péclard. 2010. 'Negotiating Statehood in Africa: Propositions for an Alternative Approach to State and Political Authority'. *Development and Change* 41(4): 539–562.

Haniffa, Farzana. 2008. 'Piety as Politics amongst Muslim Women in Contemporary Sri Lanka'. *Modern Asian Studies* 42(3): 1–29.

Hansen, Thomas Blom. 1999. *The Saffron Wave: Democracy and Hindu Nationalism in Modern India*. Princeton, NJ: Princeton University Press.

————. 2001. *Wages of Violence: Naming and Identity in Postcolonial Bombay.* Princeton, NJ: Princeton University Press.

————. 2004. 'Politics as Permanent Performance: The Production of Political Authority in the Locality'. In *The Politics of Cultural Mobilization in India*, edited by John Zavos, Andrew Wyatt and Vernon Hewitt, 19–36. New Delhi: Oxford University Press.

————. 2009. 'Governance and Myth of State in Mumbai'. In *The Everyday State and Society in Modern India*, edited by Chris Fuller and Véronique Bénéï, 31–67. New Delhi: Social Science Press.

————. 2021. 'Sovereignty in a Minor Key'. *Public Culture* 33(1): 41–61.

Hansen, Thomas Blom and Finn Stepputat. 2001. 'Introduction: States of Imagination'. In *States of Imagination: Ethnographic Explorations of the Postcolonial State*, edited by Thomas Blom Hansen and Finn Stepputat, 1–40. Durham, NC: Duke University Press.

————. 2005. *Sovereign Bodies: Citizens, Migrants, and States in the Postcolonial World.* Princeton, NJ: Princeton University Press.

————. 2006. 'Sovereignty Revisited'. *Annual Review of Anthropology* 35: 295–315.

Haraway, Donna. 1997. *Modest_Witness@Second_Millennium. FemaleMan_ Meets_OncoMouse: Feminism and Technoscience.* New York, NY: Routledge.

Hariharan, R. 2010. 'Sri Lanka Armed Forces and Dynamics of Change'. South Asia Analysis Group paper 577, update 196, 17 April 2010. http://www. southasiaanalysis.org/%5Cnotes6%5Cnote577.html. Accessed 12 December 2010.

Harris, Elizabeth. 2018. *Religion, Space and Conflict in Sri Lanka: Colonial and Postcolonial Perspectives.* London: Routledge.

————. 2019. 'Contested Histories, Multi-Religious Space and Conflict: A Case Study of Kantarodai in Northern Sri Lanka'. *Religions* 10(9): 537.

Harrison, Frances. 2012. *Still Counting the Dead: Survivors of Sri Lanka's Hidden War.* London: Portobello Books.

Harriss, John, Kristian Stokke and Olle Törnquist, eds. 2004. *Politicising Democracy: The New Local Politics of Democratisation.* Basingstoke: Palgrave.

Hasbullah, Shahul. 2001. *Muslim Refugees: The Forgotten People in Sri Lanka's Ethnic Conflict.* Nuraicholai, Sri Lanka: Research and Action Forum for Social Development.

Hasbullah, Shahul and Urs Geiser. 2019. *Negotiating Access to Land in Eastern Sri Lanka: Social Mobilization of Livelihood Concerns and Everyday Encounters with an Ambiguous State.* Colombo: International Centre for Ethnic Studies.

Hasbullah, Shahul and Benedikt Korf. 2013. 'Muslim Geographies, Violence and the Antinomies of Community in Eastern Sri Lanka'. *Geographical Journal* 179(3): 32–43.

Hashim, Ahmed. 2013. *When Counterinsurgency Wins: Sri Lanka's Defeat of the Tamil Tigers.* Philadelphia, PA: University of Pennsylvania Press.

Hayat, Maira. 2020. 'Empire's Accidents: Law, Lies, and Sovereignty in the "War on Terror" in Pakistan'. *Critique of Anthropology* 40(1): 49–80.

Heesterman, Jan C. 1985. *The Inner Conflict of Tradition: Essays in Indian Ritual, Kingship and Society.* Chicago, IL: University of Chicago Press.

Hellmann-Rajanayagam, Dagmar. 1994a. 'Tamils and the Meaning of History'. In *The Sri Lankan Tamils: Ethnicity and Identity,* edited by Chelvadurai Manogaran and Bryan Pfaffenberger, 54–83. Boulder, CO: Westview Press.

———. 1994b. *The Tamil Tigers: Armed Struggle for Identity.* Stuttgart: Franz Steiner Verlag.

Herring, Ronald. 2001. 'Making Ethnic Conflict: The Civil War in Sri Lanka'. In *Carrots, Sticks and Ethnic Conflict: Rethinking Development Assistance,* edited by Milton Esman and Ronald Herring, 140–174. Ann Arbor, MI: University of Michigan Press.

Heslop, Luke. 2014. 'On Sacred Ground: The Political Performance of Religious Responsibility'. *Contemporary South Asia* 22(1): 21–36.

Hocart, A. M. 1941 (1927). *Kingship.* London: Watts & Co.

Hodge, Paul. 2018. 'LetThemStay #BringThemHere: Embodied Politics, Asylum Seeking, and Performativities of Protest Opposing Australia's Operation Sovereign Borders'. *Environment and Planning C: Politics and Space* 37(3): 386–406.

Hoffman, Kasper and Judith Verweijen. 2019. 'Rebel Rule: A Governmentality Perspective'. *African Affairs* 118(471): 352–374.

Höglund, Kristine and Camilla Orjuela. 2012. 'Hybrid Peace Governance and Illiberal Peacebuilding in Sri Lanka'. *Global Governance* 18(1): 89–104.

———. 2013. 'Friction and the Pursuit of Justice in Post-War Sri Lanka'. *Peacebuilding* 1(3): 300–316.

Hoole, Rajan. 2001. *Sri Lanka: The Arrogance of Power: Myths, Decadence and Murder.* Colombo: University Teachers for Human Rights (Jaffna).

———. 2015. *Palmyra Fallen: From Rajani to War's End.* Colombo: University Teachers for Human Rights (Jaffna).

Hoole, Rajan, Daya Somasundaram, K. Sritharan and Rajani Thiranagama. 1992. *The Broken Palmyra: The Tamil Crisis in Sri Lanka—An Inside Account.* Claremont, CA: The Sri Lanka Studies Institute.

Hoole, Ratnajeevan. 2013. 'Jaffna's Upcoming Elections: Caste Ramifications'. *Colombo Telegraph*, 14 June 2013. https://www.colombotelegraph.com/index.php/jaffnas-upcoming-elections-caste-ramifications/. Accessed 10 April 2019.

Huang, Reyko. 2016. *The Wartime Origins of Democratization: Civil War, Rebel Governance, and Political Regimes*. Cambridge: Cambridge University Press.

Hull, Matthew. 2012a. *Government of Paper: The Materiality of Bureaucracy in Urban Pakistan*. Berkeley, CA: University of California Press.

———. 2012b. 'Documents and Bureaucracy'. *Annual Review of Anthropology* 41: 251–267.

Human Rights Watch. 2009. 'War on the Displaced: Sri Lankan Army and LTTE Abuses against Civilians in the Vanni'. http://www.hrw.org/en/reports/2009/02/19/war-displaced. Accessed 9 March 2011.

Hyndman, Jennifer and Malathi de Alwis. 2004. 'Bodies, Shrines, and Roads: Violence, (Im)Mobility and Displacement in Sri Lanka'. *Gender, Place and Culture* 11(4): 535–557.

Imtiyaz, A. R. M. 2023. 'Janatha Aragalaya: The People's Struggle in Sri Lanka'. *Journal of Governance, Security and Development* 3(2): 1–21.

International Centre for Ethnic Studies (ICES), ed. 1996. *Sri Lanka: The Devolution Debate*. Colombo: ICES.

International Crisis Group. 2017. 'Sri Lanka's Transition to Nowhere'. *Asia Report* 286. Brussels: International Crisis Group.

Ismail, Qadri. 1995. 'Unmooring Identity: The Antinomies of Elite Muslim Self-Representation in Modern Sri Lanka'. In *Unmaking the Nation: The Politics of Identity and History in Modern Sri Lanka*, edited by Pradeep Jeganathan and Qadri Ismail, 55–105. Colombo, Sri Lanka: Social Scientists' Association.

Jalal, Ayesha. 1990. *The State of Martial Rule: The Origins of Pakistan's Political Economy of Defence*. Cambridge: Cambridge University Press.

———. 1995. *Democracy and Authoritarianism in South Asia: A Comparative and Historical Perspective*. Cambridge: Cambridge University Press.

Jayasundara-Smits, Shyamika. 2022. *An Uneasy Hegemony: Politics of State-building and Struggles for Justice in Sri Lanka*. Cambridge: Cambridge University Press.

Jayatilleka, Dayan. 2000. 'Crisis of Devolution: 1988–1989'. In *Pursuit of Peace in Sri Lanka: Past Failures and Future Prospects*, edited by Kingsley de Silva and Gerald Peiris, 87–130. Kandy: International Centre for Ethnic Studies.

———. 2013. *Long War, Cold Peace, Conflict and Crisis in Sri Lanka*. Colombo: Vijitha Yapa.

Jayawardena, Kumari. 1986. *Feminism and Nationalism in the Third World*. London: Zed Books.

Jayaweera, Neville. 2014. *Jaffna: Exorcising the Past and Holding the Vision—An Autobiographical Reflection on the Ethnic Conflict by Neville Jayaweera, Government Agent of Jaffna, 1963–1966*. Maharagama: Ravaya Publishers.

Jazeel, Tarik and Kanchana Ruwanpura. 2009. 'Dissent: Sri Lanka's New Minority?' *Political Geography* 28(7): 385–387.

Jeeweshwara Räsänen, Bahirathy. 2015. '"Caste and Nation-Building" Constructing Vellalah Identity in Jaffna'. PhD diss., Gothenburg University.

Jeffrey, Alex. 2013. *The Improvised State: Sovereignty, Performance and Agency in Dayton Bosnia*. Oxford: Wiley-Blackwell.

Jeffrey, Alex, Fiona McConnell and Alice Wilson. 2015. 'Understanding Legitimacy: Perspectives from Anomalous Geopolitical Spaces'. *Geoforum* 66: 177–183.

Johansson, Andreas. 2019. *Pragmatic Muslim Politics: The Case of Sri Lanka Muslim Congress*. Cham: Springer.

Justin, Peter Hakim and Willemijn Verkoren. 2022. 'Hybrid Governance in South Sudan: The Negotiated State in Practice'. *Peacebuilding* 10(1): 17–36.

Kantorowicz, Ernst. 1997 (1957). *The King's Two Bodies: A Study in Mediaeval Political Theology*. Princeton, NJ: Princeton University Press.

Keenan, Alan. 2022. 'For Lanka, A Long Road to Democratic Reform Awaits'. Crisis Group Op-Ed, 25 July 2022. https://www.crisisgroup.org/asia/south-asia/sri-lanka/lanka-long-road-democratic-reform-awaits. Accessed 12 June 2023.

Kelly, Tobias. 2006. 'Documented Lives: Fear and the Uncertainties of Law during the Second Palestinian *Intifada*'. *Journal of the Royal Anthropological Institute* 12(1): 89–107.

———. 2008. 'The Attractions of Accountancy: Living an Ordinary Life during the Second Palestinian *Intifada*'. *Ethnography* 9(3): 351–376.

Kirsch, Scott and Colin Flint, eds. 2011. *Reconstructing Conflict: Integrating War and Post-War Geographies*. Farnham: Ashgate.

Klem, Bart. 2011. 'Islam, Politics and Violence in Eastern Sri Lanka'. *Journal of Asian Studies* 70(3): 730–753.

———. 2012. 'In the Eye of the Storm: Sri Lanka's Front-Line Civil Servants in Transition'. *Development and Change* 43(3): 695–717.

———. 2014. 'The Political Geography of War's End: Territorialisation, Circulation, and Moral Anxiety in Trincomalee, Sri Lanka'. *Political Geography* 38(1): 33–45.

————. 2015. 'Showing One's Colours: The Political Work of Elections in Post-War Sri Lanka'. *Modern Asian Studies* 49(4): 1091–1121.

————. 2018. 'The Problem of Peace and the Meaning of "Post-War"'. *Conflict, Security and Development* 18(3): 233–255.

————. 2020. 'Sri Lanka in 2019: The Return of the Rajapaksas'. *Asian Survey* 60(1): 207–212.

Klem, Bart. Forthcoming. 'Unravelling the Constitutional Settlement: Devolution, Democracy and Patronage in Eastern Sri Lanka.' Accepted by *Contemporary South Asia*.

Klem, Bart and Sidharthan Maunaguru. 2017. 'Insurgent Rule as Sovereign Mimicry and Mutation: Governance, Kingship and Violence in Civil Wars'. *Comparative Studies in Society and History* 59(3): 629–656.

————. 2018. 'Public Authority under Sovereign Encroachment: Community Leadership in War-Time Sri Lanka'. *Modern Asian Studies* 52(3): 784–814.

Klem, Bart and Dinesha Samararatne. 2022. 'Sri Lanka in 2021: Vistas on the Brink'. *Asian Survey* 62(1): 201–210.

Klem, Bart and Bert Suykens. 2018. 'The Politics of Order and Disturbance: Public Authority, Sovereignty and Violent Contestation in South Asia'. *Modern Asian Studies* 52(3): 753–783.

Knoerzer, Shari. 1998. 'Transformation of Muslim Political Identity'. In *Culture and Politics of Identity in Sri Lanka*, edited by Mithran Tiruchelvam and C. S. Dattathreya, 136–167. Colombo: International Centre for Ethnic Studies.

Korf, Benedikt. 2006. 'Who Is the Rogue? Discourse, Power and Spatial Politics in Post-War Sri Lanka'. *Political Geography* 25(3): 279–297.

————. 2009. 'Cartographic Violence: Engaging a Sinhala Kind of Geography'. In *Spatialising Politics: Culture and Geography in Post-Colonial Sri Lanka*, edited by Cathrine Brun and Tarik Jazeel, 100–121. New Delhi: Sage.

Korf, Benedikt, Michelle Engeler and Tobias Hagman. 2010. 'The Geography of Warscape'. *Third World Quarterly* 31(3): 385–399.

Krasniqi, Gëzim. 2019. 'Contested States as Liminal Spaces of Citizenship: Comparing Kosovo and the Turkish Republic of Northern Cyprus'. *Ethnopolitics* 18(3): 298–314.

Krishna, Sankaran. 1999. *Postcolonial Insecurities: India, Sri Lanka and the Question of Nationhood*. Minneapolis, MN: University of Minnesota Press.

Kunnath, George. 2012. *Rebels from the Mud Houses: Dalits and the Making of the Maoist Revolution in Bihar*. London: Routledge.

Kuttig, Julian and Bert Suykens. 2020. 'How to Be Visible in Student Politics? Performativity and the Digital Public Space in Bangladesh'. *Journal of Asian Studies* 79(3): 707–738.

Kyris, George. 2022. 'State Recognition and Dynamic Sovereignty'. *European Journal of International Relations* 28(2): 287–311.

Laffey, Mark and Suthaharan Nadarajah. 2016. 'Securing the Diaspora: Policing Global Order'. In *The Global Making of Police: Postcolonial Perspectives*, edited by Jan Hönke and Markus-Michael Muller, 114–131. London: Routledge.

Lecomte-Tilouine, Marie, ed. 2013. *Revolution in Nepal: An Anthropological and Historical Approach to the People's War*. Delhi: Oxford University Press.

Leigh, Darcy and Cynthia Weber. 2018. 'Gendered and Sexualized Figurations of Security'. In *Routledge Handbook of Gender and Security*. https://www.taylorfrancis.com/chapters/edit/10.4324/9781315525099-7/gendered-sexualized-figurations-security-darcy-leigh-cynthia-weber. Accessed 20 June 2023.

Lewer, Nick and Muhammed Ismail. 2011. 'A Voice in the Political Process? Creating Political Space for a Muslim Contribution to Peace in Sri Lanka'. In *Aid, Conflict and Peacebuilding in Sri Lanka*, edited by Jonathan Goodhand, Benedikt Korf and Jonathan Spencer, 119–131. London: Routledge.

Little, Adrian. 2008. *Democratic Piety: Complexity, Conflict and Violence*. Edinburgh: Edinburgh University Press.

———. 2014. *Enduring Conflict: Challenging the Signature of Peace and Democracy*. London: Bloomsbury.

Little, Suzanne, Samid Suliman and Caroline Wake, eds. 2023. *Performance, Resistance and Refugees*. Abingdon: Routledge.

Loganathan, Ketesh. 2006. 'Indo-Lanka Accord and the Ethnic Question: Lessons and Experiences'. In *Negotiating Peace in Sri Lanka: Efforts, Failures and Lessons*, edited by Kumar Rupesinghe, 1:69–102. Colombo: Foundation for Coexistence.

Lombard, Louisa. 2020. *Hunting Game: Raiding Politics in the Central African Republic*. Cambridge: Cambridge University Press.

Lubkemann, Stephen. 2008. *Culture in Chaos: An Anthropology of the Social Condition of War*. Chicago, IL: University of Chicago Press.

Ludsin. 2012. 'Sovereignty and the 1972 Constitution'. In *The Sri Lankan Republic at 40: Reflections on Constitutional History, Theory and Practice*, edited by Asanga Welikala, 289–340. Colombo: Centre for Policy Alternatives.

Lund, Christian. 2006. 'Twilight Institutions: Public Authority and Local Politics in Africa'. *Development and Change* 37(4): 673–684.

Mac Ginty, Roger and Oliver Richmond. 2016. 'The Fallacy of Constructing Hybrid Political Orders: A Reappraisal of the Hybrid Turn in Peacebuilding'. *International Peacekeeping* 23(2): 219–239.

Malik, Anushay. 2018. 'Public Authority and Local Resistance: Abdur Rehman and the Industrial Workers of Lahore, 1969–1974'. *Modern Asian Studies* 52(3): 815–848.

Mampilly, Zachariah. 2011. *Rebel Rulers: Insurgent Governance and Civilian Life during War*. Ithaca, NY: Cornell University Press.

Mampilly, Zachariah and Megan Stewart. 2021. 'A Typology of Rebel Political Institutional Arrangements'. *Journal of Conflict Resolution* 65(1): 15–45.

Manogaran, Chelvadurai. 1994. 'Colonization as Politics: Political Use of Space in Sri Lanka's Ethnic Conflict'. In *The Sri Lankan Tamils: Ethnicity and Identity*, edited by Chelvadurai Manogaran and Bryan Pfaffenberger, 84–125. Boulder, CO: Westview Press.

Marttila, Tomas. 2016. *Post-Foundational Discourse Analysis: From Political Difference to Empirical Research*. Basingstoke: Palgrave Macmillan.

Mathur, Nanayika. 2015. *Paper Tiger: Law, Bureaucracy, and the Developmental State in Himalayan India*. Cambridge: Cambridge University Press.

Matthews, Bruce. 1982. 'District Development Councils in Sri Lanka'. *Asian Survey* 22(11): 1117–1134.

Maunaguru, Sidharthan. 2021. '"Homeless" Deities and Refugee Devotees: Hindu Temples, Divine Power and Sri Lankan Tamil Communities'. *American Anthropologist* 123(2): 552–564.

Maunaguru, Sidharthan and Jonathan Spencer. 2013. 'Tigers, Temples, and the Remaking of Tamil Society: Report from the Field'. *Religion and Society* 3(1): 169–176.

Maunaguru, Sitralega. 1995. 'Gendering Tamil Nationalism: The Construction of Woman in Projects of Protest and Control'. In *Unmaking the Nation: The Politics of Identity and History in Modern Sri Lanka*, edited by Pradeep Jeganathan and Qadri Ismail, 158–175. Colombo: Social Scientists' Association.

McConnell, Fiona. 2016. *Rehearsing the State: The Political Practices of the Tibetan Government-in-Exile*. Chichester: Wiley Blackwell.

McGilvray, Dennis. 2008. *Crucible of Conflict: Tamil and Muslim Society on the East Coast of Sri Lanka*. Durham, NC: Duke University Press.

McGilvray, Dennis and Mirak Raheem. 2007. 'Muslim Perspectives on the Sri Lankan Conflict'. Policy Studies 41. Washington, DC: East-West Center.

Meagher, Kate. 2012. 'The Strength of Weak States? Non-State Security Forces and Hybrid Governance in Africa'. *Development and Change* 43(5): 1073–1101.

Menkhaus, Ken. 2006. 'Governance without Government in Somalia: Spoilers, State Building and the Politics of Coping'. *International Security* 31(3): 74–106.

Michelman, Frank. 1998. 'Constitutional Authorship'. In *Constitutionalism: Philosophical Foundations*, edited by Larry Alexander, 64–98. Cambridge: Cambridge University Press.

Michelutti, Lucia. 2010. 'Wrestling with (Body) Politics: Understanding Muscular Political Styles in North India'. In *Power and Influence in South Asia: Bosses, Lords, and Captains*, edited by Pamela Price and Arild Ruud, 44–69. Delhi; London: Routledge.

Michelutti, Lucia, Ashraf Hoque, Nicolas Martin, David Picherit, Paul Rollier, Arild Engelsen Ruud and Clarinda Still. 2018. *Mafia Raj: The Rule of Bosses in South Asia*. Stanford, CA: Stanford University Press.

Mihlar, Farah. 2019. 'Religious Change in a Minority Context: Transforming Islam in Sri Lanka'. *Third World Quarterly* 40(12): 2153–2169.

Mines, Mattison. 1994. *Public Faces, Private Voices: Community and Individuality in South India*. Berkeley, CA: University of California Press.

Mitchell, Timothy. 1991. 'The Limits of the State: Beyond Statist Approaches and Their Critics'. *American Political Science Review* 85(1): 77–96.

Mohideen, M. I. M. 2006. *North-East Muslim Question and Peace Process in Sri Lanka*. Maharagama: Impulse Printers & Publishers.

Mongia, Radhika. 2007. 'Historicizing State Sovereignty: Inequality and the Form of Equivalence'. *Comparative Studies in Society and History* 49(2): 384–411.

———. 2018. *Indian Migration and Empire: A Colonial Genealogy of the Modern State*. Durham, NC: Duke University Press.

Moore, Sally Falk. 1978. *Law as Process: An Anthropological Approach*. London: Routledge and Kegan Paul.

Morris, Errol. 2003. *The Fog of War: Eleven Lessons from the Life of Robert S. McNamara*. Documentary film, Sony Pictures Classics.

Mountz, Alison. 2011. 'The Enforcement Archipelago: Detention, Haunting, and Asylum on Islands'. *Political Geography* 30(3): 118–128.

Mukherjee, Mithi. 2010. *India in the Shadow of Empire: A Legal and Political History, 1774–1950*. Delhi: Oxford University Press.

Murray Li, Tania. 2005. 'Beyond "the State" and Failed Schemes'. *American Anthropologist* 107(3): 383–394.

Natali, Cristiana. 2008. 'Building Cemeteries, Constructing Identities: Funerary Practices and Nationalist Discourse among the Tamil Tigers of Sri Lanka'. *Contemporary South Asia* 16(3): 287–301.

Navaro-Yashin, Yael. 2003. '"Life Is Dead Here": Sensing the Political in "No Man's Land"'. *Anthropological Theory* 3(1): 107–125.

———. 2012. *The Make-Believe Space: Affective Geography in a Postwar Polity.* Durham, NC: Duke University Press.

Nithiyanandan, V. 1987. 'An Analysis of Economic Factors Behind the Origin and Development of Tamil Nationalism in Sri Lanka'. In *Facets of Ethnicity in Sri Lanka,* edited by Charles Abeysekere and Newton Gunasinghe, 100–170. Colombo: Social Scientists' Association.

Nordstrom, Carolyn. 1997. *A Different Kind of War Story.* Philadelphia, PA: University of Pennsylvania Press.

———. 2004. *Shadows of War: Violence, Power, and International Profiteering in the Twenty-First Century.* Berkeley, CA: University of California Press.

Nuhman, M. 2002. *Understanding Sri Lankan Muslim Identity.* Colombo: International Centre for Ethnic Studies.

Ochoa Espejo, Paulina. 2020. *On Borders: Territories, Legitimacy, and the Rights of Place.* Oxford: Oxford University Press.

Orjuela, Camilla. 2008. 'Distant Warriors, Distant Peace Workers? Multiple Diaspora Roles in Sri Lanka's Violent Conflict'. *Global Networks* 8(4): 436–452.

Pahuja, Sundhya. 2011. *Decolonising International Law: Development, Economic Growth and the Politics of Universality.* Cambridge: Cambridge University Press.

Paley, Julia, ed. 2008. *Democracy: Anthropological Perspectives.* Santa Fe, NM: School of Advanced Research Press.

Parashar, Swati. 2018. 'The Postcolonial/Emotional State: Mother India's Response to Her Deviant Maoist Children'. In *Revisiting Gendered States: Feminist Imaginings of the State in International Relations,* edited by Swati Parashar, 57–173. Oxford: Oxford University Press.

———. 2019. 'Colonial Legacies, Armed Revolts and State Violence: The Maoist Movement in India'. *Third World Quarterly* 40(2): 337–354.

Peace, Norbert. 2009. 'Disciplining the Body, Disciplining the Bodypolitic: Physical Culture and Social Violence among North Indian Wrestlers'. *Comparative Studies in Society and History* 51(2): 372–400.

Peebles, Patrick. 2006. *The History of Sri Lanka*. Westport, CT: Greenwood Press.

Pegg, Scott. 1998. *International Society and the De Facto State*. Aldershot: Ashgate.

———. 2017. 'Twenty Years of de facto State Studies: Progress, Problems, and Prospects'. In *Oxford Research Encyclopedia of Politics, edited by William Thompson*. https://oxfordre.com/politics/view/10.1093/acrefore/9780190228637.001.0001/acrefore-9780190228637-e-516. Accessed 20 June 2023.

Pegg, Scott and Pål Kolstø. 2015. 'Somaliland: Dynamics of Internal Legitimacy and (Lack of) External Sovereignty'. *Geoforum* 66: 193–202.

Peiris, Pradeep, ed. 2021. *Is the Cure Worse Than the Disease? Reflections on COVID Governance in Sri Lanka*. Colombo: Centre for Policy Alternatives, 13 August 2021. https://www.cpalanka.org/is-the-cure-worse-than-the-disease-reflection-on-covid-governance-in-sri-lanka/. Accessed 29 June 2023.

Perera, Nihal. 1997. 'Territorial Spaces and National Identities: Representations of Sri Lanka'. *South Asia: Journal of South Asian Studies* 20(S1): 23–50.

Pettygrew, Judith. 2013. *Maoists at the Hearth: Everyday Life in Nepal's Civil War*. Philadelphia, PA: University of Pennsylvania Press.

Pfaffenberger, Bryan. 1990. 'The Political Construction of Defensive Nationalism: The 1968 Temple-Entry Crisis in Northern Sri Lanka'. *Journal of Asian Studies* 49(1): 78–96.

Piliavsky, Anastasia, ed. 2014a. *Patronage as Politics in South Asia*. Cambridge: Cambridge University Press.

———. 2014b. 'India's Demotic Democracy and Its "Depravities" in the Ethnographic *Longue Durée*'. In *Patronage as Politics in South Asia*, edited by Anastasia Piliavsky, 154–175. Cambridge: Cambridge University Press.

Preltz-Oltramonti, Giulia. 2017. 'Trajectories of Illegality and Informality in Conflict Protraction'. *Caucasus Survey* 4(3): 85–101.

Price, Pamela and Arild Engelsen Ruud. 2014. *Power and Influence in India: Bosses, Lords and Captains*. New Delhi: Routledge.

Price, Pamela and Dusi Srinivas. 2014. 'Patronage and Autonomy in India's Deepening Democracy'. In *Patronage as Politics in South Asia*, edited by Anastasia Piliavsky, 217–236. Cambridge: Cambridge University Press.

Provost, René. 2021. *Rebel Courts: The Administration of Justice by Armed Insurgents*. Oxford: Oxford University Press.

Purushotham, Sunil. 2015. 'Internal Violence: The "Police Action" in Hyderabad'. *Comparative Studies in Society and History* 57(2): 435–466.

———. 2021. *From Raj to Republic: Sovereignty, Violence, and Democracy in India*. Stanford, CA: Stanford University Press.

Rajamanoharan, Sivakami and Kumaravadivel Guruparan. 2013. 'Four Years on, Genocide Continues off the Battlefield'. *Open Democracy.* https://www.opendemocracy.net/opensecurity/kumaravadivel-guruparan-sivakami-rajamanoharan/four-years-on-genocide-continues-off-bat. Accessed 19 February 2019.

Rasaratnam, Madurika. 2016. *Tamils and the Nation: India and Sri Lanka Compared.* London: Hurst.

Rasaratnam, Madurika and Mara Malagodi. 2012. 'Eyes Wide Shut: Persistent Conflict and Liberal Peace-Building in Nepal and Sri Lanka'. *Conflict, Security and Development* 12(3): 299–327.

Reynolds, Andrew. 2002. *The Architecture of Democracy: Constitutional Design, Conflict Management, and Democracy.* London: Oxford University Press.

Richards, Paul. 1996. *Fighting for the Rain Forest: War, Youth, and Resources in Sierra Leone.* Oxford: James Currey.

———, ed. 2004. *No Peace No War: An Anthropology of Contemporary Armed Conflicts.* Athens, GA: Ohio University Press.

Roberts, Michael. 2014. 'Encompassing Empowerment in Ritual, War and Assassination'. *Social Analysis* 58(1): 88–106.

Rogers, John. 1994. 'Post-Orientalism and the Interpretation of Premodern and Modern Political Identities: The Case of Sri Lanka'. *Journal of Asian Studies* 53(1): 10–23.

Rose, Nikolas. 1999. *Powers of Freedom: Reframing Political Thought.* Cambridge: Cambridge University Press.

Rothchild, Donald and Philip Roeder, eds. 2005. *Sustainable Peace: Power and Democracy after Civil Wars.* Ithaca, NY: Cornell University Press.

Rupesinghe, Kumar, ed. 2006. *Negotiating Peace in Sri Lanka: Efforts, Failures and Lessons.* Vols. 1 and 2. Colombo: Foundation for Coexistence.

Rutherford, Blair. 2004. '"Settlers" and Zimbabwe: Politics, Memory, and the Anthropology of Commercial Farms During a Time of Crisis'. *Identities* 11(4): 543–562.

Rutherford, Danilyn. 2012. *Laughing at Leviathan: Sovereignty and Audience in West Papua.* Chicago, IL: Chicago University Press.

Russel, Jane. 1978. 'The Dance of the Turkey-Cock: The Jaffna Boycott of 1931'. *Ceylon Journal of Historical and Social Studies* 8(1): 47–67.

Ruud, Arild Engelsen. 2009. 'Talking Dirty About Politics: A View from a Bengali Village'. In *The Everyday State and Modern India*, edited by Chris Fuller and Véronique Bénéï, 115–136. New Delhi: Social Science Press.

Ruwanpura, Kanchana. 2016. 'Post-War Sri Lanka: State, Capital and Labour, and the Politics of Reconciliation'. *Contemporary South Asia* 24(4): 351–359.

Sahlins, Marshall. 2008. 'The Stranger-King or, Elementary Forms of the Politics of Life'. *Indonesia and the Malay World* 36(105): 177–199.

Samararatne, Dinesha. 2019. 'Proposals for a New Bill of Rights in Sri Lanka: Narrow Debates, Unmarked Challenges'. *Round Table* 108(6): 667–678.

———. 2022. 'The People in the Palace'. *Verfassungsblog*, 15 July 2022. https://verfassungsblog.de/the-people-in-the-palace/. Accessed 28 June 2023.

Sampanthan, R. 2012. 'The *Ilankai Thamil Arasu Katchi* (Federal Party) and the Post-Independence Politics of Ethnic Pluralism: Tamil Nationalism before and after the Republic—An Interview with R. Sampanthan'. In *The Sri Lankan Republic at 40: Reflections on Constitutional History, Theory and Practice*, edited by Asanga Welikala, 933–960. Colombo: Centre for Policy Alternatives.

Samuel, Kumudini. 2003. 'Activism, Motherhood, and the State in Sri Lanka's Ethnic Conflict'. In *Feminists under Fire: Exchanges across War Zones*, edited by Wenona Giles, Malathi de Alwis, Edith Klein and Neluka Silva, 167–180. Toronto: Between the Lines.

Sánchez Meertens, Ariel. 2013. 'Letters from Batticaloa: TMVP's Emergence and the Transformation of Conflict in Eastern Sri Lanka'. PhD diss., Utrecht University.

Saravanamuttu, Paikiasothy. 2003. 'Sri Lanka: The Best and Last Chance for Peace?' *Conflict, Security and Development* 3(1): 129–138.

Sarvananthan, Muttukrishna. 2007. 'In Pursuit of a Mythical State of Tamil Eelam: A Rejoinder to Kristian Stokke'. *Third World Quarterly* 28(6): 1185–1195.

———. 2016. 'Elusive Economic Peace Dividend in Sri Lanka: All that Glitters Is not Gold'. *GeoJournal* 81(4): 571–596.

Sathananthan, S. 2013. 'The Meanings of Wigneswaran'. *Colombo Telegraph*, blogpost, 31 July 2013. https://www.colombotelegraph.com/index.php/the-meanings-of-wigneswaran/. Accessed 22 May 2021.

Satkunanathan, Ambika. 2012. 'Whose Nation? Power, Agency, Gender and Tamil Nationalism'. In *Sri Lankan Republic at 40: Reflections on Constitutional History, Theory and Practice*, edited by Asanga Welikala, 612–660. Colombo: Centre for Policy Alternatives.

———. 2016. 'Collaboration, Suspicion and Traitors: An Exploratory Study of Intra-Community Relations in Post-War Northern Sri Lanka'. *Contemporary South Asia* 24(4): 416–428.

————. 2022. 'The Aragalaya versus Struggles: A Story of Inclusions and Exclusions'. *Economic and Political Weekly* 57(52). https://www.epw.in/journal/2022/52/commentary/%C2%A0aragalaya%C2%A0versus-struggles.html. Accessed 28 June 2023.

Saunders, Cheryl and Anna Dziedzic. 2012. 'Parliamentary Sovereignty and Written Constitutions in Comparative Perspective'. In *The Sri Lankan Republic at 40: Reflections on Constitutional History, Theory and Practice*, edited by Asanga Welikala, 476–506. Colombo: Centre for Policy Alternatives.

Schaap, Andrew. 2004. 'Political Reconciliation through a Struggle for Recognition?' *Social and Legal Studies* 13(4): 523–540.

Schalk, Peter. 1994. 'Women Fighters of the Liberation Tigers in Tamil Ilam: The Martial Feminism of Atel Palacinkam'. *South Asia Research* 14(2): 163–195.

————. 1997a. 'The Revival of Martyr Cults among Ilavar'. *Temenos* 33: 151–190.

————. 1997b. 'Historisation of the Martial Ideology of the Liberation Tigers of Tamil Ealam (LTTE)'. *South Asia: Journal of South Asian Studies* 20(2): 35–72.

Schmitt, Carl. 2005 (1922). *Political Theology: Four Chapters on the Concept of Sovereignty.* Translated by George Schwab. Chicago, IL: University of Chicago Press.

Schonthal, Benjamin. 2016a. *Buddhism, Politics and the Limits of Law: The Pyrrhic Constitutionalism of Sri Lanka.* Cambridge: Cambridge University Press.

————. 2016b. 'Environments of Law: Islam, Buddhism, and the State in Contemporary Sri Lanka'. *Journal of Asian Studies* 75(1): 137–156.

Scott, David. 1995. 'Colonial Governmentality'. *Social Text* 43 (Autumn): 191–220.

Sen, Atreyee. 2007. *Shiv Sena Women: Violence and Communalism in a Bombay Slum.* London: Hurst.

Sen, Atreyee and David Pratten, eds. 2008. *Global Vigilantes: New Perspectives on Justice and Violence.* New York, NY: Columbia University Press.

Sen, Sudipta. 2002. *Distant Sovereignty: National Imperialism and the Origins of British India.* London: Routledge.

Seoighe, Rachel. 2016a. 'Inscribing the Victor's Land: Nationalistic Authorship in Sri Lanka's Post-War North-East'. *Conflict, Security and Development* 16(5): 443–471.

————. 2016b. 'Discourses of Victimization in Sri Lanka's Civil War'. *Social and Legal Studies* 25(3): 355–380.

———. 2017. *War, Denial and Nation-Building in Sri Lanka: After the End.* Basingstoke: Palgrave Macmillan.

Shah, Alpa. 2013. 'The Tensions over Liberal Citizenship in a Marxist Revolutionary Situation: The Maoists in India'. *Critique of Anthropology* 33(1): 91–109.

———. 2019. *Nightmarch: Among India's Revolutionary Guerrillas.* Chicago, IL: University of Chicago Press.

Shani, Giorgio. 2007. *Sikh Nationalism and Identity in a Global Age.* London: Routledge.

Shastri, Amita. 1990. 'The Material Basis for Separatism: The Tamil Eelam Movement in Sri Lanka'. *Journal of Asian Studies* 49(1): 55–77.

Sherman, Taylor, William Gould and Sarah Ansari. 2011. 'From Subjects to Citizens: Society and the Everyday State in India and Pakistan, 1947–1970'. *Modern Asian Studies* 45(1): 1–6.

Siegel, James T. 1998. *A New Type of Criminal in Jakarta: Counter-Revolution Today.* Durham, NC: Duke University Press.

Silva, Tudor Kalinga. 2020. 'Nationalism, Caste-Blindness, and the Continuing Problems of War-Displaced Panchamars in Post-War Jaffna Society'. *Caste: A Global Journal on Social Exclusion* 1(1): 51–70.

Silva, K. Tudor, P. P. Sivapragasam and Thanges Paramsothy, eds. 2009. *Casteless or Caste-Blind? Dynamics of Concealed Caste Discrimination, Social Exclusion and Protest in Sri Lanka.* Copenhagen; New Delhi; Colombo: International Dalit Solidarity Network; Indian Institute of Dalit Studies; Kumaran Book House.

Simpson, Audra. 2014. *Mohawk Interruptus: Political Life across the Borders of Settler States.* Durham, NC: Duke University Press.

Simpson, Gerry J. 1996. 'The Diffusion of Sovereignty: Self-Determination in the Post-Colonial Age'. *Stanford Journal of International Law* 32(2): 255–286.

Singh, Bhrigupati. 2012 'The Headless Horseman of Central India: Sovereignty at Varying Thresholds of Life'. *Cultural Anthropology* 27(2): 383–407.

Sitrampalam, S. K. 2005. 'The Tamils of Sri Lanka: The Historic Roots of Tamil Identity'. In *Dealing with Diversity: Sri Lankan Discourses on Peace and Conflict,* edited by Georg Frerks and Bart Klem, 231–274. The Hague: Clingendael.

Sivarajah, Ambalavanar. 2007. *The Federal Party of Sri Lanka.* Chennai: Kumaran Book House.

Sörensen, Mayken Jul. 2016. *Humour in Political Activism: Creative Nonviolent Resistance.* London: Palgrave Macmillan.

Sosnowski, Marika. Under review. 'The Bureaucratic Revolution'.

Spencer, Jonathan. 2003. 'A Nation "Living in Different Places": Notes on the Impossible Work of Purification in Postcolonial Sri Lanka'. *Contributions to Indian Sociology* 37(1–2): 1–23.

———. 2007. *Anthropology, Politics, and the State: Democracy and Violence in South Asia*. Cambridge: Cambridge University Press.

———. 2008. 'A Nationalism without Politics? The Illiberal Consequences of Liberal Institutions in Sri Lanka'. *Third World Quarterly* 29(3): 611–629.

———. 2012. 'Performing Democracy and Violence, Agonism and Community, Politics and Not Politics in Sri Lanka'. *Geoforum* 43(4): 725–731.

———. 2016. 'Securitization and Its Discontents: The End of Sri Lanka's Long Post-War?' *Contemporary South Asia* 24(1): 94–108.

Spencer, Jonathan, Jonathan Goodhand, Shahul Hasbullah, Bart Klem, Benedikt Korf and Tudor Silva. 2015. *Checkpoint, Temple, Church and Mosque: A Collaborative Ethnography of War and Peace*. London: Pluto.

Spivak, Gayatri. 1988. 'Can the Subaltern Speak?' In *Marxism and the Interpretation of Culture*, edited by Cary Nelson and Lawrence Grossberg, 271–313. Basingstoke: Macmillan.

Staniland, Paul. 2012. 'Organizing Insurgency: Networks, Resources and Rebellion in South Asia'. *International Security* 37(1): 142–177.

———. 2014. *Networks of Rebellion: Explaining Insurgent Cohesion and Collapse*. Ithaca, NY: Cornell University Press.

Stengs, Irene. 2008. 'Modern Thai Encounters with the Sublime: The Powerful Presence of a Great King of Siam through His Portraits'. *Material Religion* 4(2): 160–171.

Stern, Maria. 2005. *Naming Security – Constructing Identity: 'Mayan-Women' in Guatemala on the Eve of 'Peace'*. Manchester: Manchester University Press.

Stern, Paul and Daniel Druckman, eds. 2000. *Conflict Resolution after the Cold War*. Washington, DC: National Academy Press.

Stokke, Kristian. 2006. 'Building the Tamil Eelam State: Emerging State Institutions and Forms of Governance in LTTE-Controlled Areas in Sri Lanka'. *Third World Quarterly* 27(6): 1021–1040.

———. 2007. 'War by Other Means: The LTTE's Strategy of Institutionalising Power Sharing in the Context of Transition from War to Peace – A Response to Muttukrishna Sarvananthan'. *Third World Quarterly* 27(6): 1021–1040.

———. 2010. 'The Soft Power of a Small State: Discursive Constructions and Institutional Practices of Norway's Peace Engagement'. *Power, Conflict and Democracy Journal* 2(1): 137–173.

Stokke, Kristian and Jayadeva Uyangoda, eds. 2011. *Liberal Peace in Question: Politics of State and Market Reform in Sri Lanka*. London: Anthem Press.

Strauss, Julia and Donald Cruise O'Brien, eds. 2007. *Staging Politics: Power and Performance in Asia and Africa*. London; New York, NY: I. B. Tauris.

Sumathy, Sivamohan. 2001. *Militants, Militarism and the Crisis of (Tamil) Nationalism*. Marga Monograph Series on Ethnic Reconciliation, no. 22. Colombo: Marga Institute.

———. 2016a. 'A Spoonful of Sugar: The Quest for Survival and Justice'. In *The Search for Justice: The Sri Lankan Papers*, edited by Kumari Jayawardena and Kishali Pinto-Jayawardena, 296–368. New Delhi: Zubaan.

———. 2016b. 'Territorial Claims, Home, Land and Movement: Women's History of Violence and Resistance'. In *The Search for Justice: The Sri Lankan Papers*, edited by Kumari Jayawardena and Kishali Pinto-Jayawardena, 369–399. New Delhi: Zubaan.

Sur, Malini. 2021. *Jungle Passports: Fences, Mobility, and Citizenship at the Northeast India–Bangladesh Border*. Philadelphia, PA: University of Pennsylvania Press.

Suykens, Bert. 2010. 'Diffuse Authority in the Beedi Commodity Chain: Naxalite and State Governance in Tribal Telangana, India'. *Development and Change* 41(1): 153–178.

———. 2018. '"A Hundred Per Cent Good Man Cannot Do Politics": Violent Self-Sacrifice, Student Authority, and Party-State Integration in Bangladesh'. *Modern Asian Studies* 52(3): 883–916.

Suykens, Bert and Aynul Islam. 2013. '*Hartal* as a Complex Political Performance: General Strikes and the Organisation of (Local) Power in Bangladesh'. *Contributions to Indian Sociology* 47(1): 61–83.

Sylvester, Christine, ed. 2011. *Experiencing War*. London: Routledge.

———. 2013. 'Experiencing War: A Challenge for International Relations'. *Cambridge Review of International Affairs* 26(4): 669–674.

Tambiah, Stanley. 1996. *Leveling Crowds: Ethno-Nationalist Conflicts and Collective Violence in South Asia*. Berkeley, CA: University of California Press.

Tamil United Liberation Front (TULF). 1988. *Tamil United Liberation Front: Towards Devolution of Power in Sri Lanka—Main Documents August 1983– October 1987*. Madras: TULF.

Terpstra, Niels and Georg Frerks. 2018. 'Governance Practices and Symbolism: De Facto Sovereignty and Public Authority in "Tigerland"'. *Modern Asian Studies* 52(3): 1001–1042.

Thamizhini. 2021. *In the Shadow of a Sword: The Memoir of a Women Leader in the LTTE*. Translated by Nedra Rodrigo. New Delhi: Yoda Press, Sage and Select.

Thangarajah, Yuvi. 2012. 'The Poetics and Politics of Democracy: State and Governance in the East'. In *Reframing Democracy: Perspectives on the Cultures of Inclusion and Exclusion in Contemporary Sri Lanka*, edited by Jayadeva Uyangoda and Neloufer de Mel, 152–200. Colombo: Social Scientists' Association.

Thanges, Paramsothy. 2014. '"Will It Disappear, If You Stop Talking About It?" A Question on Caste and Ethnicity in Jaffna'. *Colombo Telegraph*, 21 June 2014. https://www.colombotelegraph.com/index.php/will-it-disappear-if-you-stop-talking-about-it-a-question-on-caste-and-ethnicity-in-jaffna/. Accessed 10 April 2019.

———. 2015. 'Caste and Camp People in Jaffna: Landownership and Landlessness'. *Colombo Telegraph*, 8 December 2015. https://www.colombotelegraph.com/index.php/caste-camp-people-in-jaffna-landownership-landlessness/. Accessed 10 April 2019.

Thiranagama, Rajani. 1992. 'No More Tears Sister: The Experiences of Women'. In *Broken Palmyrah: The Tamil Crisis in Sri Lanka—An Inside Account*, edited by Rajan Hoole, K. Sritharan, Daya Somasundaram and Rajani Thiranagama, 305–330. Claremont, CA: Sri Lanka Studies Institute.

Thiranagama, Sharika. 2010. 'In Praise of Traitors: Intimacy, Betrayal and the Sri Lankan Tamil Community'. In *Traitors: Suspicion, Intimacy and the Ethics of State-Building*, edited by Sharika Thiranagama and Tobias Kelly, 127–149. Philadelphia, PA: University of Pennsylvania Press.

———. 2011. *In My Mother's House: Civil War in Sri Lanka*. Philadelphia, PA: University of Pennsylvania Press.

———. 2013. 'Claiming the State: Postwar Reconciliation in Sri Lanka'. *Humanity: An International Journal of Human Rights, Humanitarianism and Development* 4(1): 93–116.

Thiruchelvam, Neelan. 2000. 'The Politics of Federalism and Diversity in Sri Lanka'. In *Autonomy and Ethnicity: Negotiating Competing Claims in Multi-Ethnic States*, edited by Yash Ghai, 197–215. Cambridge: Cambridge University Press.

Thompson, Helen. 2006. 'The Case for External Sovereignty'. *European Journal of International Relations* 12(2): 251–274.

Thurairajah, Tanuja. 2022. 'Performing Nationalism: The United Nations Human Rights Council (UNHRC) and Sri Lankan Tamil Diasporic Politics in Switzerland'. *Geographical Journal* 188(1): 28–41.

Together Against Genocide. 2015. 'The ICTY Srebrenica Genocide Analysis: Implications for Sri Lanka's 2009 "No Fire Zones"'. 8 July 2015. http://www.tamilsagainstgenocide.org/read.aspx?storyid=155. Accessed 19 February 2019.

Trawick, Margaret. 1997. 'Reasons for Violence: A Preliminary Ethnographic Account of the LTTE'. *South Asia* 20 (issue supp. 001): 153–180.

———. 2007. *Enemy Lines: Warfare, Childhood, and Play in Batticaloa*. Berkeley, CA: University of California Press.

True, Jacqui. 2018. 'Bringing Back Gendered States: Feminist Second Image Theorizing of International Relations'. In *Revisiting Gendered States: Feminist Imaginings of the State in International Relations*, edited by Swati Parashar, 33–48. Oxford: Oxford University Press.

Uyangoda, Jayadeva. 2007. *Ethnic Conflict in Sri Lanka: Changing Dynamics*. Policy Studies 32. Washington, DC: East-West Center.

———. 2011. 'Travails of State Reform in the Context of Protracted Civil War in Sri Lanka'. In *Liberal Peace in Question: Politics of State and Market Reform in Sri Lanka*, edited by Kristian Stokke and Jayadeva Uyangoda, 35–62. London: Anthem Press.

———. 2022. 'Bringing Democracy Back Through People's Power'. *Groundviews*, 16 August 2022. https://groundviews.org/2022/08/16/bringing-democracy-back-throughpeoples-power/. Accessed 28 June 2023.

———. 2023. *Democracy and Democratisation in Sri Lanka: Paths, Trends and Imaginations*. Vols. 1–2. Colombo: Bandaranaike Centre for International Studies.

Uyangoda, Jayadeva and Neloufer de Mel, eds. 2012. *Reframing Democracy: Perspectives on the Cultures of Inclusion and Exclusion in Contemporary Sri Lanka*. Colombo: Social Scientists' Association.

Vaishnav, Milan. 2017. *When Crime Pays: Money and Muscle in Indian Politics*. New Haven, CT; London: Yale University Press.

Vaitheespara, Ravi. 2009. 'Towards Understanding Militant Tamil Nationalism in Sri Lanka'. In *Pathways of Dissent: Tamil Nationalism in Sri Lanka*, edited by Rainford Cheran, 33–54. Thousand Oaks, CA: Sage.

Vandekerckhove, Nel. 2011. 'The State, the Rebel and the Chief: Public Authority and Land Disputes in Assam, India'. *Development and Change* 42(3): 759–779.

Van der Borgh, Chris. 2012. 'Resisting International State Building in Kosovo'. *Problems of Post-Communism* 59(2): 31–42.

Venugopal, Rajesh. 2018. *Nationalism, Development and Ethnic Conflict in Sri Lanka*. Cambridge: Cambridge University Press.

Verkaaik, Oscar. 2004. *Migrants and Militants: Fun and Urban Violence in Pakistan*. Princeton, NJ: Princeton University Press.

Von Benda-Beckmann, Keebet. 1981. 'Forum Shopping and Shopping Forums: Dispute Processing in a Minangkabau Village in West Sumatra'. *Journal of Legal Pluralism* 13(19): 117–159.

Walker, Rebecca. 2013. *Enduring Violence: Everyday Life and Conflict in Eastern Sri Lanka*. Manchester: Manchester University Press.

Watson, C. W. 1997. '"Born a Lady, became a Princess, Died a Saint": The Reaction to the Death of Diana, Princess of Wales'. *Anthropology Today* 13(6): 3–7.

Watts, Nicole. 2010. *Activists in Office: Kurdish Politics and Protest in Turkey*. Seattle, WA: University of Washington Press.

Weber, Cynthia. 1995. *Simulating Sovereignty: Intervention, the State and Symbolic Exchange*. Cambridge: Cambridge University Press.

———. 1998. 'Performative States'. *Millennium* 27(1): 77–95.

Wedeen, Lisa. 1999. *Ambiguities of Domination: Politics, Rhetoric, and Symbols in Contemporary Syria*. Chicago, IL: Chicago University Press.

———. 2003. 'Seeing like a Citizen, Acting like a State: Exemplary Events in Unified Yemen'. *Comparative Studies in Society and History* 45(4): 680–713.

Weerakoon, Bradman. 2004. *Rendering unto Caesar: A Fascinating Story of One Man's Tenure under Nine Prime Ministers and Presidents of Sri Lanka*. Colombo: Vijitha Yapa.

Weiss, Gordon. 2011. *The Cage: The Fight for Sri Lanka and the Last Days of the Tamil Tigers*. London: The Bodley Head.

Welikala, Asanga. 2012a. *The Sri Lankan Republic at 40: Reflections on Constitutional History, Theory and Practice*. Colombo: Centre for Policy Alternatives.

———. 2012b. 'The Failure of Jennings' Constitutional Experiment in Ceylon: How "Procedural Entrenchment" Led to Constitutional Revolution'. In *The Sri Lankan Republic at 40: Reflections on Constitutional History, Theory and Practice*, edited by Asanga Welikala, 145–200. Colombo: Centre for Policy Alternatives.

———. 2016. *A New Devolution Settlement for Sri Lanka: Proceedings and Outcomes*. Conference of Provincial Councils, Centre for Policy Alternatives, Colombo. https://www.cpalanka.org/wp-content/uploads/2016/11/PC-conference-report.pdf. Accessed 20 November 2023.

———. 2020. 'The Dismissal of Prime Ministers in the Asian Commonwealth: Comparing Democratic Deconsolidation in Malaysia and Sri Lanka'. *Political Quarterly* 91(4): 786–794.

Whelan, Frederick. 1983. 'Prologue: Democratic Theory and the Boundary Problem'. *Nomos* 25: 13–47.

Whitaker, Mark. 1997. 'Tigers and Temples: The Politics of Nationalist and Non-Modern Violence in Sri Lanka'. *South Asia: Journal of South Asian Studies* 20(1): 201–214.

———. 2007. *Learning Politics from Sivaram: The Life and Death of a Revolutionary Journalist in Sri Lanka*. London: Pluto Press.

Wickramaratne, Jayampathy. 2014. *Towards Democratic Governance in Sri Lanka: A Constitutional Miscellany*. Colombo: Institute for Constitutional Studies.

———. 2019. 'Legal Issues'. In *Thirty Years of Devolution: An Evaluation of the Workings of Provincial Councils in Sri Lanka*, edited by Ranjith Amarasinghe, Asoka Gunawardena, Jayampathi Wickramaratne, A. Navaratna-Bandara and N. Selvakkumaran, 107–190. Colombo: Institute for Constitutional Studies.

Wickramaratne, Jayampathy and Lakshman Marasinghe, eds. 2010. *13th Amendment: Essays on Practice*. Pannipitiya, Sri Lanka: Stamford Lake.

Wickramasinghe, Nira. 2006. *Sri Lanka in the Modern Age: A History of Contested Identities*. London: Hurst.

———. 2009. 'After the War: A New Patriotism in Sri Lanka?' *Journal of Asian Studies* 68(4): 1045–1054.

———. 2014. 'Sri Lanka in 2013: Post-War Oppressive Stability'. *Asian Survey* 54(1): 60–66.

Wijayalath, Ayesha. 2022. 'The Aragalaya Awakens People's Sleeping Sovereignty'. *Groundviews*, 8 October 2022. https://groundviews.org/2022/08/10/the-aragalaya-awakens-peoplessleeping-sovereignty/. Accessed 28 June 2023.

Wilson, A. Jeyaratnam. 1994a. 'The Colombo Man, the Jaffna Man, and the Batticaloa Man: Regional Identities and the Rise of the Federal Party'. In *The Sri Lankan Tamils: Ethnicity and Identity*, edited by Chelvadurai Manogaran and Bryan Pfaffenberger, 126–142. Boulder, CO: Westview Press.

———. 1994b. *S.J.V. Chelvanayakam and the Crisis of Sri Lankan Tamil Nationalism, 1947–1977: A Political Biography*. London: Hurst.

———. 2000. *Sri Lankan Tamil Nationalism: Its Origins and Developments in the Nineteenth and Twentieth Centuries*. London: Hurst.

Wilson, Alice. 2016. *Sovereignty in Exile: A Saharan Liberation Movement Governs*. Philadelphia, PA: University of Pennsylvania Press.

Winslow, Deborah and Michael. D. Woost, eds. 2004. *Economy, Culture, and Civil War in Sri Lanka*. Indianapolis, IN: Indiana University Press.

Witsoe, Jeffrey. 2013. *Democracy against Development: Lower-Caste Politics and Political Modernity in Postcolonial India*. Chicago, IL: Chicago University Press.

Women's Action Network. 2013. 'Is This the Beginning of Women's Political Representation in the Northern Provincial Council?' https://groundviews. org/2013/09/25/is-this-the-beginning-of-womens-political-representation-in-the-northern-provincial-council/. Accessed 20 June 2023.

Yep, Ray, ed. 2013. *Negotiating Autonomy in Greater China: Hong Kong and its Sovereign before and after 1997*. Copenhagen: NIAS Press.

Yuval-Davis, Nira. 1997. *Gender and Nation*. London: Sage.

Zurn, Christopher F. 2010. 'The Logic of Legitimacy: Bootstrapping Paradoxes of Constitutional Democracy'. *Legal Theory* 16(3): 191–227.

Index